1998

Mary,

Merry Christmas. Andy

 W9-BVH-867

The
Freedom
Quilting
Bee

Nancy Callahan

The Freedom Quilting Bee

The
University
of
Alabama
Press
Tuscaloosa and London

Copyright © 1987 by
The University of Alabama Press
Tuscaloosa, Alabama 35487
All rights reserved
Manufactured in the
United States of America

Library of Congress Cataloging-in-Publication Data

Callahan, Nancy.
    The Freedom Quilting Bee.

    Bibliography: p.
    Includes index.
    1. Freedom Quilting Bee (Organization: Alabama)—
History.   2. Quilting—Alabama—History—20th century.
3. Afro-American quiltmakers—Alabama—History.
4. Civil rights in art.   I. Title.
NK9112.C34   1987   976.1′3800496073   86–4369
ISBN 0-8173-0310-3

British Library Cataloguing-in-Publication Data is available.

Material in this book
was previously published
by the author in "Helping
the Peoples to Help Them-
selves," *The Quilt Digest* 4
(1986), pp. 20–29.

To Estelle Witherspoon
and her sister members of
the Freedom Quilting Bee,
past, present, and future; and to
the Reverend Francis X. Walter.

Contents

The Freedom Quilting Bee

The Women of the Freedom Quilting Bee

Color Plates

(following page 116)

Maps

Preface

On a Sunday afternoon in December 1969, I attended the opening reception for an exhibit by the Freedom Quilting Bee at Stillman College, in Tuscaloosa. Although the group had been formed almost four years earlier by black women in Wilcox County as a means toward economic survival, I had only learned of the Bee from publicity about the exhibit in my hometown.

Because my grandmother and other family members were quilters, all my life I had been exposed to and interested in quilts as an art and craft. But those at Stillman attracted me as no others ever had. They were adventurous, those Stars and Monkey Wrenches and Courthouse Steps. They were brilliant and beautiful, but in a way far different from those I had known. For instance, the color black, which I had never before seen in quilts, was frequently employed. The schemes of color—black mixed with white, black with yellow, and red on white—provided stark contrasts. In addition, rich use was made of the pure, primary hues, quite unlike the softer pastels of my past.

But those quilts also told much about their makers—members all in the struggle for civil rights. They were obviously women of enormous confidence and courage, whose daring spirits provided the sustenance by which they had prevailed. What I did not realize then but came to learn years later was the powerful history behind each showpiece in the exhibit.

Some of the quilts sold; the others went home to the Black Belt. And, for more than a decade, the back side of my soul felt a magnetic pull toward the Freedom Quilting Bee, a deep longing to visit and learn more about it. On September 9, 1980, I made the trip, traveling forty miles below Selma to a place called Route One, Alberta. A week later, I suddenly decided to write a book about the Bee.

Granted, the co-op had been publicized in the most sophisticated newspapers and magazines of the East. But the Bee was about civil rights as much as anything. And, in all the efforts to document that phase of our nation, the quilters had somehow been overlooked.

Even before Selma and the national outcry of sympathy for black voting rights set off in that city, the women who later organized the Freedom Quilting Bee had been star players in local civil rights. They went to church and heard Martin Luther King, Jr., preach. They organized among themselves. They aired their convictions to the white elected officials. They marched and spent their time in jail. And they, too, were part of the march to Montgomery.

Then, in the aftermath of Selma, Reverend Francis Walter went to the area to work for civil rights and claimed their cause for his own. He led the women as they built an economic bulwark that has lasted for two decades.

Ironically, the Freedom Quilting Bee has been, until now, one of the best-kept secrets in all Alabama. Surely it is too positive, too inventive, and too inspiring to remain anonymous. Its members should not live and die and never make the pages of history.

So I began my book by interviewing many of the quilters, some who work at the co-op now, and others who have retired but still are members. I visited their homes, met their families, and saw firsthand the way in which they live. Some of the interviews were conducted at the sewing center, where the women earn their daily bread.

On several trips to Birmingham, I interviewed Father Walter in his church office and spent hours in the study of his home, poring over reams of written materials he had collected during his work with the Bee and that had lain idle in boxes under his bed since his days in civil rights. I took notes from the personal journal he had maintained during his life in the movement and gleaned information from six years of newsletters published by the Selma Inter-religious Project, the group he had headed.

Because numerous New Yorkers were early promoters of the quilters, I traveled there and talked to them. Other supporters lived too far away for personal visits—in Chicago, California, Detroit, and elsewhere—so I interviewed them over the telephone. I also conducted personal interviews in various Alabama towns.

All these interviews were tape-recorded, even those on the telephone, and then transcribed word for word. Some of the out-of-state interviewees even sent me memorabilia they had acquired during their work with the Freedom Quilting Bee, including letters, news releases, and promotional brochures.

I spent time at the Birmingham Public Library, sifting through papers from the first seven years of the Bee. In that collection are letters to and from Father Walter that verified or corrected dates and other information obtained in oral interviews. Also there are magazine and newspaper articles, swatches of fabric, quilt orders, and invoices. The huge number of orders on file at the library from every part of the country, as well as some from abroad, is a testament to the national renaissance of interest in quilting in American decor that the Bee helped to bring about during the 1960s.

In addition, the library possesses a series of files on the history of Gee's Bend, one of the Wilcox County communities supporting the Freedom Quilting Bee. That material, including letters, research reports, and old history journals, along with other data in the Alabama Department of Archives and History, in Montgomery, and the Auburn University Library, facilitated my coverage of Wilcox County history.

First of all, this book tells the story of the fight for local civil rights in the Alabama Black Belt and the manner in which a group of impoverished, uneducated black women used that movement as a platform from which to turn a century-old art form into a viable economic enterprise that radically changed their lives. It is also an account of the method whereby Freedom's quilts and other products were marketed in other parts of the country by those whose cultures were totally different from that of the blacks in Wilcox County. And, in addition, it provides an opportunity to become acquainted with the quilters themselves—to learn directly from these plucky, unsung heroines of the things about life that really count.

Across these pages, two names stand out: Francis Walter, the priest, and Estelle Witherspoon, Freedom's longtime manager. Read of them with special interest, for, without Father Walter, the Freedom Quilting Bee would never even have existed; and, without Mrs. Witherspoon, it would never have lasted this long.

Nancy Callahan

*The
Freedom
Quilting
Bee*

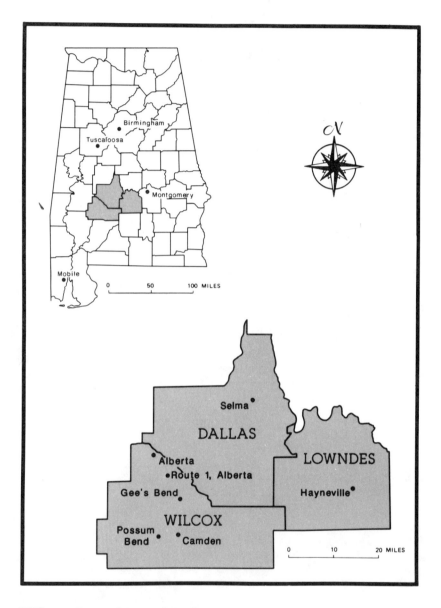

Wilcox, Lowndes, and Dallas
counties in the
Alabama Black Belt

1   *From Civil Rights to Patchwork Quilts*

On December 9, 1965, Francis X. Walter, a white Episcopal priest and newly appointed head of an Alabama civil rights project, was driving through Wilcox County, deep in the Alabama Black Belt. He was accompanied by Everett Wenrick, a white Episcopal seminarian from the North and fellow civil rights worker.

Father Walter was on a mission to document cases of harassment by whites of blacks who had been involved in the civil rights movement. Because they had demonstrated for their right to vote, countless black families were being thrown off their land. Some were even facing jail terms if they did not pay long-term bank loans that unexpectedly had been declared due. Father Walter was to collect his evidence and turn it in to the Federal Bureau of Investigation, which would prosecute those whites through newly enacted civil rights legislation.

Venturing through Possum Bend, first settled in the late 1800s but on this occasion not even a speck on the Alabama road map, the twosome came to a dead end and encountered a pig trail, skiffs, and the Alabama River. At a nearby cabin, a clothesline was gaily garbed with three magnificent quilts. Inside was their maker, a lone black woman, at work on yet another.

Long interested in folk art, Walter was caught by the quilts' bold, inventive op art designs. He immediately conceived an idea: the selling of quilts could increase pride and participation among local black women in the civil rights movement. But the seed of his notion took root and flourished far beyond his wildest expectations as the Freedom Quilting Bee, a handicraft cooperative known nationwide.

This is the story of that Bee, a celebration of two decades of the economic independence of black women in one of the poorest and most isolated counties in America. It is not a typical story one might associate with a labor coalition, the women's movement, or a folk-art industry, because the Freedom Quilting Bee is not typical. If anything, it is improbable. And, given a set of circumstances different from the ones that cushioned its beginning, it never would have come into being.

One of only a handful of all-black women's cooperatives in the nation, this unschooled but talented body of quilters has become a source of inspiration to cooperatives everywhere. It also remains as one of the most positive outgrowths ever spawned by the civil rights movement in Alabama.

Late in the 1960s, while still in an embryonic stage, the Freedom Quilting Bee captured the energies and imagination of the New York world of interior design and then sparked a nationwide revival of interest in patchwork quilts. Members have exhibited at the Smithsonian and prestigious folk craft fairs. Their works have been featured in major fashion as well as home design magazines and have been sold through New York's premiere department stores. They have generated a handsome mail-order business and continue to sell through an Eastern co-op affiliate.

But, most of all, the quilters are at work in steady jobs, in their own business, in their own community, providing significant, supplementary incomes for their families. Mostly former fieldhands whose fingers have been callused by decades of cotton chopping begun as early as childhood, the Freedom quilters are skilled artisans and self-styled business executives, who, largely through their own determination, vision, and pride, are keeping aflame an artistic endeavor that extends back in the black culture of Wilcox County for 140 years.

A Heritage of Slavery and Agriculture

To know the Freedom Quilting Bee and the women who have sustained it is to know Wilcox County, since the early 1800s an anchor of agriculture in the Alabama Black Belt, so-called for the rich, dark soil that spurred the multicountied region's economic success.

Almost from the time this geographical zigzag of a county was first settled in south-central Alabama between 1800 and 1810, the black population has vastly outnumbered that of the whites. Before the Emancipation Proclamation, the county was dominated by white plantation owners and worked by black slaves. After slavery times, many of the large plantations were split into smaller, white-owned farms. In some areas, cotton succumbed to soybeans and cattle, more lucrative enterprises requiring less labor, and to pulpwood. As a result, masses of out-of-work blacks moved to the cities, especially in the North, to work. Most who remained stayed on the farms. Some were sharecroppers and others rented from the whites or lived on the land through white charity.

It was a racially segregated life in which the political, economic, social, and cultural mores were clearly dictated by the whites and in their best interests. It was a case of rich versus poor, white versus black, lettered versus unlettered, and those who voted versus those who could not. By the beginning of 1965, black registered voters in Wilcox County were almost nonexistent. Lacking a political voice, black people had no hope of rising above their second-class status.

The Black Belt Becomes Focus of National Civil Rights

As 1965 progressed, though, the civil rights movement peaked in the Alabama Black Belt. Racially generated deaths and community demonstrations occurred. On March 7, or "Bloody Sunday," voting rights marchers in Selma, the seat of Dallas County that touches the north of Wilcox, were beaten and gassed by Alabama troopers and Dallas County deputies.

On March 15 President Lyndon Johnson responded by announcing his plans to submit to Congress a voting rights bill. Then, on March 21–25, Martin Luther King, Jr., head of the Southern Christian Leadership Conference (SCLC), led marchers from Selma, unofficial capital of the Black Belt, to Montgomery, capital of Alabama, to campaign for black voting rights. For almost half a year, the Black Belt was the national focus for black civil rights and figured daily in major headlines as well as on nightly radio and television network news.

Church Groups Form Selma Inter-religious Project

Finally, on August 6, President Johnson signed the Voting Rights Act. But, in the aftermath of the Selma-to-Montgomery march, several participating religious groups wanted to keep alive the spirit of the movement in a tangible way. It was a time in national politics of great optimism. The Kennedy and Johnson administrations had set the stage for a proliferation of private civil rights groups at the community level; leaders and followers were rising from the tiniest and most backwoods of Southern hamlets. A beehive network had been started between Southern blacks and white liberals from the North; between local civil rights groups and the federal government. Comings and goings were on a grand scale and were grounded in hope.

What resulted was the Selma Inter-religious Project (SIP), a denominational coalition that sought to continue the relationship molded during the Selma-to-Montgomery march by representatives of those faiths as well as of Black

Belt civil rights activities. The four national sponsors were the Synagogue Council of America and divisions of the National Catholic Conference for Inter-racial Justice, the National Council of Churches of Christ, and the Unitarian-Universalist Association. Other member affiliates were units within the Episcopal Church, the Methodist Church, the Union of American Hebrew Congregations, the United Church of Christ, the United Presbyterian Church in the U.S.A., and "a denomination which prefers to remain anonymous."

Priest Heads Selma Project

Named executive director of the Selma Inter-religious Project was Reverend Francis X. Walter, an Alabama native son who most recently had been priest-in-charge of Grace Episcopal Church, in Jersey City, New Jersey. He later recounted his coming back to Alabama on December 6, 1965, in the first issue of his *S.I.P. Newsletter,* a vehicle through which he communicated with national proponents of Black Belt civil rights. "Go to Selma," he was told by a representative of the National Council of Churches of Christ. "Meet the Episcopal seminarian, Jon Daniels. He'll introduce you around. Ask questions and look. See if the people want a continued ministry representing the religious groups. See if you think you are the man to do it."

The call came on July 28, 1965, to Decatur, a Tennessee River city in North Alabama, where Father Walter was doing summer supply work for three churches. Less than a month after the call, he was in Selma, talking about the project with the local people and armed with a civil rights commitment that had begun while he was a teenager in Mobile. His host was absent, for Jonathan M. Daniels, twenty-seven, of Keene, New Hampshire, was in jail. A white student at the Episcopal Theological Seminary in Cambridge, Massachusetts, he had heeded the call from Dr. King for civil rights volunteers to come to the Black Belt. Receiving seminary permission to study by correspondence, he had arrived at Selma in March to work for understanding between the area's black and white Christians. He was supported financially and in spirit by the Atlanta-based Episcopal Society for Cultural and Racial Unity.

Living in a Selma black-housing project, Daniels took part in the March demonstrations there and in voting rights organizing in nearby Lowndes County. By August he was planning a return to Cambridge. But, on the 15th, he was arrested in the Lowndes County town of Fort Deposit at the end of a demonstration. He had not been demonstrating, but simply passing out literature encouraging blacks to register to vote. Regardless, he was arrested, then transferred to a jail in Hayneville, a country town of 900, forty miles southeast of Selma. Others arrested and imprisoned in that town with him were three young black women; a white Catholic priest from Chicago, Father James Morrisroe; and a young black man named Stokely Carmichael, who was head of the Student Non-Violent Coordinating Committee (SNCC).

After arriving in Selma, the brown-haired, bespectacled Father Walter went to Hayneville to meet and visit with Daniels and the others who were behind bars. He was accompanied by a black Episcopal priest, on the staff of the Episcopal Society for Cultural and Racial Unity, who had brought bail money for Daniels. However, the group in jail decided that either all or none would be released on bail. There was not enough money for all of them, so Daniels chose to remain in confinement. On August 21, two days after the visit, the prisoners were released under curious circumstances. The sheriff would not allow them to call Selma for transportation, and he denied their request to stay at the jail. They were forced away from the courthouse by threats.

On earlier occasions, the owner of The Cash Store, a grocery 500 yards from the courthouse, had allowed the activists to buy food. That was the only place in town where they felt safe. So they went there. The owner was absent, but Tom Coleman, a white special deputy in his early fifties who was a Highway Department engineer, was inside behind a dark screen door. As the group approached the store, he pushed the door open and fired an automatic shotgun. Daniels was killed and Father Morrisroe was seriously injured.

An all-white Hayneville jury found Coleman not guilty of slaying Daniels and wounding Father Morrisroe. The owner of The Cash Store stayed out of the county at least until after the trial. Later, a Montgomery federal judge ruled that the arrest of the young churchman and his associates had been illegal.

Immediately after the killing, Father Walter remained in Selma temporarily and unofficially to aid with telephone calls and secretarial work kindled by the tragedy. Upon his return to Decatur, he elected to stay in Alabama and work against racism.

Father Walter's Background

Francis Xavier Walter was born on December 22, 1932, in Mobile, where he grew up. In 1950 he entered Spring Hill College, a Catholic institution two blocks from his home. In four years, he received his bachelor of arts degree and was accepted by St. Luke's Episcopal Seminary at the University of the South in Sewanee, Tennessee, to study for the priesthood. In 1957 he received his degree in divinity, was ordained as a priest, and spent the next two years as a fellow and tutor at General Theological Seminary, in New York City.

One of his subsequent appointments was as rector of St. James' Church, in Eufaula, Alabama, but he left there in 1961 and was refused work in Alabama by the bishop of the Episcopal church in the state because of his interpretation of the gospel with regard to racism. From 1963 until the summer of 1965, he was with Grace Church, in Jersey City.

The murder of Jonathan Daniels served as a catalyst that goaded the young priest to accept a leadership role in civil rights, for the death produced nationwide resentment toward the social inequities of the Black Belt.

When called back to Alabama, Father Walter had just left a ghetto church near the Jersey City waterfront. A fashionable, white Episcopal parish of the 1840s, by the 1960s the congregation was almost entirely black and Puerto Rican, with only a handful of whites. A living textbook in racial problems and minority attitudes, Grace Church taught Father Walter about blacks, especially the young ones, the sons and daughters of Southern parents, who were thoroughly ashamed of their background when the massive voting rights campaign had not even surfaced. According to Father Walter,

If the young blacks in that congregation wanted to insult somebody, fighting words, at least of a milder sort, were, "Your mama eat turnip greens," or "biscuits" or some such. They were deeply ashamed of being black. They didn't have any sense of racial pride and it was soon apparent that they couldn't really be whole individuals, couldn't have a whole individual psyche until they were proud of their race, of their people.

The sit-in movement in the South had an electric effect in the ghettos. People told me that when they moved up North formerly, they hid the fact that they had moved up. They didn't want to be looked upon as ghetto newcomers.

But right after the sit-ins of '59 and '60, people would proudly announce when they got into the ghetto that they had just arrived from Alabama or Mississippi, because everybody was saying, "Man, you one of those Freedom Riders?" And people would invent a civil rights past for themselves if they didn't have one. "Yeah, we're from Alabama. We was in that mess." Big heroes on the block, whereas a couple of years before, they would hide their arrival: "Oh, we've been up here for years, man."

One time we had a church social function and I cooked biscuits. The girls and boys really made fun of me because I knew how to make biscuits and because I would even associate myself with a biscuit. I felt a great sense of tragedy and a foreboding that this nation was going to pay for that.

They used to see Tarzan movies downtown and that was their only connection with Africa—a white man lording it over a bunch of people made up with black face jumping around a movie set in loin cloth. That also was their view of nature, which is another thing: They hated the green and living world and they were afraid of it, afraid even of a cow. They were ghetto kids.

I once showed a movie at Grace Church called *Anglican Odyssey*. It was about the different Anglican churches in the world. The sisters who worked there told me, "You can't show this movie." There were scenes of natives in the movie. The sisters said, "The kids just couldn't bear to see people of their own skin color in native dress. It would be so threatening that they would freak out."

I didn't believe the sisters and was doubly determined to force them to have a good image of themselves by showing the movie. The church school assembly came apart. The children went crazy, jumped up and down on the pews and fell over backwards, ran around the church and screamed. It was hysterical laughter. But it came from their deep shame at seeing black people in native costume, and to me, it was heartbreaking.

I learned before I came back to the South what terrible psychic damage had been done to black people, and I was not at all surprised when Stokely Carmichael said, "Black Power." It was a necessity, almost.

So, as he approached his thirty-third birthday, Francis Walter exchanged his work with a ghetto church in Jersey City for a position as head of a religious group that sought to help underprivileged people in the Black Belt. Given the full blessings of the Diocese of Newark, under whose jurisdiction he had been serving as a priest, Father Walter began his new work on October 1, 1965.

Six months after the advent of his Alabama homecoming, this new man in the movement would be plagued with his first major personal and professional setback: the Episcopal bishop of Alabama would refuse to give him a license to officiate in the state as a priest, and his attempts to communicate with the diocese would be declined. Other obstacles would come in time. It would take him and his wife four years to adopt a baby because of punitive measures taken by the bishop, who claimed the head of the Selma Project's work with civil rights made him unfit for fatherhood. Eventually, the Walters would adopt a daughter and son: Margaret, born in 1969; and Andrew, born in 1971.

The couple would experience serious difficulties in obtaining an FHA loan to buy a house because of his work. They would feel their telephone was being monitored by the FBI. Federal men would call at their door and drive through the neighborhood. In 1980 Senate hearings would confirm what the Walters already knew, that the federal government had "secretly" kept tabs on civil rights groups at that time.

But, in late autumn of 1965, Father Walter settled ninety miles north of Selma in Tuscaloosa, where his wife, Elizabeth, enrolled in the art graduate program at The University of Alabama, and where the SIP was headquartered in the spare wing of a black funeral home.

Francis Walter's kinship with the movement was far different in his opinion from that experienced by legions of others who came South during that era to advance their liberal persuasions. As he explains:

To be a little simple and vicious, I believe the hippie movement grew out of the kids exposed to the civil rights movement—the white kids who had come South. And most of them had a disquieting effect on me. I was a Southern white person who had some pretensions to being a sixth-generation Alabamian. What I saw them doing was trying to deal with their identity—their past—by denying it. All these rich white kids were trying to be like black people, thinking then they would be approved by blacks. They would wear the uniform of denim coveralls the SCLC workers had picked up from the peasants of the movement, the real shock troops, the black people who really lived in Alabama.

Something repels me about a person who has had so little examination of his own past and his own roots that he can throw on the identity of another so quickly. Emotionally, I just couldn't do that. I had a knowledge of what I was—good and evil—and I didn't feel like lopping off my past. So I realized I was not going to join with the civil rights movement as director of the Selma Inter-religious Project. I couldn't. I wasn't black. You can't establish power for someone else. You can't get power and lay it at the feet of someone not prepared to take and use it.

So I was going to be an adjunct and a facilitator for black persons establishing their own rights. And maybe a facilitator for persons who could relate to my own kind: middle class whites in Alabama.

I wore what a person in my economic class in Alabama would generally wear if he were driving around
Wilcox County. I got some brown work pants, flannel
shirts and stuck a bunch of ballpoint pens in my shirt
pocket. I didn't try to look or act like a black person. I
just tried to be my great-grandfather's boy. I wasn't
going to shuck him off.

Father Walter Goes to Work

Using the $16,000 that was available for the first year's operation, Father
Walter began by making the proper contacts—individuals, other civil rights
groups, foundations, and federal employees—who were strung across the
Black Belt and lapping over into Montgomery, Birmingham, Atlanta, and
New York. Enjoying the luxury of an automobile and gasoline to keep it
running, he drove workers from place to place and helped black people
register to vote. He supervised distribution of twelve tons of school books
that were donated by sympathizers in Detroit. He tried to put white liberal
Alabamians in touch with black movement activists. And, to his surprise, he
found himself counseling white church people despite his lack of Alabama
parochial status.

Before year's end, Father Walter was focusing on Wilcox County, where
he began to collect depositions from blacks who were being evicted from
their rental homes and/or facing bank loan foreclosures for having registered
to vote or having been seen in demonstrations. "We were under the naive
notion," he remembers, "that the FBI would take this data and prosecute
people under the new civil rights law that said you cannot evict somebody
from rental property because he had registered to vote or was in a demonstration or attempted to exercise his constitutional rights."

Wilcox blacks were much a part of the Selma-to-Montgomery march and
other organized protests. After the Voting Rights Act became reality, they
registered en masse. Blacks acquired political power in Wilcox County for
the first time in this century, and were on the ballot in the 1966 spring
Democratic primary. To the white power structure, the sudden series of
events was scary and threatening. By primary time, the county had about
3,600 registered black voters, easily 1,000 more than the population of the
whites in the voting-age bracket.

Wilcox was not a wealthy county. According to the 1960 census, half the
families made less than $1,550 a year. Plumbing facilities, washing machines,
telephones, television sets, and automobiles were scarce. Half the adults did
not even have a seventh-grade education. Despite these conditions, civil rights
workers said local authorities were highly laggard in seeking federal aid,
especially from antipoverty programs administered by the U.S. Office of
Economic Opportunity.

As black registration proliferated, those involved experienced what appeared to be insurmountable personal harassment by whites, through economic intimidation and discrimination. Stores stopped extending credit to movement activists. A schoolteacher lost his job for working to register voters. A woman working full time as a domestic for twelve dollars a week lost her job and was hit with a broom because she registered. She was told that, if she "was so interested in voting," not to come back.

Banks were calling in loans on a ten-day notice to black registered voters or those blacks who were identified with the movement. Loan foreclosures on farmers had been initiated; others applying for loans suffered delays. Tenant farmers who had established years of good credit were asked to pay their due in ten days or two weeks. One father of a large family had already been jailed for failure to pay, and a debtors' prison in the county seat at Camden seemed imminent by Christmas. An eighty-two-year-old sharecropper was forced off land on which he had spent his entire life, and on which his mother had been born into slavery.

The local office of the Farmers Home Administration refused or delayed loans to displaced blacks. Thus, Wilcox blacks harbored dissent toward that federal agency, especially because nonmovement blacks were treated better. As Father Walter sensed it, blacks were no longer needed or wanted in Wilcox County, and because no federal housing was available there, the one course of action seemed to be for them to move to Detroit, Chicago, and other Northern cities. "There is a concentrated movement in Wilcox to do everything short of violence to encourage Negroes to leave," he charged in the December 6 issue of his *S.I.P. Newsletter.* "In the recent past one could say that the white structure no longer needed the Negro as a laborer but that now with the vote he is considered dangerous as a fellow citizen."

Father Walter went from one shack to another, interviewing blacks, who in many cases were given two weeks to conclude a way of life that had spanned generations. Recording those "hardship cases," he then sent the data to Washington. As he says:

We collected 70 depositions until we realized it wasn't
going to do any good. The sad thing was that the
people weren't doing anything productive. A lot of
them were not even paying rent because the whites,
out of charity, had let them stay for free; the places
were hovels and the black people had been keeping
them in repair for years anyway.

It was sour white charity. Some lived 50 miles away
and had not seen this land for 30 years. They left the
shacks there, and the people were living in them, not
even paying rent. Or maybe they did pay, whatever
they felt like doing. That was another tragedy: They

were not even busting up an economic reality. Those
people were the leftovers, not of slavery but of the
sharecropper system which took the place of slavery.
They were old ladies who had demonstrated for the
right to vote so they got thrown off.

How can you be prosecuted for evicting somebody
you've let stay on your land without paying rent? The
effect on the black people was, of course, that they had
no place to go. They were out. It's sad how desperate
and miserable these people were, but, to a person,
quiet and dignified in their misery. The FBI did nothing. The federal government prosecuted no one.

The Freedom Quilting Bee Is Born

Within this framework, the Freedom Quilting Bee was born when Father
Walter was lost and looking at a clothesline two weeks before Christmas. He
later would learn that the maker of those Possum Bend patchworks was Ora
McDaniels, but at the moment she was simply a black woman in a cabin and
at work on a quilt, whose clothesline told of her exceptional flare for color
and style.

Intent on meeting the quilter and seeing more closely her work, Father
Walter and Wenrick, who had come to the Black Belt for a year to continue
the work of Jonathan Daniels, left their car and eased toward her home far
away from the road. "After opening a barbed wire fence and going through,
I saw a woman who looked as though she had urgent business in the back-
property wood lot," he recalls. "I yelled and she just went on about her
business, so when I got half-way up to the house, there wasn't anybody
there." He would be told later that, upon seeing the two white men, the black
woman had fled to the fields to hide.

Three weeks later, Father Walter returned with Ella Saulsbury, a black
woman from the Camden side of the Alabama River and a field worker for
the Wilcox County SCLC who aided the priest in gathering testaments of
racially caused hardships. "The woman said she had run into the woods. A
white man was coming to see her and she didn't know him. She was afraid
so she had run away. She knew my black associate so it was okay for us to
sit down and talk. I asked her if she would be interested in selling some
quilts."

It was hardly an idle proposition. Father Walter and Ms. Saulsbury had
stopped by the home of another Wilcox black woman to discuss quiltmaking
soon after his clothesline encounter. He had learned the woman's rate was
three quilts for five dollars; the buyer supplied scraps and thread. Since then,
he and his SCLC coworker had been swapping ideas about marketing local

quilts in New York City, where Father Walter had a friend who had suggested a quilt auction. As the cleric explains:

> I'd had a little talk with my wife, and she came up with the original germane idea. She said, "Don't ask people to let you have these quilts so you can send them to New York and have them auctioned and give the money to the Wilcox County SCLC because nobody will trust you. People don't have any trouble trusting a dollar bill. Take a little money down there."
>
> I said, "That makes sense," because I was quick to realize black people had no reason to trust me. Their trust level was understandably low. So I would ask a woman, "How much do you normally get if you sell to somebody?" And she would say, "Oh, five dollars." I later found out that was generally the going price but rarely did they ever sell a quilt. Occasionally a white woman would say, "Make me a quilt," and give them five dollars.
>
> So I said, "Okay, we'll offer ten dollars. I'll pay you ten dollars now for this quilt and send the quilts to New York. They'll be auctioned off. Then I'll bring back whatever we make and give it to Reverend Harrell."

Dan Harrell was an SCLC national representative who was working in Wilcox County.

"The people were in a win-win situation. Ten dollars was twice as much as they'd ever got for a quilt before." And the sale of a ten-dollar quilt meant for most a 1 percent gain in annual income. "So if this crazy white man never showed up again, it really didn't matter. But my goodness, if he actually was going to do what he said, rather unheard of for white people, that would be even better. What was there to lose?"

During the next few weeks, Father Walter borrowed $700 from the Jonathan Daniels Memorial Fund, run by the Episcopal Society for Cultural and Racial Unity; bought seventy ten-dollar quilts; and shipped them to New York. "I got a number of them from Possum Bend. Then somebody said, 'The women on the other side of the river'—Wilcox being divided by the Alabama River—'over in Gee's Bend, are some really good quilters.' So I went over there and asked Reverend Harrell who I should see from the mass meeting."

"Mass meeting" was the term describing local assemblies of Southern blacks that were held periodically during the civil rights era. Organized at least at the county level, many were divided into precincts; masonic halls, churches, and homes served as gathering places. Attendants would exchange

information, organize to register as voters, sing, pray, and report on movement progress.

The name Father Walter was given was Minder Coleman, who lived in
the final stretch of Alberta, about a mile from Gee's Bend. A woman of
achievement, she had served as president of Gee's Bend Farms, Inc., a Roosevelt experiment during New Deal days under the Farm Security Administration. A member of that agency's weaving cooperative in Gee's Bend's
earlier life, she understood the concept and potential of a quilting business
for black people of her county. She grandly envisioned participants acquiring
sewing machines and a place to make the quilts. And she wanted to be
chairman. "Minder said she would get the quilts if I'd tell her whether I was
coming in the morning or the afternoon. She'd just have the quilters and their
quilts out on County Highway Number 29. As I drove by, I could buy them
right in front of people's houses."

By February 10, 1966, Father Walter had purchased patchworks virtually
from every crossroad in the county and had dipped into Selma and the small
Dallas County communities for more. On that day, he also met the quilting
brigade from Gee's Bend. They were Minder Coleman, Nellie Young, Nettie
Young, Millie Cary, Callie Young and Rose Pettway—six anxious artisans
looking forward to making a sale, testing their talents in a far-off market,
and embarking on a spectacular gamble that just might lift their lives by
higher financial gain. So enthusiastic was one quilter that she did not have
time to complete one of her offerings. But Father Walter waited for the final
stitches.

Some of those quilts were made especially for New York. Others came
from beds. Still others were pulled from storage hampers—neatly folded
family treasures sold for the need of a $10 bill. Regardless, they displayed a
rich and pulsating range of hue as well as design. Rhythmic and romantic by
name, the patterns reflected images of the familiar and long-honored elements
of black Wilcox society: her people, traditions, occupations, work implements, the natural kingdom, outer space, and the Bible. They were Grandmother's Choice, Grandmother's Dream, Pine Burr, and Chestnut Bud;
Gentleman's Bow Tie, Pig in a Pen, Monkey Wrench, and Bear's Paw; Wild
Goose Chase, Sunshine and Shadow, Double Wedding Ring, and Coat of
Many Colors. There were Star quilts of every description, an Alphabet quilt
featuring blocks lettered from A to Z, and a long list of others.

Francis Walter vividly remembers an Overall quilt, made as a Six-Point
Star: "It was a bunch of worn-out, unsewn overalls with the pieces cut, a
very moving document of a person's life because the worn spots and the
unworn spots were all there. You could see the labor that had worn out those
clothes." Among the eye-catchers were quilts with strong splotches of black
in the multicolored motifs. All-black configurations frequently dominated
white backgrounds. Also popular were two-toned quilts, not just in black-

Detail from a late 1960s quilt of black and white Stair Steps, typical of many quilts found by Reverend Francis X. Walter on beds in Wilcox County cabins. (Photo by Nancy Callahan. Quilt owned by Michael and Nathan Goodson and Willita Zoellner, Tuscaloosa, Alabama)

and-white but blue-, red-, yellow-, even brown-and-white. By contrast, others were made from rainbow ragbags of flour sacks, men's shirts, and castaway dresses.

Also part of that shipment was a broad scale of quality reflecting individuals working at their own levels. Some were brilliant showpieces blessed with tiny, even stitches and perfectly cut jigsaws sewn correctly into place. But just as astonishing were the less-than-perfect presentations, marred by their

Among the most impressive quilts discovered by Reverend Walter were the Lone Stars, also called Stable Stars, such as this one from the 1960s. (Photo by Ted Klitzke; quilt owned by Annetta Contestabile of Switzerland)

irregular, haphazard stitches and their well-intended, hit-or-miss color schemes—showpieces themselves in their crude, almost eerie, approach. As one early buyer said of the quilt whose patches were all one color except for the red block at one end, "If Picasso can do it, I guess they can, too."

Father Walter's early thought was to give a fourth of the quilt profits to the Wilcox SCLC and the other portions, after expenses, to the quilters. But, as he went from door to door, collecting the quilts and dispensing ten-dollar bills, momentum for a quilting cooperative mushroomed. He and Reverend Dan Harrell became convinced that all proceeds should go to the quilters through a cooperative.

In March the two men talked about incorporating the quilters. Father Walter set a meeting date later in the month for those interested in joining the co-op. He obtained the free services of a young Birmingham attorney, Erskine Smith, to draft an organization charter. He borrowed $300 from the Atlanta-based Southern Regional Council to buy more quilts. Somewhere along the way, the new phenomenon was anointed, appropriately, the Freedom Quilting Bee. On March 26, 1966, more than sixty quilters met in Camden's Antioch Baptist Church. They sold fifty more quilts to Father Walter, adopted a charter, elected officers, and set the foundation for an institution that was unique in black Wilcox history.

The following evening, an auction was held in a photography studio in the west sixties of New York City. This gave the Freedom Quilting Bee its first exposure away from home—to an audience so different in background, opportunity, and culture that it might as well have been from a planet uncountable light years away.

2 — Quilt Auctions in New York City

Soon after Francis Walter discovered the patch-work quilting skills among the black women of Wilcox County, he voiced his findings to an Alabama friend who was living in New York City. Tom Screven, thirty-three, was a salesman with a wholesale custom-handmade carpet concern, V'Soske Rugs and Carpets; he had worked previously in theater, antiques, and wholesale home furnishings.

Before the end of 1965, Screven heard from Father Walter about the quilts and wrote back, saying, "Send them up." He received a couple, showed them around, and noted how appealing they were to all who saw them. "There was no consciousness of quilts then," he now says. "There were none of the books, exhibitions or co-ops. I don't know how much I even knew about quilts. I was taken by his descriptions of where they came from, who was making them and the way the people lived."

Screven's eagerness to help had much more to do with who the quilters were than with the caliber of their product. A member of Alabama's "silent generation" of the 1950s, he had been an apolitical person who, a decade later, had acquired a social consciousness:

The way I remember civil rights was riding the subways to work in the morning and reading in *The New York Times* of the atrocities in my home state. Finally, it began to grab me. Here was this unrelenting horror story pounding at me every day. Here I was in this upper crust business, involved with people decorating their places in stylish, expensive ways. I was working for architects pouring incredible amounts of money into offices. I had become strongly aware of poverty, especially where I had come from.

One of the New Yorkers to whom Screven showed the quilts and described their makers was John A. Newfield, a friend from Birmingham theater days who had left his hometown in 1953 for New York. When the quilting bee was founded, Newfield was a publicist with Columbia Pictures. He explains his role:

Tom was very excited and thought there ought to be some way to get a market for them. We talked about what might be done. He said they had a lot of quilts and they were making more. He felt he could get a bunch up here and wondered if I knew how to merchandise them.

I thought it would be fascinating, and a lot of people would be interested in assisting. The thing to do was to get a number of quilts up here, set up a viewing and have an auction. I thought we could raise a fair amount of money. I would see what I could do to publicize the quilts and get something launched. One of the first things Tom said was they desperately needed cloth.

Consequently, Screven visited New York's wholesale home furnishings fabric houses, obtained free materials, and shipped them to Wilcox County. Newfield and Screven's friend, George Davis, a packaging executive, contributed money toward the freight charges. As Screven tells it:

The lines changed periodically at the fabric houses such as Scalamandre, J. H. Thorp, and Schumacher. When that happens, the showrooms have to be up to the minute, so they throw out endless samples.

I knew people who could save fabrics for the quilting bee. I explained what it was and they would give me the fabrics. V'Soske had a little stockroom where I would pitch the fabrics into boxes. I figured at some point I had sent two thousand pounds down there. I sent them Railway Express because it was the cheapest way. I scrounged up money for the shipping from friends because I wasn't making a lot. That must have gone on for a year.

A lot of the fabrics didn't work. Many were upholstery and I didn't have a great sense of the quilters' needs at that time. Unfortunately, some of those heavy fabrics did get in the quilts because the women were using what they could get. If they didn't get what they liked, they sometimes used heavier things that were hard to work with and not as satisfactory.

Meantime, progress had been made toward the auction. One of Newfield's friends was Peter Basch, a photographer whose studio was at 33 West 67th Street. Just off Central Park West, it was in an area brimming with photographers, artists, and others in the creative professions. "He had a wonderful studio," states Newfield. "It was regarded as a painter's studio apartment. The main room was two stories high with a huge north window and a balcony. It was very sizeable. I asked Peter if he would lend us his studio to display the quilts and then have the auction."

Basch said yes. Then Screven and Newfield put together a promotional sheet that they mailed and handed to people they believed would be interested. "Have A Tilt At A Quilt," said its headline. "Here is a unique opportunity for you to lend support to a worthy and urgent cause, and, in the process, acquire a totally handmade QUILT that is a genuine example of folk art." The sheet also noted:

> Probably, you have never heard of Wilcox County
> in Alabama, whose population is 80 percent Negro
> sharecroppers with an average *family* income of less
> than *$1,000 yearly.* The good ladies of these families
> have traditionally made quilts simply to keep their
> families warm, and they are currently amazed at the
> possibility that "outsiders" might actually pay money
> for their handiwork. Each quilt represents the individ-
> ual maker's variation on one of the traditional folk
> patterns, the variations determined mostly by the ma-
> terials at hand. The backings are frequently made from
> sacking, with sack labels (Purina Feed Chow, for in-
> stance) sometimes still visible. . . .
> It takes better than a week to make a quilt—when
> its creator is not working in the cottonfields—and
> whatever proceeds we are able to send may be her
> family's only source of cash until the next cotton crop.
> Civil Rights and religious leaders in Alabama are
> convinced that the formation of Cooperatives will be
> the most constructive means for immediate and long-
> range improvement of the economic status of these
> impoverished people. Only by tapping and channelling
> their great productivity potential can they achieve a
> measure of economic freedom; and this freedom will
> be the most effective means of converting Civil Rights
> legislation into an actual fact of life. . . .
> Plan now to brighten your bed and gladden your
> heart and spirit by buying a quilt on Sunday, March 27.

Newfield recalls, "I made a few phone calls and got a few very interested people to look at a couple of quilts beforehand, and they made calls. Essentially, it was word-of-mouth." A drawing card, he says, was the auction location, for Peter Basch was a well-known, respected photographer with a *Life* magazine portfolio. Another magnet was the quilts, for Screven anxiously showed them to anyone who would agree to look. On February 3 he wrote Father Walter:

> Those first four quilts are as good as sold. Several
> people I know are interested. A Negro singer I'm mad
> about, Mabel Mercer, said the other night when I
> was at a club hearing her that she'd take two. I'm really
> wildly excited over all this. The idea of being able to
> help people *directly* appeals to me very much. It's so
> much more direct than contributing to a fund or dem-
> onstrating in the street, to which I am far from
> opposed.

Screven said in the same letter that he found it painful when acquaintances did not share his feelings:

> It really amazes me how complacent people are. You
> have probably long since grown used to it. Already I
> have sensed a far-off look in more than one person's
> eye when I explained the project. Of course, some
> people have been most interested and I'm sure I'll gen-
> erate a lot of excitement, but I'm a little stunned when
> people glaze over as if they don't have any sense of
> the need they could satisfy, neither the need of your
> sharecropper family *nor* the need they themselves have.

And what were Father Walter's thoughts about Black Belt quilting while his friend was scurrying around New York with Wilcox patchworks under his arms? "In the back of my mind, I know quilting can never become a realistic or competitive business," he wrote Screven on February 2. "There's just too much labor. But in this interim time in Wilcox when no money at all is available and no jobs, it can do something perhaps more important: Teach people how to make money collectively. If a mundane shirt factory or doll factory grew out of this, I'd be more than satisfied."

March 1 came and then: "Dear Tom: I've got good news. Postcards from the wilds of Wilcox report that there are 38 quilts waiting for me to pick up. Counting the ones I left there we have 50 at least. We've also picked up a lot more quilters just by word of mouth." Included in the group was a yellow and black quilt called Tiger Stripe; many originals; and Tom's favorite, for which he paid thirty-eight dollars top bid: a checkerboard quilt of red squares alternating with white polka dots on blue—all on a white border. "At all costs," he loudly proclaimed, "put that lady on making more!"

By March 6: "Dear Francis: We have generated a good deal of excitement. Several people are so anxious they're a bit peeved we won't sell to them now, but we're determined to stage a most exciting auction with as many quilts as possible—and with none of the really special ones taken away."

Near auction time, Screven and Newfield spent many hours preparing the studio, hanging quilts on ladders and rope, draping them on whatever equipment their host would let them touch, and mounting lights to feature favorites. "We had virtually all the quilts hanging on something. It was a tall room and we hung them around the walls so they were all visible."

Auction time came on March 27. As Screven later wrote about it:

Only about 40 people showed up. I put up a pretty
bold front but I was so crestfallen. Yet the people were
really interested. The sympathy for the cause was
high and the people were surprisingly open with their
purse strings. We did have about eight bids from $25
to $45 for people who couldn't come, so that helped;
and at least four people were bidding for at least one
other person.

I feel that the people who were there are a very
valuable core of supporters, maybe more valuable than
they would have been if there had been more people.
Everyone was surprised at the quality of the quilts.
I think many thought they'd be less fine and not really
artistic.

As vengeful as it may be, I feel a certain satisfaction
that the skeptical and disinterested, who would have
loved owning one of the quilts if they'd seen them,
especially at the moderate prices they went for, lost
out and did not get one.

The forty participants purchased forty-two quilts; this left only five. As auctioneer, John Newfield was not as interested in touting the aesthetic value of the quilts as in portraying the humanity of the quilters:

The people at the auction had liberal philosophies
and were interested in the whole process of desegrega-
tion, upper mobility and opportunities for blacks.
They could afford to spend twenty or thirty dollars
for a quilt even if they didn't want one. They had
enough money to make a contribution to a good equal
rights cause and were willing to listen to our
persuasion.

The whole pitch I used was that these quilts were
done by women of sharecropper-type families, all
were black and had very bad economic fates. This was

a way to help those wonderfully talented black women
become self-supporting.

Each quilt had a number and we auctioned them in
sequence. Where the quilt was hanging I would point
out, "This is the quilt here and this is the pattern."
Tom had more intensified stories about the individual
women and quilt-making. Some of them had marvelous names, such as America Irby, Lucy Marie Mingo,
Missouria Pettway, Aolar Mosely, "Mama Willie"
Abrams and Estelle Witherspoon.

And he would mention the place where 'this person'
came from, again with marvelous little names. Then
I would beg the people on to bid. I insisted on starting
bids at twenty dollars.

Because the average quilt price was twenty-seven dollars, supplemented
by a trickling of follow-up contributions, more than $1,100 was forwarded
through Francis Walter to the new Freedom Quilting Bee.

"That auction really got us excited and I was terribly fired up about it,"
declares Screven, now of San Francisco. "The quilts went so easily." So he
and Newfield decided to hold another auction of much grander scale. It took
place on May 24 at the Community Church of New York, a Unitarian-
Universalist denomination on East 35th Street. "We didn't know where to
go or what to do. Somebody said, 'There's this liberal preacher at that church
on 35th Street.' Donald Harrington was a real mover in the early civil rights
movement in New York and his church was one of the true civil rights
leaders. He was amazingly receptive and didn't ask any questions. He said for
us to use his basement hall." Harrington donated his auditorium, the usual
fee being seventy-five dollars.

Screven and Newfield received major help this time from Monica Bayley,
who came aboard by accident. She and her husband, Edwin Bayley, lived in
the apartment directly under the Peter Basch studio. Before that first auction
began, she was coming home from a Sunday walk in Central Park and
noticed a quilt auction sign near the elevator. She owned a collection from
New England and had helped to make some. So she decided to take a look.

As Screven later wrote Father Walter, "She was about the only person we
didn't drag to or at least calculate on being at the auction." When she arrived,
bidding was in progress. But, as far as she could tell, volunteers were few
and the participants were mostly artist friends who had little money for quilts.
She bought a couple and became a volunteer on the same afternoon, for,
when Tom and company decided to hold a second auction, a place was needed
to store more quilts. Mrs. Bayley offered her large, convenient apartment.

This black and white version of the Log Cabin is also called Sunshine and Shadow. Quilts that looked like it were among those sent to the New York auctions. This one never sold because of its lumpy, hand-beaten cotton insides; it is stored in a back room at the Freedom Quilting Bee. (Photo by Nancy Callahan)

She also helped ship boxes of cloth scraps to Alabama. Although she held two jobs, she devoted countless hours to promotion of the second auction.

A woman of great stamina who was full of ideas, Monica Bayley was copy editor for McGraw-Hill art books and correspondent for *Features and News,* a Chicago syndicate. Her husband was vice-president for administration at National Educational Television. He had been the first director of information for John Kennedy's Peace Corps. Both had been journalists at home in Wisconsin.

"I had been interested in the civil rights movement for a long time," Mrs. Bayley explains. "Even in Milwaukee when they had block beautification, I helped in Urban League things. The Freedom Quilting Bee was perfectly natural for me but a different kind of project. The Selma March was such a blow. It made people feel a sense of urgency about trying to help."

Mrs. Bayley drafted a news release for New York City's print media and a public service announcement for local radio and television stations: "Lovers of folk art and good causes are invited to attend the Freedom Quilting Bee benefit auction. Now that Alabama Negroes in Wilcox County finally have the vote, help them to get economic freedom while you help yourself to get an unusual example of folk art."

Once Screven arranged for the second auction location, he saw the need for a promotional poster. Finding a printer who would donate his services was no problem, but recruiting a volunteer designer was impossible. So he did the layout himself. It was a combination of quilt designs printed in primary red on blue for a vibrating effect. "The whole op art phenomenon had been in flower. I hoped a poster of that style would capture attention of those likely to be attracted to the quilts."

His friend George Davis had a connection with a silk-screen printing company, which ran off two hundred copies, each with a strong easel back. "We put that poster all around New York's East Side. Mostly I walked to

Admission ticket and red and blue poster for the second New York quilt auction, 1966. (Courtesy, Monica Bayley, Tom Screven, Will Screven)

QUILTS
AUCTION

COMMUNITY CHURCH of NEW YORK
40 East 35th Street, N.Y.C.
TUESDAY, MAY 24, 1966 · 8:00 P.M.
HAND MADE BY MEMBERS OF THE
FREEDOM QUILTING BEE — WILCOX, ALA.

Door Prizes
Preview – 7:00 P.M.
ADMISSION: $1.00   № 2453
FOR INFORMATION: OR 5-6606

QUILTS
AUCTION
TUESDAY   MAY 24 - 8 PM
THE COMMUNITY CHURCH OF NEW YORK · 40 E 35th STREET
HANDMADE BY MEMBERS   THE FREEDOM QUILTING BEE
WILCOX COUNTY ALABAMA
PREVIEW 7:00 PM   ·   ADMISSION $1.00   DOOR PRIZES
FOR INFORMATION PHONE OR5-6606

stores where I was working. There were a couple across from Blooming-dale's." Mrs. Bayley tried placing posters, but often faced resistance:

Placing posters is interesting to me because of all
the refusals I got from business people. There was
a big car agency near us with a huge showroom and
acres of window space. It's hard to believe the man
wouldn't let me put one in. But just on chance I went
to a Chinese laundry where there was a nice window
with several other promotions. I took one in, the man
said, "Fine," and I put it right in his front window.
    I went home footsore and weary and said to my
husband, "It was discouraging because people wouldn't
let me put signs in their windows, even in places where
I trade. But this Chinese laundryman let me put one in
there." He thought it over and said, "Well, he probably
can't read English." It's ironic.

Because of Newfield's friendship with Howard Thompson, a Mississippi-born writer for *The New York Times,* a promotional paragraph appeared in that newspaper. In addition, the auction producers continued their phone calls to friends and friends of friends.

Late on auction day, when Screven and the group arrived at the church for final preparations, they found a banquet just winding down. Along with a couple of ministers, they cleared tables and washed dishes.

Staged on a Tuesday evening, a preview began at seven and the auction at eight. Admission was one dollar. Volunteers held the individual quilts on a stage during bidding. Screven was auctioneer. More than a hundred people came.

"The bidding was very lively, even extraordinary on a few quilts," Screven points out. "Charles Kriebel, a journalist in men's fashion for *Women's Wear Daily,* bid against a black lady for a quilt that was yellow and aqua. It was an amazing abstract design, as though the quiltmaker had taken almost a segment of one block and blown it up to full size. Maybe it came from a shortage of materials, or maybe they were making them quickly to get them to the city."

The top bid was $70 for an electrifying orange and blue quilt of new cotton called a Churn Dash. Among the others were a couple of black-and-white ones, sold to a city showroom of a furniture company; and a coral-and-blue rendering whose pattern could be perceived as two designs. "Some of the quilts were so original," says Mrs. Bayley, "that they looked like op art. Some of the decorators bought them for wall hangings." The second highest bid was $48 for a Rik-Rak. The lowest prices were $21 and $22.

Most of the participants were middle-aged professionals, in home furnish-

Patterns of optical illusion, such as this series of circles and stars, captured the fancy of New York auction-goers. (Photo by Ted Klitzke; quilt owned by Annetta Contestabile of Switzerland)

ings and the arts. One man came before the auction, contributed $10, and left. Through her secretary, Mayor John Lindsay's wife phoned her regrets to Screven, who had sent her an invitation. Mrs. Bayley had written most all the other major area officeholders. Her only response came from Senator Jacob Javits, who sent a telegram that arrived at the church during the auction.

Those in attendance included Gloria Lawrence, one of the few blacks there and a ranking worker in New York's Democratic party; Jack Harrellton, a writer/editor for *Look* magazine and a friend of Newfield; Lorli Willis, whose husband, Jack Willis, was with National Educational Television; Mrs. Charles Eames, whose husband was a designer with Herman Miller Furniture; favored customers of Screven, who worked with Skidmore, Owings and Merrill architects; and a representative of Lord and Taylor department store.

Stella Chasteen, wife of a New York City artist, bought at least ten quilts, as Screven remembers, "one after another, paying a little higher price." "The names on the quilts were entrancing," adds Mrs. Bayley. "Each quiltmaker would make her own little tags that would have her name, where she was from and the name of the pattern. On one of the tags the pattern name said, 'Don't know.' It was an original quilt and she didn't know what to put down because she had made up the pattern." The average price for a quilt at this auction was $28, a dollar more than at the first one.

So the purchasers carted away their Climbing Vines and Sunburst Stars and used them to warm their beds as well as decorate their living rooms, business showrooms, and office walls as palpable support of a struggle 1,200 miles to the south, where hungry, black, female field hands would be able to reach their full potential.

Midway between the auctions, Screven wrote Francis Walter: "I really feel some of those first quilts should have gone for more, because I don't think the naturalness, fineness and authenticity some of them had will ever be caught again."

Two decades later, the Freedom Quilting Bee is like a butterfly that has left its cocoon. Its contemporary quilts are flawlessly executed in proper, machine-washable polyester. Yet in some New York homes the awkward, rough-hewn pieceworks from the Screven-Newfield auctions are deemed priceless possessions. Awe-inspiring like stained-glass windows, those original Freedom quilts are rare mosaics made with material from a maternity-clothes factory in Linden, a Black Belt town down the way, where Minder Coleman once worked and acquired a mammoth warehouse of scraps from which she donated enough to fill her station wagon; from Hancock's, of Tuscaloosa, where Francis Walter bought bolts of cotton prints with borrowed money; from feed sacks sold in the farm supply stores of Selma and Camden; from blue jeans worn during labors in the field by the husbands and sons of the quilting bee women and by the women themselves; and from the overflowing treasure chest of silk, velvet, brocade, and all the other giveaways from the finest fabric houses in New York.

"The ones made of old jeans were breathtaking," Screven points out. "The pockets were taken off and you could see the pocket patches. It was sad to me. And I've seen many others get as emotional about them as I have." That blue-jean quilts were shipped at all was the result of a woman at a quilters' meeting who approached Father Walter. He later wrote Screven about it. "The old lady asked me, 'Would you buy an overhaul quilt?' I said yes so she scurried home from the church, returning with it later. I'm told only the poorest faced with no scraps at all would normally make such a quilt. I'm asking people to do it now. The denim faded in all possible shades of blue is very attractive."

That one was a Star of Bethlehem, known also as Stable Star. The degrees of worn-out, blue-jean patches of the star were fused with white, feed-sack background. Mrs. Bayley still remembers that quilt:

It was before faded denim was popular but it was beautiful. Tom and I were taken with that quilt and would like to have bought it. But we knew it would bring quite a bit in the auction. Some girl bought it. After the auction she complained about it a little bit. She said, "It's sort of primitive. Maybe I paid too much." I said, "We all would like to have that quilt." So I think she went away satisfied.

At that point Tom turned to me and said, "She doesn't know it but she just bought the whole story of the cotton fields. It's all in that quilt." We had tears in our eyes. It was that impressive.

Days after the auction, Mrs. Bayley opened her apartment to those interested in buying the unauctioned quilts at fixed rates. For a while, she continued to place her own orders with the co-op and give them as wedding presents. She also placed some quilts with educational television stations in Boston and San Francisco, where they were auctioned on the air. But she made other sales: "I used to mail to funny little places such as Coy, Gee's Bend and Alberta at the post office around the corner from where I lived. There was a nice guy in the parcel post window who used to talk to me. He said, 'I'm curious. Is this some project?' I said, 'Yes,' and told him all about it. He had a cottage some place and said, 'I'd like to help.' So I took a couple of quilts to the window and he bought one. It was a Maltese Cross design."

Today Monica and Edwin Bayley live in Berkeley, California. In one of the rooms in their home is a framed poster from an auction long ago. On their antique, king-sized bed is a blue-and-white Wild Goose Chase quilt with feed-sack backing. Made in 1966, it was the first large quilt ever produced by the co-op. Mrs. Bayley had drawn the pattern to her dimensions and sent it down for the women to follow. They also custom-made two twin-sized quilts for her. Each was a mishmash of five-inch-square patches made from cloth scraps Mrs. Bayley had saved from her own sewing projects. The backs were feed sacks. "After we moved to California our house was burglarized. Those two quilts were taken. It was so terrible, I cried. I said, 'I don't care what they took except for my Freedom quilts.' I never could replace them but I still have the big one. I take care of it and it's still very nice."

Tom Screven continued to filter New York fabric samples into Wilcox County until the quilting bee acquired contracts calling for specific materials.

On May 31, 1966, Father Walter received a check from Screven for the sale of more than seventy quilts in the amount of $2,065, netted from New York's second exposure to the black Wilcox quilt market. It was used to pay for washing machines, telephones, front porches, indoor bathrooms, bedroom furniture, clothes, high school graduation rings, and, in at least one instance, college tuition for the great-granddaughter of a slave.

3   *Gee's Bend: The Culture that Shaped the Quilting Bee*

         Francis Walter's first-year register listed 150 quilt-
ers from all parts of Wilcox County as well as a few from neighboring Dallas.
Their addresses were as varied and colorful as Possum Bend, Polk Junction,
Selma, and Coy; Camden, Minter, Hybart, and Hopewell; Gastonburg,
Browns, Alberta, Gee's Bend, and Boiling Springs. Gradually, the activity
settled in Alberta and Gee's Bend, on the northern fringes of the slowly
curving Alabama River.

The Two Albertas

     Twenty-eight miles south of Selma on Alabama Highway 22, which be-
comes Highway 5, is the entrance to sketchily settled Alberta. Barely inside
the Wilcox line, it consists of a few houses, a grocery, service station-grocery,
lounge, cotton gin, post office, and community health center operated in a
converted mobile home. The population is 135.
     The post office was established in 1888 as Alberta Station, then changed
to Alberta in 1894. During its early years, Alberta's claim to fame was a
couple of artesian wells 965 feet deep. Four miles away was Boiling Springs,
a natural curiosity that is still there and once supported a health resort.
Alberta was a thriving sawmill quarter with two cotton gins. Today, farming
and cattle prevail. Many residents find work in Selma, Camden, and elsewhere—except for those employed at the Freedom Quilting Bee, the largest
industry there.
     At Alberta, county Highway 29 heads southeastward, penetrating five or
six miles of almost total wilderness until it reaches the tiny village of Rehobeth, named for a Bible town. It supported a post office during the years

1852–1955. Older people still call it Rehobeth. For the past quarter century, though, the U.S. Postal Service has designated it Route One, Alberta.

Nine miles farther down Highway 29 is the first appearance of Gee's Bend, a 10,000-acre peninsula that dead-ends at the Alabama River as that yellow water body meanders toward Mobile and the Gulf of Mexico. Shaped like an oxbow, Gee's Bend is enclosed on three sides by the river. Its population is 1,050.

The Gee's Bend Factor

From Possum Bend to Boiling Springs, the tradition of all these communities figured strongly in the focus of the Freedom Quilting Bee. They were shared traditions established since the time of slavery. But unlike the others was Gee's Bend, one of the nation's handful of all-black communities and possibly its most isolated settlement. The Gee's Bend heritage would serve as a major factor in this quest for economic independence by black Wilcox women.

Long before Gee's Bend was ever so known, it was Indian land. It is thought that, in the sixteenth century, Spanish explorer Hernando DeSoto visited an Indian village on a creek in this area before he pushed on toward his death in Mississippi. Four hundred years later, "black" people live there who claim Indian blood. Some have Indian surnames. Others have Indian characteristics.

The first recorded white resident to live in the area was Joseph Gee, a planter from Halifax, North Carolina, who bought most of the Bend after he was more than fifty, came in 1816, established a plantation, and named the place for himself. Upon his death, in 1824, he left forty-seven black slaves at his Gee's Bend plantation. Two of his North Carolina nephews, Sterling and Charles Gee, came to Alabama in hopes of inheriting his estate. During the legal maneuverings, Sterling inherited a family estate back home and returned to live there. Charles became manager of the Gee's Bend plantation. Some people say the Bend accommodated a slave-trading operation for the Gees between Alabama and North Carolina.

In 1845 the two Gee brothers owed $29,000 to their relative Mark H. Pettway. As settlement, they gave him Gee's Bend. A year later, Pettway and his family moved there in a caravan with a hundred or more slaves. Except for one cook, the slaves literally walked from North Carolina to Gee's Bend.

The 10,000-acre bottleneck retained "Gee" for its name. But, when the blacks first entered the Bend on its river-rich soil, the last name, indeed, the new identity of each one became "Pettway." It is a name that has prevailed in Wilcox County all these years. Today, if someone from Gee's Bend is named

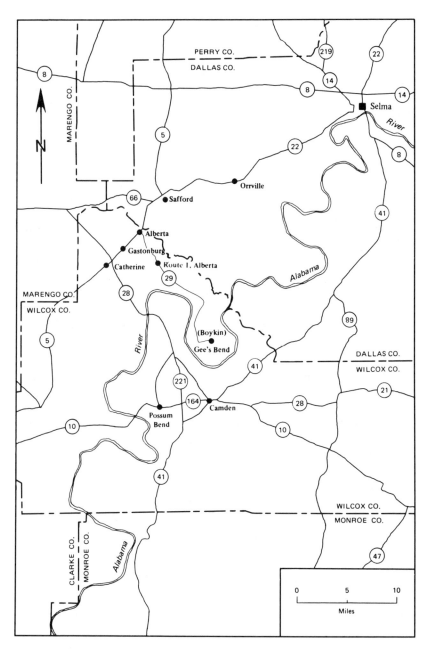

Gee's Bend and environs
along the Alabama River

Pettway, he or she is a descendant or married to a descendant of those Mark Pettway wagon-train slaves who walked from North Carolina.

The majority of current Gee's Benders share that Pettway heritage because the isolation caused by the eccentric land shape closed in by water on three sides prevented insiders from leaving, and kept outsiders from coming in. As a result, human life there for the past 140 years has involved an almost pure breed of people.

Mark Pettway emerged as one of the most successful planters in Wilcox County. Although a few white Wilcox farmers produced a modest number of cotton bales on their own, he followed the regional custom whereby the large, successful plantation owners depended on a thriving network of slaves to make a financial success of the land. For Pettway, Gee's Bend was a dukedom in the vast Southern cotton empire.

Abraham Lincoln's Emancipation Proclamation freed from slavery the black Pettways of Gee's Bend, but they remained on the bulb-like peninsula as though they were rooted in the soil. They lived in the same quarter shacks as always, tilling the same plots of earth. After emancipation, however, they mostly farmed as tenants or sharecroppers.

Members of the Pettway family held the land until 1895, when they sold their 4,000 acres and left. For the first time in half a century, no white Pettways lived at Gee's Bend. But reminders of the family were numerous, including the "big house," that spacious dwelling called Sandy Hill, where the family had lived, and a whole community of blacks who called themselves Pettway—and who stayed behind.

In 1900 a new family destined for longtime ownership entered Gee's Bend's history: the VandeGraaffs, of Tuscaloosa. Attorney Adrian Sebastian VandeGraaff acquired the land the Pettways had sold to others, then added 3,000 more acres. Until 1937, when the VandeGraaffs sold all the property to the U.S. government, they were a family of absentee landlords that caused no major changes for the tenant Pettways of Gee's Bend.

For the first sixteen years of VandeGraaff ownership, a family uncle lived at Sandy Hill as supervisor. After his death, other white, family-appointed overseers were in charge, but the VandeGraaffs made only occasional visits.

All the while, the Pettways continued to plow the furrows, pay their rent—when they could—and obtain advanced credit on supplies, when necessary, from merchants in Alberta, Camden, or Mobile. Their isolation continued, too, for, though the Bend was a mere five to seven miles from the county seat of Camden, the two were separated by a bridgeless Alabama River. A makeshift and not-so-safe ferry carried Benders into town and back when weather permitted, but it was not ideal. An alternative was the eighteen-mile land route on the narrow dirt road from Gee's Bend to Alberta, which was clouded with dust in dry weather and covered with mud in seasons of wetness; then by state highway to Catherine and a bridge crossing the river for the

Camden trek. Just one way, it was more than forty miles. The other option was to stay put.

As the Reverend Renwick C. Kennedy wrote in the *Christian Century* on September 1, 1937, "There is nothing exactly like Gee's Bend anywhere else in the United States." At that time pastor of a Camden Presbyterian church, he was the first person to call national attention to the area by writing stories for the *Christian Century* during the 1930s. He stated, "Gee's Bend represents not merely a geographical configuration drawn by the yellow pencil of the river. Gee's Bend represents another civilization. Gee's Bend is an Alabama Africa. There is no more concentrated and racially exclusive Negro population in any rural community in the South than in Gee's Bend." His descriptions of the Bend portray a people staunchly independent, self-sustaining, original, resourceful, and dedicated to their faith in God.

The Depression Hits Gee's Bend

Although Gee's Benders had never heard of Wall Street—a world away from their primitive fields—the 1929 stock market collapse brought severe change to their lush pouch of cotton and corn for the first time since Joseph Gee had come to carve out his plantation more than a century before.

Because of the Great Depression, the price of cotton fell to five cents a pound. When the Gee's Bend farmers took their crop to Camden to cover the debts they owed the merchant who had advanced them credit, the price was too low to cover those debts. So the merchant stored the cotton in his warehouse in hopes of better times. He continued to advance them credit for the next three years, but obtained chattel liens on the possessions of sixty families. He was the only one to maintain records of the entire three-year system of business.

In the summer of 1932, the merchant died. That autumn, his widow foreclosed on the Benders who owed her husband's estate. Seemingly from out of nowhere, her representatives suddenly trooped off the ferry on the large loop of land. Riding on horseback and wearing pistols on their hips, they took away everything not nailed down. The action is "liquidation" in legal language. In Gee's Bend, it was the beginning of starvation. As though the intruders were vultures disposing of their prey, they brought along wagons manned by blacks from across the river and picked the place clean.

Reverend Kennedy described how it affected one of the tenants on the bottom land in *Christian Century* on November 14, 1934: "They took his corn and potatoes, his chickens, his hogs, his plows and tools and wagon, they cut his sugar cane that was ready for the mill, they loaded his cows and tied his two mules to the rear of a wagon, and then passed on to the next family."

Like a parade, the wagonsful of liquidated goods from 68 households and more than 300 people were ushered back to the ferry, put on board, and floated to who knows where. At least they no longer had any debts. But, except for a few handsful of food and other articles stashed in leaf-covered ditches and livestock hidden in swamps, they no longer possessed anything else, either: no produce, no animals, no fowl, no wagons, no farm implements, no records of cotton stored in a Camden warehouse, no future.

Thanks to the VandeGraaffs, who were otherwise helpless in the situation, the land was rent-free. Wild plums and nuts, though not very filling, became prime food sources, along with game and fish as well as occasional beef from nearby white planters. Had it not been for the Red Cross, which provided flour, meat, and meal, during the winter of 1932–33, the people of Gee's Bend would have starved to death. W. J. (Bill) Jones, of Oak Hill, retired Wilcox County school superintendent, was Red Cross campaign manager then and assisted in rendering aid. "He just cleaned 'em out," Jones says of the merchant's heirs. "He sent wagons over there, just one after the other, and took what cotton they made, and corn, hay, potatoes and molasses. Practically all their produce. They were left starving to death. It's a picture you couldn't overdraw."

With National Guard help, foodstuffs were shipped from Birmingham to the Camden armory, then ferried to Gee's Bend to those stranded on that side of the river or distributed at the armory to any people who could cross over. The Red Cross also sent shoes. Jones and his late wife paid visits to the homes of the Gee's Bend people with a county welfare worker: "Just to describe what a terrible situation it was, on one occasion the welfare worker saw a carcass on the table and thought sure it was a dog. You just can't imagine the horror of it. Starvation was terrific."

Gee's Bend Becomes a Federal Guinea Pig

During the ensuing years, state and federal agencies stamped their presence on Gee's Bend with projects designed to pull the people to their feet. In 1935 that place and others like it were discovered by the most powerful aid agent in the country: Franklin D. Roosevelt. Thus, that cutoff collection of Pettways was given the glad hand of welcome into the New Deal. Their hundred-year-old homeland became the object of a federal drawing board of social ideas; the people became the experiments to put those ideas into practice.

In 1935 the president, through executive order, tailored a new federal agency, the Resettlement Administration, to fight chronic rural poverty. Two years later, it became part of Roosevelt's Farm Security Administration (FSA), and the Gee's Bend farmers became clients of Uncle Sam. In came plows, oxen, seed, feed, and a raft of other handouts and promises for more. In came the Washington folks, including FSA's caring, compassionate director, Dr. Will Alexander, to mix with the people. In came brief-cased officials to poll and politick the down-and-out. In came government planners to blue-print a model community as well as builders to carry that model to fruition. And in poured federal money, by the wagonload, it seemed.

By 1937 the VandeGraaffs had sold their cul-de-sac outpost to the statewide branch of Farm Security, the Alabama Rural Rehabilitation Corporation. Then the New Deal organized a cooperative farming association, Gee's Bend Farms, Inc., known locally as "the project" and at the White House as the darling of the FSA. From off the drawing board came a hundred new farms sized from 60 to 100 acres. Each had a new home, painted, screened, and topped with a leakless roof; a barn, chicken house, smokehouse, outdoor water pump, sanitary outdoor privy, fenced-in garden, and cast-iron cook stove, a first for many; and "precious" (pressure) cookers and other symbols of a higher level of life. Project members bought the homesteads with generous government loans and worked the farms on a cooperative basis, renting the crop fields from the government.

As one of the Pettways was quoted thirty years later in the Selma Project *Newsletter* on January 12, 1968, "We got $1200 loans, three percent interest and 40 years to pay." The government also loaned the Gee's Bend Project money to erect a cooperative store and cotton gin. And, compliments of Washington, like mushrooms, up sprang a blacksmith shop, gristmill, ware-house, health clinic, grammar school and nursery school staffed with teachers, a co-op office, canning centers, weaving looms and even a federally funded church doubling as a community center. A full-time nurse ministered to the people's health and taught health courses, and two physicians appeared at regular intervals. Also available were a home economist and experts on how to farm. Through purchase of cooperative memberships, Bend farmers could buy from the co-op store, use the gin and mill, work with the co-op's farm equipment and reap profits collectively obtained.

By mid-1940 construction was complete, and well-documented, for a spirited channel of government information churned out Farm Security stories for newspapers, magazines, radio programs, and addresses by public servants. A rare and talented team of federal photographers was given free-dom to capture with the camera the lives affected by Farm Security and the settings where resettlement took place. Thus, two of the nation's most able young photographers, Arthur Rothstein and Marion Post Wolcott, who went on to distinguished careers, produced more than 150 shots in this picturesque stretch of backcountry. In scenes of maypole dances, clinical exams, quilt-making, and plowing in the fields, the faces of Gee's Bend were flashed across America—classical portraits all.

The federal government did not stay in Gee's Bend as long as the white Pettways or the VandeGraaffs. In 1945 Congress abolished the Farm Security

This Gee's Bend woman and children working on a quilt were photo-graphed by Arthur Roth-stein for the Farm Secu-rity Administration in April 1937. (Courtesy, Library of Congress)

Administration, which was forced to liquidate its cooperative farms. But a new agency took form as the Farmers Home Administration (FHA), which made it possible for co-op members deemed capable of running farms to buy the land with long-term government loans.

By 1947 almost all members of Gee's Bend Farms, Inc., were buying their farms. Since 1846, it had been the same fertile soil cultivated by the same sets of hands, or at least by the heirs of those worn-to-the-bone fingers. Some of them say they bought the land, then bought it again, then again, and again: first as slaves, then as tenants, next as test-tube members of a co-op, and finally as qualified individuals fulfilling a bargain with one more government group.

In 1949 "Gee's Bend, Alabama" was no more. A post office was established in the community and somebody from somewhere named it "Boykin," after Mobile Congressman Frank Boykin, who, as far as anyone knows, had never set foot on the place. Yet, to the rock-hard residents, "Gee's Bend" will be forever. As they see it, the government was able to force a community name change, but it has no power so strong as to dent the time-enduring character of the people.

In 1962 Congress passed more legislation affecting "Boykin." A lock and dam was authorized for Miller's Ferry, just down the river. The word was that, when the dam was activated, its backwaters would turn a third of Gee's Bend into a lake. And what farmer, especially the breed from Boykin, would want to watch his land disappear, even for federally promised "flood money"?

Later came the fight for civil rights, involving boycotts, marches and Martin Luther King, trips to jail, trips to register to vote, and, at long last, trips to the polls. Such was this 10,000-acre tract by the time one of God's civil rights workers began going door to door, giving $10 bills for patchwork quilts.

The story had been different in other parts of the county, where land evictions—what first had brought Francis Walter into Wilcox County—were all too prevalent. With a few exceptions, the Gee's Benders were not evicted because they owned their land. Their homes were havens for uprooted friends and families down the way.

They would live to see their own land loss, though, in 1968, when the switch would be turned on at Miller's Ferry Lock and Dam. A third of their land would be impounded, taken away. Even the ferry, unpredictable as it was, would find the shallow new waters impossible to tread and seek refuge a county down from Wilcox. Deputy sheriff Willie Q. Pettway, owner of 66 acres of Gee's Bend farmland, lost all except 12½ acres, and one day would comment, "All I can do is sit here and look at a lake."

Despite the uniqueness of Gee's Bend, its women shared many things in common with the women from the Albertas and elsewhere who became the Freedom Quilting Bee. Away from the rest of the world, an all-black quilting tradition was born as well as bred in Gee's Bend and spilled into the souls of those who lived nearby.

A Modern Perspective on the Gee's Bend Tradition

When the Freedom Quilting Bee was organized, a close observer of its quilting tradition was Elizabeth M. Walter, who was then married to the priest who founded the folk art co-op. Born in Decatur, she attended The University of Alabama during the 1950s, received a degree from Florence

State University (now the University of North Alabama), then went to New York, where she worked in publishing as a copy editor and book jacket designer. Later she married Francis Walter. In 1966, when the co-op was formed, she was working toward her master's degree in painting. Eventually, she earned her doctorate.

In talking to the quilters, Mrs. Walter learned that they acquired their sewing supplies from traveling salesmen who came through in station wagons and converted buses. For many, the rolling store was their only source of supplies because they rarely went to town. "In 1966, these were isolated people not only in a rural setting but without access to any normal cultural influences of the 1960s except television, and just about every cabin of a Freedom Quilting Bee member had a television."

Mostly, they were self-sufficient farmers. To purchase merchandise not reaped from the soil, they made occasional, "big" trips to Selma. For their medical needs, they infrequently went to the doctor in Grove Hill, a town to the south. But their sewing supplies were procured from peddlers. Mrs. Walter continues:

And the peddlers didn't have a wide selection. The women would place their orders and the next time the peddler came around—a week or two weeks later—he would bring the material.

The women were restricted severely by their raw materials—cotton fabric, cotton batting and backing, left over, too, from scraps, because everybody also made their own clothing.

So the earliest quilts were uneven. There were some outstanding patterns with poor, cheap cotton, but not made for sale or display. They were functional objects created to keep human beings warm on corn husk mattresses covered with flour sack muslin sheets. And if you've ever slept on a corn husk mattress, it has to be the most uncomfortable thing on which you've ever slept, particularly below freezing. They would load as many as five to ten quilts on top of these beds just to stay warm.

So when Francis admired those quilts on the fences and decided to buy, the people were hesitant. What would he have wanted them for except to keep warm.

While the Bee was new, Mrs. Walter acquired a couple of quilts that tell the story not only of the Gee's Bend/Alberta quilting heritage, but also of the formative period of the co-op. One is a deep-blue-green and brown creation of abstract geometry. Plagued with poor workmanship, it has no pattern or consistency about its stitching. As she says:

I do not know who made the quilt but the woman
was restricted because she only had white thread. She
didn't even have the option of using thread of another
color. The quilt was made by an unskilled quilter who
did it as a functional piece with no intent of it ever
being displayed as a model of craftsmanship and
purpose.

But the longer you look at the design, the longer
you wish it had been in other contrasting colors, the
more you realize what an extraordinarily beautiful
piece of geometry it is.

Dr. Walter does not know the quilt's name. It probably is a variation on
Bricklayer or Courthouse Steps. To her, it is the mirror image of a tree. Its
pattern evokes all sorts of imagery. It is like two angular brown trees joined
at the tops, in a pool of blue-green water. It also has an Egyptian aura: two
lotus blossoms joined at their widest angles, or two step pyramids connected
by a bridge. Dr. Walter points out:

A two-dimensional work of art is based on color
and design. This quilt is lacking in color sense but it
has exquisite design. I have an affection for this ugly
old quilt because I am attracted to geometrical abstrac-
tion, and its severity has great appeal to me. It is logi-
cal, orderly, and has a classical simplicity I never found
in another quilt. It is unique in its serenity. To my
knowledge, this pattern never was repeated. Nor have
I ever seen it in a book.

Another feature about this quilt was rarely if ever
repeated: It was backed with white flannel. The majority were backed with cotton muslin or some plain
cotton piece. So it's a warm, soft quilt, wonderful to
raise babies on.

This was the orphan quilt. I took it to my heart and
treasured it all these years because it represents something lost immediately in the commercialization of the
Freedom Quilting Bee. Over the years, it has gained
in importance to me as a design. It has bubblegum on
it now. When I took it to be cleaned, it was the talk
of the drycleaners. It is a singular expression of the
human spirit of a woman who prevailed under adverse
circumstances.

As Elizabeth Walter saw those precommercial quilting bee patchworks,
the craftsmanship was inconsistent and the needlework varied enormously.
The quilts lacked color sophistication, possibly determined more by their

supplies than the quilters' desires. They were not designed for sale, but to please the maker.

Regardless of drawbacks, the quilts had qualities that made them outstanding and different from those produced by other cultures. According to Dr. Walter:

> What distinguished Gee's Bend quilts from all other American quilts I had ever seen was their bold patterns. They had self-confidence. They were aggressive patterns.
>
> What grabbed initially was the boldness, the aggressiveness, the assertive patterns so different from white Appalachian quilts that are tight, sometimes tedious and seem introverted. These were extroverted quilts. The contrast was evident immediately. The Gee's Bend quilts reminded me of the school of hard-edge geometry, painters such as Frank Stella and Barnett Newman. They did not conform readily to anything in traditional art other than paintings.
>
> Something about the quilt tradition seems to have allowed these women to develop their exclusive, personal pattern style. They had so little influence from outside that their quilting tradition was unique to that isolated bend of the Alabama River, in a society dating back to early nineteenth century. When the slaves were brought in, they were isolated on the plantations. If they needed quilts to warm themselves, they had available only what patterns were given to them. Perhaps they had no notion of any others.

This quilting process had probably begun in 1846, if not before. And, all the while, there was an absence of white influence and white dominance different from any other black community in Alabama. Dr. Walter believes the setting gave the blacks of Gee's Bend self-confidence and aggressiveness that came to be manifested in their quiltmaking. "It is my feeling—without historical evidence—that Roosevelt was able to go into Gee's Bend for this very reason. They had a highly articulate, competent, and well-organized black society. He knew that Resettlement could succeed in Gee's Bend."

Dr. Walter saw a deep parallel between the cooperative movement in which she had become involved and the Gee's Bend project of three decades earlier. She knew she was part of history in the making. "They had historical background on which to base this new effort. I'm enough of a historian to have seen that continuity, and I felt it strongly."

Thus was the status in early 1966 of quiltmaking in the river bend when Father Walter began to survey the bedrooms, closets, clotheslines, and fences for quilts with market potential.

Bridging Tradition with Commerce

"Everybody had their own sense of design we did not want to destroy," Dr. Walter contends. "The one thing we could change that would improve the quality of the quilts in a way that seemed least to adulterate the purity of the originals was to give the women better cotton and nice material." So Mrs. Walter drove to Birmingham, to a seconds and surplus warehouse of Alabama Mills. It was a huge, inexpensive outlet for the cotton mills of East Alabama. She was accompanied by William Hood, former resident of Birmingham and friend of the Walters who taught art at Oberlin College in Ohio. Using $100 from early quilt sales, they bought bolts of high-grade cotton fabrics with appealing, modern colors and potentially beautiful combinations. She took the materials to the quilters and gave them possibly their first chance ever to select fabrics they wanted, no strings attached.

"The women were ecstatic," Dr. Walter reflects. "They were like hens plucking over baby chicks. 'Looooooook at this. Wooooooooo.' They wanted three yards of this and five of that. It was one of the happiest moments I have ever had, to give somebody something to work with they had never seen even in their wildest imagination. So instantly, the quality of the quilts just skyrocketed." She also acquired sample swatches, swatchbooks, and drapery material from Indurall Paint Company, of Birmingham, owned by Dr. Hood's father. "And we began collecting scraps from our families and wherever we could get them because buying material was expensive and would have cut into the co-op's cost margin."

Dr. Walter's second quilt, a random patch design, was made from those Birmingham cloth bolts. It is a series of pink solids on a field of orange and yellow printed fabric, backed with muslin. The quilt should have been all squares, but is spliced with occasional rectangles. "It is not well-made because the pattern is inarticulate and not systematic. A random pattern such as this one did not have high salability, because what went first were the identifiable patterns, even though the colors were kind of hippie."

The quilt is not a rectangle but a square, so it is not the proper size for a bed. Most of the pink material is shaped in crosses. "If you read the field as the printed fabric and the motif as the pink cross, then the crosses jump at you. There are nine crosses and these odd blocks. That's why you can't follow scheme. The pattern does not work with the choice of material. But she had only two pieces of material, only the pink and the print. And this pattern would function only if she had three choices. But rather than going back to the Bee and getting the third color, she used what she had."

When the quilt was turned in, it was not standard, rectangular shape. "That was another problem," states Dr. Walter. "Initially, how do you standardize a quilt when you don't know what you're doing and you've never done it before? I got the Sears, Roebuck Catalog, opened it to sheet and bedspread sizes, wrote them on a piece of paper and gave them to Francis to send to Wilcox County. I said, 'Make the quilts this size,' at least 72 inches, to go to the size of the sheet. It was three years at least before the sizes were predictable."

Dr. Walter learned that the quilters were not only basically illiterate but had no tape measures:

> When you're making a quilt in an isolated, piney-
> woods cabin and you have a certain amount of mate-
> rial, you work with what you have. So this one came
> out square. It slides off the bed and never does tuck in,
> but the co-op bought it from the woman. I have it
> because nobody would buy it. The size was wrong,
> the pattern not readable, and it was thought to be too
> loud and garish. We wanted them more subdued and
> aesthetic. It has worn down over the years and is not as
> raucous as it was. I call it my Happy Quilt. It has worn
> well and I never tire of it.

Engaged full time in graduate studies, Elizabeth Walter was not a daily contributor to the Freedom Quilting Bee. But, as a woman of multiple skills, she was called on to meet a number of its challenges. "I saw myself within an historical event simply as one of the actors who, with a liberal bent, wanted to do the right thing as an Alabamian. I did it because I wanted to help. I was the crisis person, the last back-up person. I always took up the slack."

Mrs. Walter ultimately received her doctorate in art history from the University of Georgia, is now head of the art department at the University of North Alabama, and lives in Florence.

4

The
Quilting Bee
Obtains
Professional Help

In early 1966, while Tom Screven and friends were collecting fabrics and conducting auctions in New York, events were taking place in Wilcox County that would lead to organizing a professional business. Led by Minder Coleman, workers met in homes, made quilts, and provided training sessions for those less experienced.

Then there appeared one day in Francis Walter's mailbox a letter dated March 7 from Route One, Alberta, inquiring about the quilting program. Its author was Estelle Witherspoon, a short, ample black woman who was fifty years of age. As Father Walter came to learn, she and her husband, Eugene, were esteemed by their neighbors as the black community's most respected couple. A zesty, good-natured woman who possessed charm, leadership, and ingenious common sense, she had more formal education than most blacks of her time and place. She had been through the ninth grade—as far as one of her race could go, then had repeated the grade three more years. She was a fourth-generation quilter whose talents with needle and thread had been honed since childhood. As she recalls:

There was a friend of mine down to Boykin named Nellie Young. She called me and asked did I see this preacher going around buying quilts. I told her, "No, I didn't see him." She said, "Well, I'm going to give you his address. You write him."

So I wrote him a letter and asked him whenever he's back in Alberta to come back by my house. I'd like to talk to him. So he did, and we talked about what we thought would be best for us to do about organizing ourselves to get these quilts sold.

On April 2 the Freedom Quilting Bee was legally incorporated as a nonprofit cooperative association under state law. Officers listed were Estelle

Witherspoon, president; Minder Coleman, vice-president; Addie Nicholson, secretary; and Mattie Ross, treasurer. Chairman of the board was Callie Young.

Mrs. Witherspoon would blossom as the prime force sustaining the operation, and would rise to the front ranks of the American co-op movement. But first, Father Walter, Mrs. Witherspoon, and other leaders believed that, if the cooperative was ever to achieve a firm footing, it needed a professional manager.

The First Professional Manager

From the Southern Regional Council the Freedom Quilting Bee obtained a grant to support such a person for three months. She was Lois Deslonde (pronounced *de*LONDE), a young black woman who had been born in New Orleans and educated at Louisiana State University in Baton Rouge, where she earned a degree in home economics. Only weeks before coming to the Bee, she had been in South America, helping to organize a handcraft cooperative among the Indians. Recommended by the National Catholic Conference for Inter-racial Justice, she belonged to the Roman Catholic lay community, Caritas, in New Orleans, a group of dedicated women who took the vows of poverty, chastity, and obedience—not to be confused with the Roman Catholic relief organization of the same name.

On loan from Caritas, she arrived from New Orleans at the Tuscaloosa train depot on June 6, skilled in arts and crafts, experienced through her religious community with handcraft guilds, and loaded with equipment to facilitate her duties. By the time of her coming, the cooperative had swelled from 60 members to 125 and quilts were selling for an average of twenty dollars.

Making her home with the Witherspoons, Miss Deslonde kept books and made contact with those who could promote and market the quilters' wares. She gave sewing sessions to improve members' skills. She taught them to make many handcraft objects, matching members with talents. She formulated guidelines for quality control. She discovered and brought forth a gold mine of creative ability as well as ingenuity and a new spirit of dignity in individual accomplishment.

Making her rounds in a 1951 celery-green, jeep panel truck bought by the co-op for $150 plus $51 for a new clutch, the new manager traveled the whole of Wilcox, running nightly workshops after the women had completed their days chopping cotton, thinning corn, and harvesting squash and cucumbers. Unsure of the territory, "the jeep lady" was often stopped by waving children whose mothers had posted them as sentinels awaiting her arrival.

Under Lois Deslonde, the co-op produced eyeglass cases, potholders, aprons, and *TV Guide* covers—all done in crewel work of flowers and fruit. Corn husk doormats and white oak baskets were fabricated from natural materials near at hand; felt Christmas tree ornaments were embroidered. When a white man, a potter, joined the cooperative on a temporary basis, the stock was broadened with pitchers, churns, crocks, and dinnerware. Then, while digging through her chest, one member discovered an old sunbonnet, or "pore" bonnet. So the Freedom Quilting Bee went into the sunbonnet business, offering little girls and ladies sizes for beachwear and gardening. And, for the first time, customers could order quilts in a specific size, design, and color.

Miss Deslonde was touched by the pride shown by her pupils. "Upon entering one of their homes," she once wrote, "one is sure to find a piece of stitchery or a new quilt pattern tacked to the wall. Because the ladies are tired from working all day in the field, we try to limit classes to an hour and a half, but sometimes their enthusiasm plays havoc with the schedule."

The very attendance of these women at those gatherings after strenuous hours of labor was indicative of their faith in the co-op's potential. At one of the early sessions in the home of Gee's Bender Mattie Ross, twenty-five women were present. Work was almost impossible because of the lack of sitting room. "Next time I go to Gee's Bend," the manager wrote Father Walter in Tuscaloosa, "we'll break up into smaller groups. Meetings will be in five different homes."

The priest stresses Miss Deslonde's ingenuity:

One of her ways of working with people was to make almost everything a game. There was lot of socializing to try to get the women to express themselves artistically. She realized that if she just walked in and told people to start designing, they wouldn't do it. So she would have "tea parties."

They would have games and she would have made some little prize. Once, she passed out pencils and paper and said, "I want everyone to draw an animal." She didn't say why but she was trying to get some of their original work to design small products needed to sell in craft shops.

The Famous Freedom Hoot Owl

During that session, Maggie McCloud McMillian, of Route One, Alberta, sketched a hoot owl, a creature highly visible on the local fence posts and by the creek where she washed her clothes. Her design was used by the quilting bee as the face of countless hoot owl potholders for at least those first four years. Now retired, Mrs. McMillian thinks she made two hundred or more. "Looked like a hoot owl. Big eyes and trimmin' around it. I worked the whole thing with thread," she states as she recalls that summer. "The potholder was a gray color. I used red thread, white eyes and black for the eyeball. I tried to make it show up like an owl sittin' on a limb."

The potholders were made in a variety of colors. Their sale price was $1.50 each. Today they are collectors' items. As Father Walter says:

> It was interesting to watch all the hoot owls gathered at the Witherspoons to be packed and sent to all the stores. I could pick one up and say, "Mattie So-and-So made this one. These are hers." That's what makes handcraft production attractive, but it's also what drives marketing people crazy. If somebody says, "I want one like this one," the market can't make that guarantee. Or if they take one home and wash it, the potholder might run because the woman used a fabric that happened to be in her house.
>
> As each woman would do the potholder, the owl went through many transformations. They all had the little feathers but each would be slightly different. They would be squint-eyed, cross-eyed or with round pupils, skinny, fat or lopsided. I thought it was probably the best thing they ever did.

During Father Walter's first months with the SIP, he received a letter from Leslie DeMane, a high school student from Greenwich, Connecticut. She wanted to come to Alabama and work in the civil rights movement. With her parents' blessings and Father Walter's invitation, she arrived in mid-July to serve as an assistant to Miss Deslonde. She lived until summer's end in the home of Callie Young.

On August 6 at a park near Camden, the Bee conducted a quilt fair featuring a quilt contest, exhibit, and sale. One of the most talked-about competition entries was by Mattie Matthews, an independent quiltmaker, whose quilt portrayed four huge donkeys.

On the evening of August 24, Estelle Witherspoon staged in her home a surprise birthday party for Miss Deslonde. More than thirty people came, though most had worked long hours that day picking cotton, preparing supper, and cleaning up for a social. According to Father Walter, who made written note of her gifts after the party, Miss Deslonde received $11 in one-dollar bills in envelopes penciled with "Happy Birthday," three or four cakes, a sack of raw peanuts, two pairs of stockings, a pair of pillow slips saying "His" and "Hers," a jar of peaches, a jar of tomatoes, a sack of muscadines, a shoebox containing half a fried chicken, a one-serving box of N Corn Cereal, a patty of mashed lye hominy, and a lemon meringue pie.

Not long after she joined the quilting bee, Miss Deslonde overheard an interesting comment; a member was describing herself to her young daughter: "Your mother could have been a wonderful woman if she had had the opportunity to get an education." Lois wrote about the incident months later back in New Orleans. "This woman was not only speaking for herself but for all the other people who have not been given a chance to overcome poverty."

Now Mrs. George Ruth, Jr., of Rosharon, Texas, Lois Deslonde is remembered for molding among the quilters an exhilaration of sisterhood and solidarity. She was also an agent through which members marched a step upward from the deep-rooted demon of poverty.

5   *Freedom Sparks the "Patchwork Look"*

Less than a year after the Freedom Quilting Bee was chartered, it received its first contract with a New York City interior design firm and attracted major attention in Eastern art circles. What resulted was a national rebirth of interest in patchwork. Most of this early notice came from an unlikely chain of friendships.

Planting the seed for the contract was Monica Bayley, who had helped Tom Screven with the auctions. Her friend Doris O'Donnell was with the U.S. government in Morocco. Ms. O'Donnell had the ability to put the proper people in touch with one another. One such person was her friend Diana Vreeland, editor-in-chief of *Vogue* magazine, who in turn was a friend of Sister Parish, whose decorating company, Parish-Hadley, Inc., was among the most elite in New York.

O'Donnell Paves the Way for Parish Contract

In July 1966 Doris O'Donnell entered the life of the quilting bee and made a mammoth impact on its future. Although Monica Bayley triggered her involvement, she first learned of the co-op in Morocco, where she had been with the American Embassy. While there she was borrowed by the Agency for International Development (AID) to work with one of its consultants, Stanley Selengut, to stimulate the production of Moroccan handcrafts for export. She ultimately was hired away from the government by Selengut, whose business was native crafts and who was later to be associated with the Bee.

Before returning to the states and her new role, Ms. O'Donnell went to Rome to visit friends, among whom was writer/artist Eugene Walter, who, as it turned out, had grown up in Mobile, Alabama, and was the only first

50

cousin of Francis Walter. "In my conversation with Eugene," reports Doris O'Donnell, "I told him what I was going to be doing and he said, 'Drop everything and go straight to Alabama and see my cousin, Francis Walter, and do something about the Freedom Quilting Bee.' "

Ms. O'Donnell then asked her new employer to write Eugene Walter's cousin, which he did: "Francis Walter, Selma, Alabama." The letter was never delivered, but when Ms. O'Donnell came back to New York, the subject was revived by Monica Bayley, who told her about the volunteer work she had been doing for a quilting bee in Alabama.

At the same time, Father Walter's SIP was in grave financial difficulty. To save its life, he flew to New York for fund-raising. "At the moment, the Selma Inter-religious Project is flat broke," he would be quoted in an August column by syndicated writer Inez Robb. "The trouble is that too many white people believe that the voting rights bill solved everything, and that there is no need for additional financial support. Nothing could be farther from the truth. . . . I have a house and a wife, and no pay check so far this month."

On July 27 Father Walter, Tom Screven, and a few others met in New York with Doris O'Donnell. Through her auspices, Ms. O'Donnell and Father Walter met the next day with her boss, Stanley Selengut, and his toy designer, Sara Stein. Destined to become a key to the quilting bee's marketing approach, the crafts entrepreneur promised to send down toys for the quilters to fabricate so he could assess their potential in his operation.

Later in the day, Ms. O'Donnell arranged an interview for Father Walter with Inez Robb. The result was a nationally run column describing the Freedom Quilting Bee—the group's first cross-country publicity. By the 30th, Father Walter was in Washington telling his story to Ms. O'Donnell's mother and stepfather: Doris Fleeson, the respected capital journalist and first woman to become a syndicated political columnist in this country; and Dan Kimball, retired secretary of the navy, former president of Aerojet-General, and at that time chairman of the company's executive board. Kimball made two promises: he would buy a hundred quilts for his factory store in Sacramento, and he would send two representatives to the Black Belt to study and recommend possibilities for economic development.

Within a month, fifty quilts were on their way to California. Meantime, Ms. O'Donnell had put Father Walter in touch with more figures who could promote his co-op: Washington journalist Mary McGrory; Daniel Schorr, the CBS correspondent; and Norman Sherman, press secretary to Vice-President Hubert Humphrey.

Father Walter flew back to Alabama, but Ms. O'Donnell continued to arouse interest in the quilters within her realm of acquaintances. She talked to Sally Victor, a New York City milliner whose hat designs possibly could be produced by Freedom—"bonnets for rain or shine." Ms. O'Donnell gave one of the quilts, a black-and-white Chestnut Bud by Lucy Marie Mingo, of

Gee's Bend, to Diana Vreeland, with whom she had worked on a promotion in Morocco. "She thought it was sensational," recalls Ms. O'Donnell. "When I mentioned the Freedom Quilting Bee, she said, 'Doris, do you believe in the occult?' She had dictated a memo that very day to the effect that American handcrafts are the coming thing in the fashion world. She was most anxious to be helpful. She got in touch with Sister Parish, rang me up and said, 'I think we might be able to put something together.'"

Ms. O'Donnell also placed quilt orders with the Bee for several of her New York friends. Bobby Short, the noted black singer/pianist, bought a black-and-white Monkey Wrench. Hugh Auchincloss, the writer, purchased a Tree of Life in dark blue on robin's egg blue. Douglas Newton, director of the Museum of Primitive Arts, acquired a king-sized quilt in red, white, and yellow.

Ms. O'Donnell visited a New York clothing manufacturer, Milton Solomon, and talked him into sending nine winter coats valued at $500 to the rural Alabama quilting community. But a moral question emerged: how does one distribute nine coats among 150 poor people? The co-op officers found a solution: the coats were given to the first ones who produced a certain number of quilts up to standard by a set deadline.

As Francis Walter wrote Solomon:

> We have found that encouragement, appreciation
> and esteem go a lot farther in encouraging fine crafts-
> manship than any amount of money. Money to tenant
> farmers is not completely pleasant to receive. It carries
> overtones of being that which symbolizes their bond-
> age and exploitation. Indeed, until the Freedom Quilt-
> ing Bee began marketing quilts outside Alabama, the
> women around Selma had no idea theirs was a craft
> worthy of appreciation by folk artists or interior deco-
> rators. It was what you did to keep warm if you were
> poor.

By October, Ms. O'Donnell was in Wilcox County, making the quilters aware of the work quality expected of them in New York commerce and getting a feel for the culture behind their newborn industry. Late on the first evening of her stay, members came to the Witherspoon home from their day in the fields to meet their New York visitor:

> I remember Mrs. Witherspoon said, "We will begin
> our meeting in the usual way with a song," and the
> women sang a hymn. Then Dan Harrell said a prayer.
> At that point I was to explain why I was there. It was
> so difficult. Here I was looking at those hard-working

people from an entirely different world. How could I
explain that I came from New York? How could I
explain Diana Vreeland or Sister Parish?

Dan Harrell spoke of the need to find a place for the
women to work together efficiently on a regular basis.
There had been some question about a building in
town made of native wood. Harrell said, "That simply
won't do because anybody could set a match and it
would go up overnight." In effect, he was saying, "We
don't have support in that community. When you work
here, Eugene Witherspoon's dog will go out and bark
if the sheriff comes up and we'll all know." But where
the proposed building was, there was no such
protection.

That night when I went to bed in the Witherspoon
home, the one book in the room where I slept was
James Agee's *Let Us Now Praise Famous Men*. I read it
by the light of the naked light bulb and the description
in that book was exactly what I was in: two rooms
divided by a dog trot, a typical sharecropper's house."

Ms. O'Donnell tried to gear the quilters toward mass merchandising. She
told them to preshrink cotton material before cutting it and to measure
carefully the cloth squares to make them even. She did not want them to lose
the ethos or artistry of their handiwork, yet she knew the public market
meant quality control. She emphasized product duplication so the women
could use their talents time and again rather than on limited, "one-shot"
opportunities. She envisioned a consumer beholding a quilt made by the
collective and saying, "I want one just like that one," then receiving one of
the same dimensions, color scheme, and pattern.

A quiltmaker she was not, but Doris could turn a fine seam, which gave
her great pleasure and pride. She found the quilts "stunning" and their color
display especially distinctive:

I can tell a Freedom Quilting Bee quilt from an
Appalachian quilt as quickly as the snap of a finger
because of the color strength in the Freedom quilt.
The technical term is "high chroma," the use of primary colors at their most intense contrast. The quilts
had a dynamism resulting from their combination
of geometry and brilliance in juxtaposition of primary
colors. What struck me when I first saw them was
that as patchwork quilts so many of them were black-
white, red-white, dark blue-white. Such opposition
gave them a wonderful, almost Mondrian design.

Gambles and Disappointments

Two months after Doris O'Donnell left Wilcox County, the Freedom Quilting Bee saw the first tangible results of her labors: the arrival of a box from Sally Victor containing three hat patterns. If the quilters could interpret those patterns the way the designer intended, construct the hats accurately, and return them to New York in time for a spring hat showing on December 17, 1966, the cooperative had a chance for a large contract. But the patterns arrived late—on December 9—and the quilters had never before made designer hats. Three days of round-the-clock flurry produced a shipment by December 12, but a contract never resulted.

Elizabeth Walter, who worked closely with Estelle Witherspoon to prepare the shipment, thinks back to those fast-paced moments:

It was a desperate, frustrating effort to have those
hats done in 72 hours. They were to be pieced together
and sewn not unlike a rain hat with gores coming up
to a point. I had never made a hat in my life. It was
a good idea so I just sketched a pattern on newsprint
or white craft paper. Mrs. Witherspoon and I did the
best we could and the whole thing was a flop.
Sally Victor was disappointed in the craftsmanship
and design. It was not what she had in mind and she
said it would never sell. Under the circumstances, she
was right. It was just one of those things we tried that
was not successful. The whole thing was, "You just
do it and let me see if I can buy it," strictly on specula-
tion. But at the time, we were too naive to respond
otherwise.

More disappointments occurred. The enormous order of quilts from Aerojet-General fell through because they were not approved for sale by the state of California. They did not include manufacturer's registration, obtained under a certificate issued by that state. So the fifty were returned to Alabama.

Meanwhile, the quilters had made dozens of felt Christmas tree ornaments that could not be sold. "We had to pay the women for all those ornaments, then nobody bought them," Elizabeth Walter declares. "I have 150 of them. Over the years they have been eaten by the moths."

Through Dan Kimball's friendship with Vice-President Humphrey, federal contacts came to Alabama as promised to discuss with Father Walter the feasibility of Black Belt economic development. What the federal authorities envisioned, however, was a factory in Selma where workers would make bombs for use in Vietnam. According to Father Walter, "A factory represent-ative came down and said they had had wonderful success in Arkansas with an all-woman factory. They were packing steel balls in cannisters with jelly gas and it really perked up the economy. Can't you imagine Mrs. Witherspoon packing little steel balls for the war? So we told them we weren't interested."

Freedom Wins a Parish-Hadley Contract

Before the end of 1966, though, one of Ms. O'Donnell's other feelers jelled as a $750 contract for the Freedom Quilting Bee with Parish-Hadley. As a result of this relationship, there occurred a nationwide revival of the use of patchwork quilts and patchwork material in interior decor. Mrs. Henry Parish II, known as "Sister," and her partner, Albert Hadley, have for decades directed one of the most prominent interior design firms in New York City and gained a reputation for "the undecorated look." During the Kennedy administration, Mrs. Parish did the interior design for the White House. In fact, she and Jacqueline Kennedy were the first to achieve historical accuracy in the state rooms, using only authentic pieces that had been there at some period during the life of the structure.

Upon learning of the Freedom Quilting Bee, Mrs. Parish was struck with the aesthetic potential the quilts offered her projects. She found them appealing as American craftsmanship. She liked knowing she could give productivity to a group who needed work. A longtime lover of quilts, she decorated her own homes with her personal collection. She had also placed quilts in her clients' homes, using them as bedspreads or cutting old ones apart and using the fabric as ottoman upholstery.

Mrs. Parish considered quiltmaking to be a dying art and regarded the Freedom Quilting Bee as the first organized group bringing it back to life. So she sent an order to Route One, Alberta, for patchwork fabric. Heading the venture was thirty-two-year-old James Wagnon, an Oklahoman new at Parish-Hadley who was in charge of special projects. As a child in the late 1930s, he had observed the "older ladies" of his community, his grandmother included, in quilting bees. Even then, he knew the mechanics of quiltmaking. "But at that point in Oklahoma we had reached the stage of turning up our noses at this folksy, craftsy thing," he now recalls. "We didn't understand the sophistication or the chicness of a quilt."

Wagnon viewed the wares of the Alabama group far differently, as objects of great beauty suitable in the most sophisticated interiors. Examining the early samples, the firm was especially taken with "the beautiful crudeness" of the work. "It wasn't highly refined in design or workmanship," says Wagnon, today a decorator with his own business, "but their beautiful crudeness was part of what attracted us to the quilts. I talked with Mrs. Parish about that point. She said, 'I think we can do so much with these people. We can help them and be a good market for them. I don't want to change their natural ability or their soul, but to make the quilts more suitable for our use, perhaps we can adapt some of the designs.' "

Which is what Wagnon was told to do, and to adapt "the color waves" to suit the tastes of the firm's clients:

> We were in the beginning of a period when lots of clear colors were coming into style—clear greens, acid greens, bright oranges and yellows. All those bright colors were being used together, a technique not in vogue before. Until then, the color palettes for decorating had not been quite so sharp. Mrs. Parish had been well known for mixing lots of patterns in decoration, although it was not the trend. Her point of view toward decorating always was the English country approach. She had a talent for mixing lots of patterns, and using pattern on pattern, which was certainly not the vogue but has now become popular.

So Mrs. Parish would use the quilted material from the Freedom Quilting Bee as part of her pattern-on-pattern approach. Her firm would use many of Freedom's own designs, but would introduce to the group "modified, classical quilt designs," or patterns changed slightly and using contemporary color schemes.

Jim Wagnon acquired the co-op's patterns. Using colors and fabrics specified by Parish-Hadley, he cut pieces of cloth, pasted them in mock-up designs, and mailed them to Wilcox County. As he describes his procedures:

> There is a place on 34th Street called Ashil that sold inexpensive cotton material. I would spend hours in Ashil going through the dress materials, looking for modern colorings of patterns like the old calicos and even the ginghams in small scale so the quilting would have a bit of feel of the old things but at the same time have the new colorations. The people at Ashil thought I was out of my mind. Finally, I had to explain what I was doing. "Patchwork quilts?," they said. "Nobody makes patchwork quilts anymore." But I had such fun finding beautiful little fabrics, then going back to the studio, clipping and scheming colors and getting combinations worked out.
>
> One pattern was Thistle. At that time the Freedom Quilting Bee was doing it in a scale probably typical of the classical scale of design. Mrs. Parish especially liked that pattern so we blew it up. The thistle head became three times its normal size. The

leaves were very angular and angry, so we blew them
up much larger.

Another pattern was Rik-Rak, based on a series of
stripes and zigzags. Rik-Rak was one of our most
commercially successful designs. We had it made often
as curtains and upholstery fabric.

Parish-Hadley supplied the quilters with the fabrics because the firm
wanted its own exclusive color schemes. Members of the co-op were responsible for cutting and piecing together the material, in some cases quilting
it, then shipping it to New York. From Wilcox County came quilts for use
as bedspreads or as quilts, quilt-patterned pillows, curtain material, and
upholstery material to cover sofas, chairs, and benches—all to grace some of
the finest and most carefully selected interiors in the country.

The Paley/Burden Orders

The first order was for the summer home of William Paley, chairman of
the board of Columbia Broadcasting Company, and his wife, Babe. The
second was for the New York City home of their daughter, Amanda Burden.
Mrs. Paley selected a bright orange-on-yellow patchwork decor that ran
through her house on Squaw Lake, using Chestnut Bud, a pattern that is
traditional with black Wilcox quilters but is no longer being made. Mrs.
Burden chose Gentleman's Bow Tie as the focal point of her baby's nursery,
for curtains, a quilt, and a pillow in pink, blue, and white.

Before the Paley venture could begin, however, Elizabeth Walter was
summoned to help because the size of the order required quilting frames
unlike any the quilters had ever used. She explains:

Sister Parish suggested to Francis that the best way
to make quilts fashionable in the United States was to
put them in someone's home and write an article about
them. She suggested making eighteen feet of quilted
fabric to upholster Babe Paley's sofa. Not realizing
what would be involved, Francis said, "Yes, we'll try
and do that." But eighteen feet was a different format
in dimensions from anything they had ever worked
with.

None of us knew what we were doing. So I had to
devise a quilting frame to accommodate a fabric large
enough for the women to work on it.

Traditionally, the quilting frames in those black homes were hung by ropes
from the ceiling, usually in front of the fireplace, and were let down when

ready for use. Many homes that lacked closets acquired valuable storage space on top of double beds as children moved away. In those cases, quilting frames were stored on the beds. The Paley task failed to fit any existing frame, regardless of its circumstance. "I had no first-hand experience with quilting frames," Dr. Walter continues, "but what distressed me was the effort of the women to put the quilt in the frame."

Typically, at their corners the quilting frames had been nailed or screwed together:

So I said, "Why not put a wing nut on there?" It was so much easier to undo a wing nut. I figured out the lumber dimensions, got a drill and bit, put wing nuts in the corners, dropped a bolt down in each corner and made a roller to accommodate the material the women quilted. They could roll the material up and only have out in the frame what they were actually working on.

They told me how wonderful I was. It was labor-saving and a much more efficient device, but I think they immediately went back to the other way as soon as that order was over. It never occurred to them to put wing nuts on their own frames. It was traditional thinking despite improved technology.

Once the length problem was under control, the quilters were at work on the two orders by the first of February 1967. For this one job, they worked regular hours for one month. The Paley order, seventy-five feet in length, was finished by March 1, prompting a grand-scale celebration. The material was hung in front of the home of Mattie Ross, whose cramped dwelling was the workplace for it all. The project was photographed, packed, and taken to Selma for shipment.

In addition to displaying the material outside for the pleasure of passersby, the ecstatic quilters provided dinner that day for anyone in Gee's Bend who wanted to come by the Ross home to observe the artistry close at hand. Among the unexpected guests were the rural route postman and a crew of loggers, all white. The victory dinner was fried catfish and chicken, deviled eggs, potato salad, sweet potato pie, and purple lemonade.

The Burden commission was conducted in the home of Catherine Robinson, of Route One, Alberta. She had cut and pieced a baby quilt for Sally Victor, so she was selected as one of six to put together the Burden order. Because she weighed more than 450 pounds and could travel only by pickup truck, the others elected to work in her home. The project was difficult. Knotted strings were used instead of yardsticks because only one of the women could read. Although the knots were in proper positions, each of the six panels was too short and had to be redone.

But, by the time that job and all the others arrived at Parish-Hadley, the quilters' New York sponsors had no qualms about quality. Jim Wagnon states:

> When it came to us, it was ready. Qualitywise, it was very good. The workmanship was often crude, but we liked that. In comparison to another group I worked with later on called Mountain Artisans [a now-defunct West Virginia quilting cooperative], the workmanship of the Freedom Quilting Bee was cruder but much more attractive. The Mountain Artisans tried to be too refined and they missed somehow. The crudeness of the (Freedom Quilting Bee) quilt made it so appealing.

Wagnon once visited Wilcox County to see the workers firsthand, an event that endeared the co-op members to the former New York banker but thrust him into the turbulent Black Belt racial climate. As he says:

> There was a county fair going on in Selma. I went with two young black ladies. I wasn't in the least bit aware that my going out with two black ladies might be any problem. We arrived at the fair and you would have thought we were from Mars. People were standing and looking and uttering awful things of disgust. Never in my life have I experienced the insults they flung at us as we walked by. I'll never forget it.
>
> There was one stand where they did woodcarving, something I thought Parish-Hadley might use. So I walked up with these two girls. We were commenting about it and the man who was running the booth said, "Listen here, you Yankee. If you think you're gonna come down here with these black girls, try to mix it up, take my crafts to New York and make a profit out of it, you're wrong." He insulted me, kicked me out and wouldn't let me stand around and look. It was really an experience.

By comparison, "I had a great affinity for the quilters, the way they worked, the love they put into the work and for the fact that economically, they were so hopeful about what their work for Parish-Hadley would do for the local families. With my coming from New York they knew they were going to get lots of work. It gave them hope of employment and making a little extra money. Psychologically, it seemed to make them very happy."

The Quilters Lock Arms with the Arts

In early 1967, while Freedom's first Parish-Hadley project was underway, the co-op achieved its first acclaim from members of the Eastern art community.

On February 14, 1967, the opening of the new art gallery at The University of Alabama was marked by a showing of the works of abstract expressionist Lee Krasner of New York City. Ms. Krasner was the widow of the world-renowned American painter Jackson Pollock, one of a handful of the twentieth century's major contributors to abstract expressionism and a founder of action-style painting. Pollock had attracted much attention for dripping and spattering paint on a surface rather than applying it through conventional brushing methods. Part of an awesome creative partnership who put much energy into her husband's career, Ms. Krasner was quite a painter in her own right; her individual exhibition in London the previous fall had won critical praise.

Lee Krasner came to Tuscaloosa for the opening reception and three days at a campus arts festival. The Art Department chairman, Dr. Theodore Klitzke, had become strongly interested in the quilters and showed Ms. Krasner color slides of their work.

Lee Krasner died on June 19, 1984. Before her death, she talked about her experience with the Freedom Quilting Bee. "I got very excited about it," she recalled her first impression, "and asked where the quilts were being made. Learning that it was fairly close by in a place called Alberta/Gee's Bend, I asked if I could go down and have a look, and if it would be possible for me to get some of those quilts."

A friend of Dr. Klitzke, Father Walter arranged for Ms. Krasner to be taken to the site. Among those with her on the trip was Donald McKinney, president of New York's Marlborough Gallery, which handled her paintings and arranged for her Tuscaloosa exhibition. She described her first contact with the South:

Gee's Bend was quite an experience in itself and I
shall long, long remember it. At some point on the
trip I wondered if we could stop some place for coffee.
Someone in the car said, "Yes, there's a place fairly
close by. We'll stop there, but please, under no conditions are you to discuss where we're going or what
we're going to do," which frightened me a bit. We

went in, had our coffee and never discussed where we were going. Then we got back in the car and continued driving.

As we drove farther and farther toward Gee's Bend, the place really became frightening because at some point, someone in the car said, "That house we just passed was the last place with a telephone in relation to where we're going," and we were still not at Gee's Bend. Finally, we arrived at somebody's house and went in. I shall *never* forget it.

We went into this room where there was a stretcher (quilt frame) the full space of the room. Women were seated against the walls of the room, working on a quilt. It was quite a sight to behold: to have the door opened and to be confronted with I don't know how many women sitting around, working on this quilt.

I was standing in the doorway and Reverend Walter introduced me as Miss Krasner who had an exhibition at The University of Alabama. Then he started to tell me all their names. It was the same name that kept going around for four, five, or six times. At last, another name came in. I said, "How did you get here?" Then everyone laughed and the whole thing became very relaxed.

I was very taken with what I had seen. I asked about this and that and ordered three quilts. While I was in the house I saw on the mantelpiece a shell. I collect shells, so after everyone relaxed, I asked where the shell came from. They said, "Right down here at the river." I asked, "Is there any way I may get such a shell? I'd love to take one back with me." Somebody said, "My husband will be home soon and he has a lot of them in back of the house. He'll give you some." So I was driven to the woman's house. The poverty was beyond description. There was a pile of shells in the back yard and I was allowed to select one.

When the man went off to put the shell in a bag, I asked Reverend Walter, "Can I pay him for this? When I buy a shell on Madison Avenue in New York, I pay for it." He said, "Under no condition are you to offer him money." So I accepted the shell, thanked him very kindly and we drove back to Tuscaloosa.

There was a little girl at the house where I got the shell. On the way back to Tuscaloosa I said to Reverend Walter, "In what way can I repay the man for the shell? Can I do anything for that little girl?"

When I returned to New York I thought the best

thing would be to send her a book and make sure the
heroine of the story was not a blue-eyed blonde. I had
quite a time finding such a book but I did find it and
I sent it to her with a note. I received a response saying
she had taken the book to school and it had caused a
good deal of happy commotion. I also spoke to several
people in New York about those wonderful quilts. So
indeed, Gee's Bend is very implanted in my mind.

Lee Krasner talked about the Freedom Quilting Bee with everyone she
saw, praising the artistic merits of the quilters and urging purchase of the
quilts. "I accepted them instantly," she spoke of their artistry. "They were a
craft of the highest order. They were magnificent." One of her listeners was
art historian Henry Geldzahler, then curator of twentieth-century art with
New York's Metropolitan Museum of Art. He ordered quilts for himself and
showed them to his friends, who placed orders of their own. At one point,
he met with Father Walter to discuss the co-op and see its samples. As he
explains:

I was touched by the quality of the work. I'm a
curator of museums so I'm very involved with quality,
but helping the Freedom Quilting Bee was not a question strictly of quality. There was a human question,
of people making something with their own hands
and having the possibility of making money out of
their own aesthetics. Their aesthetic values didn't have
to be mine for me to honor what they were doing. I'm
not a crafts expert but I can tell strong, bold and controlled design when I see it and those qualities in the
quilts were very good. So I was doubly happy to help.
I'd read enough newspaper articles and Southern
literature to know there was a very warm, rich vein of
black Southern culture that hadn't been tapped and
hadn't had a way of expressing itself in my life. I just
got shivers of good feeling for being able to do something. If you're cynical, you call it liberal claptrap. If
you're a humanist, you say it's holding hands. That's
how I felt about it, holding hands.

Until her death, Lee Krasner still had her shell from the banks of the
Alabama River and displayed the keepsake on her bedroom chest. Held in
various lights, it shimmered softly in pink, purple, and green like art deco, a
form to which she was especially drawn.

Ms. Krasner also kept her three quilts from Alberta/Gee's Bend. One is a
creation of white flowers, possibly tulips, on a dark brown background. Her

other quilts, made by Mattie Ross, are of the Crow's Foot design and were sent to Ms. Krasner after she had left Alabama. "Work has begun on your two 'crow foot' quilts," Francis Walter wrote to the artist. "It will be a while before you receive them because the pattern is unusual. Only one woman, Mrs. Mattie Ross, really does it well. This is the season when people are in the fields and Mrs. Ross does farm. But rest assured, you will get them."

Ms. Krasner was so attracted to the quilts' beauty that she discussed with Geldzahler the possibility of an exhibit by the Freedom Quilting Bee at the Metropolitan Museum of Art. The idea never jelled, but, as she told it, "That was how I felt about the work I saw down there."

Ms. Krasner's Marlborough representative, Donald McKinney, now director of another gallery, Hirschl and Adler, continues to hold on to his three quilts, including one made from flour sacks. "I was impressed by the honesty and simplicity of the quilts," he states. "They were simple yet sophisticated. I could feel the honesty and warmth. I dislike cuteness and they weren't cute. There was strength in those quilts."

Geldzahler now does writing and curatorial work on his own. Although he uses one of the quilts to decorate a daybed in his living room, he has worn out many. "I used them to keep me warm. And they did."

Two Milestone Years

The first two years in the life of the Freedom Quilting Bee, 1966 and 1967, were amazing in terms of job orders and volunteer energies. Between its founding in March 1966, and the end of the calendar year, the co-op provided $5,500 in profits to its members, amassed mostly from the sale of $20 and $25 quilts. The top earner made more than $200, a substantial and personally beneficial sum when compared with her six-day-a-week work as a cook and maid, for which she earned $12 a week, about $600 a year. In fact, the co-op raised family income for some by as much as 25 percent.

When the sixty or so members gathered in Alberta's Pine Grove Church on April 15, 1967, to hold their first annual membership meeting, leaders reported that within the first year the organization had grossed an income of $10,158. Of that amount, $8,200 was paid to the members; a couple earned more than $300 each.

As the Bee's potential became more obvious, its leaders embarked on a two-part goal: to hire a full-time professional manager and to erect a small structure where the women could work together rather than fragmented at home. In June 1967 a grant of $5,000 was received from the New York Foundation that enabled the group to seek a manager for one year.

Then, as word spread, the quilters were visited by a folk art consultant to the Smithsonian Institution, who arranged to have Bee leaders invited to the

Smithsonian's Folklife Festival during the first week of July on the Mall in Washington. Their task there: to stage a working quilt exhibit. So Father Walter drove from Wilcox County to the nation's capital a van carrying four quilters, twenty-five quilts, and a frame. For four days, international spectators blended with potters, blacksmiths, basket weavers, and quiltmakers— representing Eskimos from Alaska, Indians from out West, hill people from Appalachia, and black women artists from the heart of Dixie.

By August the quilters had hired the professional staff person: Mary Brooks, a young white woman from Athens, Georgia, and a graduate student in art at the University of Georgia. For the next twelve months—the most challenging in the co-op's history—she and Estelle Witherspoon would work together as comanagers of the organization.

In addition, the Freedom Quilting Bee was the focus of promotions that would be seen seasons later in home design magazines the nation over.

Meanwhile, a higher-quality product and a new surge of enthusiasm had sparked the quilters to raise their rates, if modestly. The going price for a single quilt became $25; a double quilt, $30; a double coverlet size, $35; and a king size ("you send size"), $50.

"Cotton picking and fall work in the fields will soon be over," wrote Francis Walter in his *Newsletter* on September 19. "Quilt-making will commence in earnest in time for Christmas sales."

Ascendancy of the Patchwork Look

While quilt sales and future plans were going in their own directions, the 1967 arrangement between the Freedom Quilting Bee and Parish-Hadley was a mixture of magic. It inaugurated a new look, the patchwork look, in the nation's interior decor. As Sister Parish reflects, "It was the beginning of the revival of quilts in this country. Everyone went through their closets, got out their grandmothers' quilts that had been packed away for years and put them back on the beds." Wagnon adds: "That the Freedom Quilting Bee was doing it and that they became a medium for us to work through was a significant factor. The Appalachian project that came along later, the Mountain Artisans, was a direct result of the Freedom Quilting Bee's first initial impact on this market."

In 1968 and 1969 patchwork had a high priority among American trend setters. Sometimes the Freedom quilters were credited, sometimes not. Diana Vreeland, intent on making quilts high fashion, promoted the concept in *Vogue* with months of quilt layouts by Parish-Hadley. In one scene, a wicker-bamboo chair had a red-and-white quilted cotton seat that had been pieced by the Freedom Quilting Bee. In another, *Vogue* spotlighted Parish-Hadley's national network of "skilled but housebound women" who provided the firm with afghans, wooden tables, ribbon-covered pillows and material made from patchwork. That "look" was a room in which quilting was in every aspect of the decor. Again, *Vogue* ran a picture of a "superb velvet quilt" available for $135 at Bloomingdale's and on exhibit at the Hallmark Gallery. Named as maker was the Freedom Quilting Bee.

During those couple of years, *House and Garden* also pushed patchwork. In a Christmas Eve supper scene, the table covering was a tomato red-and-white checkered quilt by the Freedom Quilting Bee. Flanked by two small end tables topped with holiday wreaths, it was laden with crystal and silver from Tiffany's. Pages later, a story on Christmas parties included a photograph of "a brilliant patchwork quilt" as a holiday luncheon tablecloth. The centerpiece was an iron and silver peacock from Morocco. The quilt, an unlabeled blue, green, and light brown Rik-Rak, had been made in Wilcox County.

Once more, *House and Garden* featured the quilts, this time spread on the grounds of a summer estate, all set for a picnic. Midst the fruit, wine, and sandwich fixings were baby-sized Coats of Many Colors, known in that story as "banquettes." In the back of the issue, shopping information listed the Freedom Quilting Bee and its address at Route One, Alberta.

The "patchwork look" marched on. The Freedom quilters enjoyed publicity, admiration, job orders, and extra money for their families. The co-op was deluged with written requests, many of which could not be handled. Also, material scraps and clothing arrived from across the country.

Although Parish-Hadley can be attributed with initiating national emphasis on patchwork, the firm suffered criticism. A 1968 story in *The New York Times* reported Mrs. Parish's efforts to recruit low-income artisans across the country. It said her company paid the Freedom quilters $1 an hour for the hand-pieced material, then charged its clients $70 a yard.

Letters to the editor of *The Times,* verbal outcries, and other protests reprimanded Parish-Hadley for making money off poor people. Wagnon recounts his reaction:

That made us very sad because exploiting poor people was the farthest thing from our motives. The article said the quilters were getting minimum wage or a dollar an hour or whatever it was at the time and that we were selling the fabric for $70 a yard to our clients, which is true. But we were not making anything more than a normal business profit, which was not a very high-margin profit.

The reason for the great difference in the two figures was that at a dollar an hour, it took many hours just to make one yard of fabric. Also, we were supplying the material, which added to the cost. And we didn't

even charge for the design. We weren't trying to make
money from the design. Our input to the whole project
was to help with the design so it would be successful.
It really did get very distorted.

For the most part, Parish–Hadley concluded its contract with the Freedom
Quilting Bee somewhere in 1969, not because of any lessening of quality.
"Ours was a limited volume," Wagnon explains. "We had made the quilting
statement for a year or so. We didn't like to repeat ourselves too much. I think
we helped them a great deal from the standpoint of their becoming known.
As a result, they got busy with larger jobs."

Although Parish–Hadley abandoned quilting and pursued another look,
its interest in Freedom prevailed. "Very often we had extra materials left over
from projects," Wagnon points out. "We would pile them in boxes and give
them to the quilting bee. I remember sending down bundles of scraps every
time we would clean out. We would send them at our own expense and were
delighted to do it because we knew they could use the materials."

By 1970 Bloomingdale's in New York, the nation's premiere department
store, had conducted a campaign featuring quilts and quilted items produced
exclusively by the Freedom Quilting Bee. Full-page advertisements that
appeared in *The New York Times* and other promotions exposed still another
level of shoppers to the reemergence of patchwork as a notable form of
beauty.

Later, Sister Parish continued the trend a bit through *House and Garden*. In
April 1971 the magazine featured the interior of an island home she had
decorated in Maine. Sprawling on a sofa was one of Freedom's Eight-Point
Star quilts. Reclining on the quilt-draped sofa were two quilted pillows of
the same pattern.

On May 5, 1972, *Life* magazine came out with "Craze for Quilts," a
multipage picture layout that further spread the gospel. According to the
story, "The current craze for quilts is part of the burgeoning interest in crafts.
But it also reflects modern taste in abstract art." On the first page were two
large photographs. At right was Sharon Percy Rockefeller, showing a portion
of her home with its quilted walls and furniture made by Mountain Artisans,
the co-op network she had been promoting. At Mrs. Rockefeller's left was
Luella Pettway, of Gee's Bend, at work on a Zig-Zag at the Freedom Quilting
Bee. To those aware of the gulf historically separating their two levels of
opportunity, the likeness of a Rockefeller and a Pettway on the same page of
a national magazine was incredible.

Diana Vreeland, now special consultant to the Costume Institute of the
Metropolitan Museum of Art, still owns the Chestnut Bud she obtained
through her Doris O'Donnell connection, along with another similar in

design she later bought from the Bee. One of the quilts continues to reside on her bed.

Sister Parish also has a couple of the early quilts at her Maine farmhouse. In hues of dark brown and black, each is dominated by a big red ball that she claims "the women interpreted as the sun or the moon."

One of the co-op's most talented members made the Parish quilts. Evicted the previous summer, she and her husband had built a new house, where only one thickness of yellow pine separated them and the weather. They used her proceeds to insulate and seal a room in their home.

6   The Quilting Bee Goes Commercial

After its first two years, the Freedom Quilting Bee abandoned its free-spirited approach to creativity as well as salesmanship and went commercial. During the late 1960s, Sister Parish continued to promote the quilters in her own circle of contacts, but a man named Stanley Selengut was the catalyst that transformed the one-of-a-kind quilting production into a look-alike assembly for mass appeal. As a result, 1968 is remembered by the quilters as the year Stanley Selengut arrived in town.

Selengut: The Man for the Job

Another of the Doris O'Donnell sources, Selengut had a penchant for producing and marketing native crafts, with which he had attained enormous success. He became the co-op's sales representative and carried out a masterful merchandising plan that put the quilts in stores across the country and put money into their makers' pockets. He also guided to fruition a community sewing center, where the quilters work to this day.

Selengut, who was thick-mustached and nearing forty, had been born in 1929 in the Bronx of Jewish parents. He joined the U.S. Marine Corps at age seventeen. Not yet twenty when he was discharged, he passed a high school equivalency test and enrolled in a junior college. Later, he attended night school at New York University and earned a degree in civil engineering. He then worked for a company manufacturing small vacation houses.

A man who sought adventure, Selengut read about the Pan-American Highway and began to make trips to South America over the route. It was dotted with exotic Indian crafts native to the continent. On one trip, he was charmed by a collection of Andean face masks the Indians were using cere-monially. These masks were the kind that completely covered the head, save for slits at the eyes and mouth.

Selengut Associates introduced the novelty to the world as the Andean ski mask. Luckily for him, skiing had just become popular, and the market for ski clothing had not been fully explored. He embarked heavily in wholesaling to the ski industry, tailoring a certain style or look for a native-craft product, contracting native villagers to make the product according to his terms, buying it from the makers and selling it around the globe.

At the peak of his operations, Selengut employed 2,000 people. In the process, he dramatically changed the lives of the villagers with whom he worked because most existed in an economy where money was not the mode of exchange. They altered his life as well, for he became an authority on stitchery, garment-making, rug-weaving, the design of cloth products, and similar areas of knowledge.

After those days, Selengut's ability to turn native crafts into salable products thrust him into relationships with the U.S. State Department, the Zuni Indians, the U.S. Office of Economic Opportunity, the Poor People's Corporation of Mississippi, General Learning company, and the gift section of *Holiday* magazine. If anyone on the planet knew how to serve as broker for a homegrown creation—be it an Ecuadorian hat, a Moroccan caftan, or a quilt from Gee's Bend—Stanley Selengut was the man.

It had been a year and a half earlier, in 1966, when Doris O'Donnell had taken Francis Walter into Selengut's New York City office, lined with crafts from across the earth. At that time, Selengut was concentrating on early learning; he had designed and developed early learning educational products for children. He also owned the construction company making his products. He recalls the incident:

This minister with a white collar came walking into my office one day with a bunch of quilts in his hands. He said he had heard about my abilities to develop and market craft products. He was wondering if I could help him market these quilts.

Then he explained that the quilts were done by black ladies near Selma, many of whom had been involved in the civil rights movement and had been dislocated from their homes. There was no employment for many of these people. They were trying desperately to make a basic living but they had very little skills. Some skills they did have went into making these patchwork quilts. Now, they were trying to market their quilts. He was having trouble selling them

even for fifteen dollars a piece because he just couldn't
find a market.

He asked me to look at the quilts. Some were nice-
looking and some were ugly. I said, "Why is there
such discrepancy?" He said, "They're made from scraps
of cloth. If we get a nice bunch, the quilts can be very
handsome; if we get an ugly bunch, the quilts are
ugly."

I also said, "Some seem to be beautifully made but
in others, the workmanship looks terrible." His reply
was, "Some of the ladies are really good seamstresses
and some sew very poorly."

I told him, "It would be hard for me to help you.
Most of the work I do is in wholesaling to stores in
quantities. There is no way I could possibly take a
product as inconsistent as this to a store and market it.
I'd have to be able to present them with something
for which they could buy two dozen, and I would
have to deliver two dozen of something that looks like
the sample. With no supervision and by basing your
total production on handout scraps of fabrics, even
bits and leftovers from manufacturing mills, there is
no way I could market a consistent product."

Then he asked if there was some way I could help. I
said, "You need a basic budget to start with, because
the least I would need would be enough money to get
a basic fabric inventory to make a standard product,
then sell that standard product."

I said, "You need a budget for fabrics and a budget
to send a designer down to color-coordinate and show
the ladies how to make the quilts with combinations
of the new fabrics. Then, I probably could help because
we could start work on a consistent product.

Armed with this advice, Father Walter returned home, aware that the
quilters lacked the money to invest in Selengut's knowledge of product
development. Neither had they yet acquired the unity and trust among
themselves to make it work. And, besides, the last thing they wanted was
the feeling they had traded the power to run their organization for a one-
time promise of a little extra money.

Almost two years elapsed. Parish-Hadley would not last forever. Then,
the Selma Inter-religious Project acquired for the quilters a grant through
the Southern Consumers Cooperative, in Lafayette, Louisiana, that enabled
Selengut to become involved with the Bee.

Selengut Comes to Wilcox County

On January 16, 1968, he arrived in Wilcox County. Accompanying him were Sara Stein, a toy designer, and Joseph Rodd, a furniture designer and specialist in woodwork production. They made a presentation that evening at a Gee's Bend church. Two days later, Southern Consumers "hired" Selengut Associates, providing the co-op a $2,000 management subsidy grant and a $5,000 low-interest loan. The purpose of the grant/loan was to give the quilting bee a chance to demonstrate that twenty-five or thirty members could raise their income from 25 cents to a dollar an hour in one year.

Mrs. Stein would train the group and Selengut Associates would purchase needed fabric. The co-op would acquire a new inventory of quilts and related products designed by Mrs. Stein, present it to stores, and win contracts. Selengut agreed to work for expenses only, a testament to his personal commitment to the cause. "The ladies can look forward to quilting satin and silk and making more money than they ever have off the land," wrote Francis Walter in his February 1968 *Newsletter.* "But ladies," he cautioned, "learn not only how to sew but how to manage, how to keep books, how to run your own show."

Freedom Works for Bloomingdale's

One of the first things Selengut did was to take an armload of Wilcox quilt swatches into Bloomingdale's. Jody Bradshaw, a home furnishings fashion coordinator, became so excited that she decided to conduct a full promotional event on quilted products by the Freedom Quilting Bee. "So I went back to Gee's Bend, Alabama," Selengut says, "with a $20,000 order. It created chaos. They had no organization to supervise it, no way of dealing with it. They didn't have a building and everybody was making quilts each in their own little area."

Selengut had already bought "exotic" sample fabrics and sent them down with Sara Stein, along with instructions that she color-coordinate the traditional patterns with his specified fabrics rather than the scraps the quilters were accustomed to using. "You could take any design," the tall, gentle New Yorker explains, "develop it with velvets and Liberty of London paisley fabrics and have a very exotic look." Which is exactly what he did, over and over again.

So much for the individual scrap works of days and years gone by. Goodbye forever to quilts made from Cuban sugar sacks and overalls and little-girl dresses and shirts worn out from cornstalk pulling. Enter instead that expensive and beautiful Egyptian cotton called Liberty of London. As Francis Walter says:

There is no way to take an authentic religious or utilitarian object, turn it out by the profit motive and not alter its construction. If you make a broom, you just make it and use it, then you make another broom in another year. If you carve a little household god every few generations, you are not going to produce them all alike if some white man comes along and tells you he will buy as many as you can make.

So Stanley came in with the hard financial study and said, "All right, you want to make quilts. They should be authentic but they must also be well-made. They can't be sloppy. You can't make them with scraps any more because when people dry-clean the quilts, they might stain and the buyers will be furious."

We used Liberty of London prints and the women had to sew to a certain standard. As art objects, the Henry Geldzahlers and the Lee Krasners no longer wanted the quilts. But still, they were authentic. Sara Stein introduced some variations of traditional quilt designs which were amazing and beautiful. Then she selected fabrics and color patterns. One of them, the Jacob's Coat (Coat of Many Colors) still is produced in her basic fabric-design selection.

Sara Stein Runs Quilting School

When Stanley Selengut teamed up with the Freedom quilters, Sara Bonnett Stein, of Pound Ridge, New York, had been a designer for a number of his projects, including educational toys. She owned a couple of old quilts, but was not a quiltmaker. She was a seamstress, however; she could embroider; and she knew how a quilt was made.

First, Mrs. Stein studied quilt books. Then she toured New York City's Museum of Modern Art, where she conceived ideas for contemporary design. She found an art catalog saying op art was in style. So op art became a source of inspiration. Then she began to work out samples of quilt patterns.

By mid-January, 1968 Sara was at a church in Gee's Bend, Alabama, her first trip to the South since a childhood visit to North Carolina. She showed the local people a set of toys she had recently invented in hopes they would want to start a small toy-making industry:

They were whimsical and sophisticated handmade wooden toys, but obviously for do-nothing rich folks. Just novelty. Funny stuff. So I made a presentation to one of the blankest audiences I've ever seen.

"Mama Willie" Abrams studies the lush Liberty of London fabric acquired by Stanley Selengut.

(1972 photo by Reverend Arthur Rivard; courtesy, Fathers of St. Edmund, Selma, Alabama)

One of the toys was a cat. You pushed her tail up and two little kittens came down. Another was a Pinocchio kind of acrobat that twirled and did acrobatics on a stick. And there was a grasshopper. You pulled a ring, he would leap in the air and come back down.

They were articulated but handmade, handpainted toys for adults, but they couldn't have had any meaning to those people. Stanley had said, "Take down your toys," and Francis Walter had said, "Take down your toys. Everybody will love them." I was doing what I was told to do, but my presentation was from outer space. It didn't grasp the people there in any way.

Three months later, on April 19, Mrs. Stein returned to Wilcox County and spent more than a week conducting a sewing school for members of the Freedom Quilting Bee. She was accompanied by her husband, Martin D.

Stein, an architect with Urbahn Associates, in New York City, and three sons. The Stein family stayed with Callie Young, board chairman, and her husband, Ed. "The children were grown and they had a guest house, believe it or not. They actually had an extra shack. We stayed in the guest house and had our meals with the Youngs or during the day with the quilting bee." Headquarters for the Stein sewing school was the home of Estelle Witherspoon. The New York designer says it was "a double cabin with a dog trot in between, and so leaky they had to keep moving the quilts around every time it rained."

Mrs. Stein had been briefed by Father Walter about local conditions and was told not to expect more that what was there:

Prior to meeting him, I really didn't know anybody lived in this country that was outside of a money economy, that was outside of communication with the rest of the world. Francis Walter had told me that when they exhibited at the Smithsonian—one of their big entries into the outside world—they were put into a hotel, turned the faucet on in the bathtub and had no idea how to turn the faucet off. They had to get help from the management because they never had seen running water.

It was another world. Gee's Bend still was twenty miles to the nearest telephone and the per capita income was under $300 a year. It wasn't a cash economy and the goal Stanley and I set was to earn minimum wages, in those days $1.25 an hour.

One of the difficulties we had was the concept of hourly wage because that didn't strike them as just. They felt somebody who was half blind, arthritic, and terribly slow at sewing should get the same amount as somebody who could do it quickly and turn out more quilts. There were so many suffering members of the community and they felt these women needed help as much as anybody else. So whether hourly wage ever made sense to anybody, I don't know.

Stanley and I felt if they wanted as a community to make the Freedom Quilting Bee profitable in any sense, they would have to use their fastest women, turn out quilts as quickly as they could and not rely on people who were slow or who didn't make quilts good enough to sell, which was another problem. Hourly wage was a brand new concept. Their idea was that you were paid for the quilt whether it took you a long time or a short time.

Sara Stein discovered many other community facets far different from those of her own environs:

After a day's work I would help Mrs. Young with the vegetables and planting time. There was no water anywhere. We had to haul water in big milk cans, water each plant dipper by dipper, out in the fields, then lug water back.

I grew up, in the summers at least, in a farming community where there wasn't running water. But there was an artesian well with a hand pump. That's what they had, a pump at the kitchen sink, a pump out in the fields. They didn't know about elevators or running water. They couldn't comprehend what Bloomingdale's might want from an order or that the company might want consistent sizes, and they certainly had no idea of the quality Bloomingdale's would want.

They didn't know that beds came in singles, doubles, and queen sizes, that you must have different-sized quilts to fit the beds and that a quilt must go over the bed edge a certain amount. They didn't know how to measure. We had to knot strings for them, using a different string for each quilt size so they could measure the finished product to make sure they got it right.

Most of their scissors literally were broken off, so dull and so old that they had never been able to cut through more than one layer of cloth at a time. It was a wonder they could even do that. I couldn't work their scissors at all. They were hopeless.

Their thimbles had been used for so long that the tops were worn through. All indentations were actually holes with three or four indentations still there that they could push against the needle.

Mrs. Stein does not believe the women realized the handicap of inferior equipment:

It always had been that way. I think they could conceive of having a better pair of scissors, a new pair of scissors, or another thimble. But there was a feeling also that somehow nothing could change and nothing could be done to correct the situation.

If a bench broke, they didn't repair the bench. The men didn't have basic carpentry skills you would expect from almost anybody. When they made a bench, for instance, it would have no bracing. They didn't know

how to brace a bench. They had to learn to do those
things we at first assumed everybody knew.

The quilters had good cotton thread but they used
flour bags for the backing as always. A lot of their
quilts were made with bluejeans and were pretty, but
would not have been accepted by Bloomingdale's.
They would beat or bat cotton from their own fields
to make batting. They would beat it and flail it to
try to make it flat and smooth. Of course, it never was
smooth. There were places with no batting, places
where it was lumpy or too thick, and it was very hard
to quilt through. They also had crude quilting frames
but that was fine because they were serviceable and
it didn't seem to me that you could go in and change a
whole bunch of things.

We got them good scissors. We showed them how
to cut through six layers of cloth at a time, which was
absolutely news. We made permanent Masonite patterns that didn't wear out and they could make the
patterns on top.

We got thimbles with great trouble because their
fingers were so spaded from field work, flattened and
large at the ends. No thimble would fit that you would
go to a store and buy. You had to go directly to a
thimble company. I believe they were size twelve. I
wear a size six so you can imagine. That was partly
why they couldn't replace their old thimbles belonging
to their grandparents: they just couldn't get big ones.

Mrs. Stein did not give a high rating to the artistic merits of most of the
quilts she saw at the Freedom Quilting Bee. She remembers one woman
who had a flair for color and some who had a facility for balanced design.
"Bluejean quilts are always beautiful because all the shades of blue work well
together."

But, mostly, Sara thought the quilts were ugly. Although the traditional
designs were striking, the women had to take what cloth they could obtain,
much of it poor quality. The quilts were finished badly with unattractive
backing:

They didn't know how to miter a corner, and in the
quilting, they would get to the end of a thread, snip
it and start another one slightly overlapping. Little
threads were always sticking out. They never used
knots in their quilts, so unraveling threads were always
present. We taught them how to make knots, pull

them through the back so they would be hidden inside
and wouldn't unravel later.

They used some of the beautiful patterns. One
woman specialized in the Texas Star. Most of the
women couldn't handle the tiny diamond patches required of a Texas Star, but she could. Another worked
in assorted rectangles but she had a real sense of design.
They had done the Log Cabin and other nice designs.
They weren't the finer designs but if we had gone
into the finer designs, they never would have gotten
through a quilt and made money off of it. So we tried
to stick with the simple ones.

Once a package of designs had been put together that was acceptable to
Bloomingdale's, Mrs. Stein set forth every detail by which the co-op members
were to make their quilts. She bought their material and specified what cloth
would go with what pattern. She gave each woman a shoe box of the squares
she was to use. When the quilter was finished with those squares, she would
report to Mrs. Witherspoon. Someone else might be chosen to assemble the
squares into the quilt top. Another person or a group of the best quilters
might do the quilting of that creation, and a different worker might do the
binding:

Each person had been responsible for the whole
production of the quilt. Some did terrible binding,
some did terrible quilting, and some terrible patching.
So we tried to divide the labor or match individual
talents with specific jobs.

My impression was that the older women had difficulty learning. Mrs. Witherspoon was the one who
had a business grasp of how such a thing might work,
and she seemed to understand division of labor and
hourly wage. The younger women learned what I was
talking about. Many of them had had other jobs so
they were more experienced, but there weren't very
many younger ones. A whole generation was missing.
They were grandparents and grandchildren. All the
children were working in Detroit, New York, and
Chicago.

I worked with those in their sixties and seventies,
maybe some in their fifties. There were little kids.
They would sit there quietly. And then there were a
few women in their twenties and thirties who had had
a rough time in Detroit or New York and had come
back to live on the farm again.

Mrs. Stein found it hard to tell whether or not she was truly teaching:

> I would see evidence either that somebody didn't
> want to do what I said or hadn't understood what
> I said, but everything was always "yes," quickly as the
> snap of a finger. Some things I could see click right
> away. When somebody could cut six pieces of cloth at
> once instead of just one piece, or when they had thim-
> bles to work with, they obviously were delighted and
> that was genuine. But in the time I was there, I believe
> one quilt was pieced. I didn't even see a final product
> that first time.

Although she corresponded with Estelle Witherspoon for a time, her nine days of quilting instructions left no time for cultivating solid relationships. And besides: "I think they were so guarded against whites coming in from outside with the bouncy optimism of the liberal thinking they could change things, that the guardedness would have been impossible to penetrate except over a long period of time."

Mrs. Stein had a closer look at the life of board chairman Callie Young than that of the others, for she stayed in her home. As she recalls:

> I was surprised to find chamber pots. There wasn't
> even an outhouse. When my family summered in
> Connecticut before we built a house on the property,
> we just lived in a barn. The first thing my father did
> was build an outhouse. But they didn't have outhouses.
> So we were stuck that first morning with pots we
> didn't know what to do with. I had to ask Callie what
> to do with the contents of the pot and she just told
> me as long as it was over the fence where the chickens
> couldn't get at it, that was fine. So we dumped it over
> the fence.
>
> They had scavenger chickens, something I never had
> seen. They were raised completely on whatever might
> be left from the meal and whatever insects the chickens
> could get for themselves. There was no such thing as
> chicken food or dog food. The dogs ate whatever
> scraps were left.
>
> Callie Young was pretty good at mimicking Francis
> Walter. The women liked him and he was a wonderful
> help to them but they found him very funny because
> they felt he acted like a woman. In the morning he
> made his own bed. I'm sure they found me funny and
> learned to mimic me as soon as my back was turned,
> too.

But we shared the same experience raising children, changing diapers and getting mad at husbands. All of that is life as usual wherever you go. But it was a revelation that a group of people in prosperous America lived under such grotesque handicaps in what was to me another world and another age with no experience of what I considered everyday life.

Sara Stein found the children raised quite differently from the way she mothered her own sons. Except for the Witherspoons' daughter, Louise, age nine, who became friends with the designer's seven-year-old son, Lincoln, she saw only the very young, including many three-year-olds. She says:

My children must have appalled the community. Their children, for instance, would come in and sit while their mothers sewed. I mean *sit* with their hands folded in their laps for hours. It's inconceivable that middle class white children could ever do that. Our children are trained or encouraged to be curious, to explore and ask questions.

Those children didn't open their mouths, get up, or do anything. And they were praised for being good. It was a totally different concept of childrearing. If they had gotten up, that would have been bad, naughty. They weren't punished severely. I think it would have been, "Now you sit down."

Our children wanted desperately to take home some anoles, the small lizards that live there. It was nearly time for us to go and we hadn't succeeded in catching any. We offered fifty cents to any child who could catch us one. We did get a few but they thought we were out of our minds for wanting those lizards.

"I felt there was an enormous disparity between women and men," Mrs. Stein continues:

Francis Walter explained that because the women didn't work as much in the fields when they were children, they got a lot more education than the men did. They went to school. They had real handwriting. Maybe the spelling was not too good. Maybe the grammar wasn't perfect, but they could write a letter. They could talk. Their vocabularies were much larger than those of the men.

The boys worked in the fields and unlike a lot of rural communities where the school schedule is ad-

justed to seasons of planting and plowing, I don't believe theirs was adjusted for the working boys. So
they just skipped a lot of school because they had to
work. My impression was that the men were quite
uneducated and inarticulate.

This story also comes from Reverend Walter. The
summer before I was there, a young white woman had
come to help them. She took to sitting in the afternoons with a young black boy from the community
who was about her age. They were doing nothing
at all but sitting on the porch and talking after work in
the afternoons. Apparently he was more intelligent
than most and more interested in world topics. She
was an educated young woman. The people of the
community didn't mind their sitting on the porch, but
when they discovered she was using mouthwash, they
were appalled at her potential immorality, because
mouthwash ads are geared to win you the favors of the
opposite sex. They couldn't see any reason but a sexual
motive for using mouthwash; they were furious and
it was real trouble.

This was how inexperienced they were. Although
they may have had a television, there was no way for
them to interpret what was happening on it.

During her days at the Bee, Mrs. Stein saw only two or three television
sets, two pickup trucks, no automobiles, no washing machines, and no clothes
dryers. Each home had one combination electric light socket and outlet on
the ceiling.

On a cheerier note, she came to learn that the co-op members were "women
of business." Conducting meetings according to rules, with a chairwoman
who required people to speak in order, was an aspect of that life the quilters
enjoyed. "They had really caught on to being businesslike and liked its
discipline. I sat in on a general meeting at which some decisions were made.
It was very orderly and run by Estelle with a firm hand. They were very
good at that. I was curious whether women working together on church
affairs might have been a forerunner to the ease with which they took to
such a role."

Mrs. Stein never envisioned that the Freedom Quilting Bee would endure
two decades and possibly longer: "I probably felt it would ultimately fail
because of the differences between their outlook of what they could do and
how to do it and the rest of the world's outlook of what constitutes a
commercial product."

Financially, Mrs. Stein's work was voluntary. Her plane tickets to Alabama
were paid with the Southern Consumers grant, but she and her husband paid

for his trip and that of their children. Martin Stein also used the time as part of his vacation. Her designs were gratis; so were her time and talent, both in New York and Alabama.

Then why did she do it? "Because I wanted to see if it could be done. I always want to get people doing more and understanding that they have tremendous capabilities. I would have stuck with it a lot longer if there had been a way and an opportunity. But it got too much into the need for promotion and sales, which I'm not interested in."

The Bloomingdale's Campaign

Promotion and sales were Selengut's forte, as revealed by the contract he arranged with Bloomingdale's. He did not do it alone, though. Jody Bradshaw, the department store's representative, became one of the Bee's most staunch adherents. Born in 1939 in Manhattan, Ms. Bradshaw began a twelve-year career at Bloomingdale's in 1960. Possessing a strong design-school background, she spent half her time as a buyer, mostly of modern furniture; the other half, as a home furnishings fashion coordinator. Her job was helping to select salable, good-taste merchandise. She also worked with manufacturers to design products for Bloomingdale's.

"Sometimes I designed the product," she says. "Sometimes the manufacturer's designer designed a product with my set of directions. But product design was my specialty and I had done it literally around the world. I had also worked with handcraft around the world."

During the late 1960s, Bloomingdale's had major priorities in Europe. Ms. Bradshaw obtained rugs from Portugal, woven bedspreads from Spain, ceramics from France and Italy, and glassware from Italy:

> I would spend three months of the year going
> around Europe working with large manufacturers but
> also going from one little town to another, wherever
> the local tradespeople had a particular expertise. I
> worked with lots of craft people, little craft unions
> who had organized so they could produce a fair
> amount of product. We really couldn't buy one of this
> and one of that and one of another thing, but we would
> work with craft people who could produce something
> in volume so a department store could buy it. I never
> had had that experience in this country. The people I
> worked with here were large manufacturers.

Stanley Selengut enabled Ms. Bradshaw to work at last with American handcrafts. At the time he made his bid with Bloomingdale's, she was the soft goods expert charged with the sale of fabricated items. As she describes the incident:

He came in with a huge shopping bag full of little swatches. I didn't know whether he was married, single or anything else but the minute he walked through the door, I knew I was going to marry him.

He pulled out these quilts, or swatches, really, showing what the ladies did. What intrigued me about these samples was that they were a very old, authentic American art form which I had never before seen in bright, up-to-date fabrics. All I had ever seen had been antique quilts in shops.

It seemed to me an exciting statement welding the old and the new. There was one whole set of swatches done just in velvets which was exquisite. Others were in very bright-colored prints. Probably the most exciting was a Star pattern. Large stars. There was a number of traditional patterns but again, what set them aside was the use of these wonderful new fabrications.

I, of course, saw it as a merchant. Was this a product we could sell? We were a very large department store with a number of branch stores and I wanted to make sure this was something viable for the Freedom Quilting Bee and for Bloomingdale's. What it boiled down to was: Could they produce enough if we sold it in great volume? Could they produce the quality control we would need? If we were to show a sample pattern, would the quilt come out the way the customer expected it? The product was hand-done and naturally was going to vary depending on what hands made it.

I talked to Stanley in these terms and he said, "Why don't you come down and see for yourself?"

I was on my way to Europe so at first I had one of my assistants begin some recoloration and redesign work. Many of the designs were exquisite the way they were but Bloomingdale's felt we were a fashion leader and we had a tremendous grasp on the forecast of colors that were to come. We wanted to add our expertise to this old and new art form. Through these quilts, we would forecast colors that would be used in home furnishings and make the quilts even more exciting.

Eventually I got every one of the home furnishings soft goods buyers together. We jointly decided to do an overall store campaign using the Freedom Quilting

Bee's products, that we would sell quilts, placemats,
aprons, pillows and any quilted item that made sense
in a home furnishings world.

The venture was Ms. Bradshaw's true foothold in American handcrafts.
"It was very stimulating for me to lend my expertise to help somebody in
my own country," she beams.

Sale of the items began in 1969; the storewide promotion, where applicable,
occurred the next spring. The event brought Ms. Bradshaw to Alberta/Gee's
Bend several times:

I worked with the ladies from the point of their
cutting the swatches and sewing them together, to the
finished product, saying, "Well, this is really great
but it came out three inches too long for an apron. So
next time we have to make it three inches shorter."

What I tried to do was help them adapt what they
were making to be more salable to our customers. I
couldn't teach them how to build a quilt. Sure, I knew
how to build a quilt but they knew that a lot better
than I did. What I did lend them was my expertise in
terms of which fabrics, color combinations, and patterns would likely be more salable in today's world. I
also worked with products they hadn't made before,
such as placemats and aprons, to broaden their range
of prices.

I never will forget one of the first samples we did. It
was an apron that came out two inches too long. There
couldn't have been anybody any more unhappy than I
because for those ladies, the fabrics were gold. At
the onset, I had cut the fabric, shown them the correct
size, I made the apron and it came out too long.

In all my years of product design, I don't think I've
ever felt worse. I had wasted two inches of their fabric
and it broke my heart. Every sample had to come out
perfectly because otherwise I would have felt as though
I was robbing them of their fabric.

Samples usually don't come out perfectly the first
time, but we made less mistakes on those samples than
I ever made before or have made since because they
communicated to me how serious they were, how
much this all meant to them and how much they cared
about the fabrics. Of all the places I've worked in the
world, I've never been under pressure any heavier, not
to waste one inch of their fabric.

I grew to love those people very much. One of the

preconceived notions I had before working with them
was a natural prejudice that people who are poor probably are poor because they are lazy. I don't think I
went down there with that thought in mind but what
flabbergasted me was that those people were poor
not because they were lazy or stupid, but because they
lived in a part of the world where they just didn't have
the opportunity to make a real living. No one had
given them an opportunity.

It was a naive, stupid notion because I was used to
lack of opportunities in Europe, but when I began
to work with those ladies, I was overwhelmed at how
loving, bright, honest and hardworking they were,
and untinged by so much of what society or political
situations can do. I never came across a group of people
who cared more.

A Resurgence of Interest in Quilts

As part of its quilting promotion, in June 1969, Bloomingdale's ran a full-
page advertisement in *The New York Times*. It featured an artistic layout of a
couple of bedrooms decorated with quilting. Covering one of the beds was
the Double Wedding Ring, a traditional pattern among the more talented
black quilters of Wilcox County. The second bed showcased a paisley burst
of Stars and Stripes, another pattern of accomplishment among the area
quilters. The advertisement stated:

Come to our patchwork paradise. See quilts, cover-
lets, pillows, patchworked in sumptuous acetate velvets,
paisleys, calicos and other cotton prints, plump with
polyester or kapok filling. All lavished with fine stitchery and quilting, done by patient hands, with the authentic beauty of by-gone leisurely times. Made here in
America, all the designs, which are exclusively ours,
are faithful reproductions of historic 18th century patterns. All are treasures, to use and prize now and hand
down as future heirlooms.

Prices ranged from $180 for a Wedding Ring full coverlet to $11 for a small
pillow.

By the time the promotion was in progress, Ms. Bradshaw had changed
positions with the company and had left the sale of the quilts to others. But
she was well aware of consumer attitude toward the project:

The store viewed it as one of the most exciting promotions it had ever had. Afterwards, I watched that
whole American resurgence of interest in quilts. It
came after that promotion. I firmly believe that resurgence was a result of our promotion because
Bloomingdale's is a trend setter. Bloomingdale's kicked
off quilting in the United States as an "in" kind of
new art. There were a couple of other groups doing
quilts at the time, but the combination of the Freedom
Quilting Bee and Bloomingdale's was the largest factor
that kicked off that whole thing. Their getting together
was the impetus, without question.

The co-op's relationship with the store was only for a short term, for the
time came for new trends and new promotions. As Ms. Bradshaw explains:

Sears does have long contracts, and Macy's has long
contracts sometimes, but the way most stores buy,
their contract is their order copy. You write an order
and you get supplied. You continue writing an order
as long as it sells and as long as you want to carry it.

There was no contract in the sense that Bloomingdale's agreed to buy from the Freedom Quilting Bee x
number of quilts forevermore. What typically happens
when you start a promotion is that you buy what you
think you're going to need. However, what happens
with a trend-setting department store—and Bloomingdale's is *the* trend-setting department store in the
country—is that the store, always of necessity, must
have a new trend. The next season, because everyone
looks to Bloomingdale's for a new trend, the store
must come up with one. It must stimulate the customers who shop there because they want to get
something different.

Bloomingdale's does one or two storewide promotions a year. That doesn't mean items from a past promotion might not be carried over. That would depend
on how well the items sold, the individual buyers
who generally get tired of the product before the public
does because they look at it every day, and other factors. Handcrafted items by their very essence are
slightly more difficult to handle. It's not as easy as
buying something out of a cookie cutter, although
Bloomingdale's really is not interested in buying out of
a cookie cutter, or buying because of the simplicity of
a purchase.

Bloomingdale's went on to focus its attention on Indonesia, Morocco, the People's Republic of China, and other countries as well as new concepts, themes and enticements—all to whet customer appetite. But, for a spell in 1969–70, quilting was a major thrust in the store's domestic area. And, as Ms. Bradshaw remembers the event, it started a style with consumers coast-to-coast. Stanley Selengut shares that feeling: "We were the ones who started making quilting fashionable. We were copied all over the place. A lot of the Appalachian groups got into the act but we were the ones who started the whole movement." And Francis Walter recalls only too well the designers—with drawing pads—at the quilters' tent at the Smithsonian Folklife Festivals. "They would be drawing our designs—Sara Stein's designs—which were not patented."

Also, during that time, Father Walter attended a clergy conference, where he spotted a minister's wife wearing a dress splotched with hoot owls:

Our hoot owls covered the dress! It was the one
Maggie McMillian drew with a pencil on an ordinary
piece of letter paper. The hoot owls on that dress were
the same size as the ones on our potholders. The designer had put them all over a black background as
a printed material. It was not illegal but someone had
stolen the design. I asked the lady where she got the
material. She said, "I got it at Hancock's and I made
myself this dress."

So there was something in the air that gravitated
toward the artistry of these black women at that time,
and of quilting in general. People such as Sister Parish,
Diana Vreeland and others sensed that, took it in their
teeth and went with it.

Other Commercial Projects

The Selengut era was prolific for the Freedom quilters. Besides the Bloomingdale's order, the cooperative was at work on other sales. On July 4–7, 1968, the Bee was represented for the second time at the Smithsonian Folklife Festival. "Recognition and interest came like balm from Gilead," Father Walter told the readers of his *Newsletter* later that month.

Then in August 1968 the Atlanta-based Federation of Southern Cooperatives sponsored a booth in a New York trade show, wholesaling regional wares to boutiques and gift shops. A charter member of the organization, the Freedom Quilting Bee participated and grossed $3,000. During that same month, another of New York's department stores, Lord & Taylor, began to carry Freedom quilts. Later in the fall, members exhibited their products during a two-week promotion of American folk culture at the St. Louis department store Famous Barr.

In 1969 Selengut sealed a mail-order merchandising arrangement with *Life* magazine. The company paid $7,500 for quilts and "dashikis," the African-inspired ornamental garbs made by Freedom. The two items were sold along with goods from the Poor People's Corporation of Mississippi in a new test offering called Life's Treasures.

In March of that year, *Woman's Day* ran a story on the group. The result: more than a thousand letters, many of which were passed on to Mountain Artisans, the white, West Virginia quilting co-op, because the Freedom quilters could not handle that many. Also in March, the Bee staged the groundbreaking for its new sewing center (see Chapter 7). By early summer, the group was at home in its very own building, and by autumn the quilters were fast at work on "the largest quilt in the world."

"The Largest Quilt in the World"

Commissioned by E. I. du Pont de Nemours & Co. (Inc.), of Wilmington, Delaware, and arranged by Selengut, the quilt was constructed for Sakowitz, a large department store in Houston, Texas. The store annually staged a festive fall promotion, and in 1969 it was to focus on American folkways by keynoting ethnic contributions to the nation's heritage. Sakowitz officials wanted the storefront decorated with a piece of Americana that would immediately identify the promotional theme. A spectacular patchwork quilt was the obvious choice. Sakowitz then appealed to du Pont because the company's Dacron 88 fiberfill was used widely as quilt filling. The natural candidate to produce the oversized quilt was the Freedom Quilting Bee, known nationwide for perpetuating this American craft.

Du Pont contacted Selengut, who put the company in touch with Estelle Witherspoon. The request: a patchwork quilt in a random arrangement of equally sized squares. This sounds simple enough, but the dimensions were hardly routine: twenty feet wide by forty-four feet long, or about one-fourth the size of a basketball court. Despite the cumbersome size and the almost impossible deadline, Mrs. Witherspoon accepted the order without the bat of an eye. "All we had to do was furnish the labor," says she. "They paid us $2,500, and you know, back then $2,500 was some money."

Du Pont shipped to the quilting bee hundreds of swatches of material, thread, and filling, made, of course, by du Pont. The quilters cut the swatches into fifteen-inch squares, arranged them for optimum aesthetic affect, and stitched them together. They used literally thousands of tiny stitches to fuse the layers together. As a final grand embellishment, they were given a golden fabric shaped as an American eagle to appliqué on the center facing.

The huge quilt was ready for delivery two weeks before the deadline—a feat that stunned both du Pont and Sakowitz. But, as Estelle Witherspoon told a du Pont writer whose feature about the project came out in the January–February 1970 issue of the *Du Pont Magazine:* "We just called in everybody who could come by truck or foot or horseback and told 'em to get to it."

Gerald Montaigne, a du Pont textile fiber man, claimed in that story, "We can't substantiate it, but it must be just about the largest handmade quilt in history." Mrs. Witherspoon's comments support this view:

Ooooooooh, that was really a large quilt. We had to
roll it and roll it and roll it. It had such large rolls on
it, you could hardly reach your arms over the rolls.
See, what we did was put so much of it down, work
on that much, and roll it up.
We would have eight ladies working on it one day,
and the next day we would have eight more. The third
day we would go back and get those first eight. We
would just rotate them around to give them all some
work. It took us about three weeks to do it.

The quilt was so large when completed that it had to be taken outside the sewing center and folded in the yard. "The people from du Pont came down for several days and made pictures of everybody here," Mrs. Witherspoon explains. "When we finished it they came down, picked it up, and took it back in a big old truck."

Ropes and pulleys raised the gargantuan vertical quilt to the facade of the department store, where it stayed for two weeks, then was taken down, crated, and returned to du Pont. Some people believe it should have been given to the Smithsonian, but its fate was far different. The quilt toured the United States for a while, and then Mrs. Witherspoon accepted du Pont's offer to return it to the co-op. To pay an overhead debt, members cut it into eighteen small quilts and sold them for ten dollars each. As Mrs. Witherspoon now looks on the incident, "We were so much poorer then than we are now, and $10 worth of quilts was a great help."

Sitting behind a desk in her office at the sewing center, the effervescent administrator points to a photo of the extraordinary quilt on a bulletin board. Once used to grace a page of *Du Pont Magazine,* the picture shows a multicolored patchwork hanging from the second story of the Sakowitz store, centered with an American eagle.

Does Mrs. Witherspoon ever wish she had kept the quilt intact? "I wish I had kept a part of it anyway. I wish I could have. But we were so poor. They told me we could do anything we wanted with the quilt. We just wanted to keep the picture."

More and More Like a Business

Meanwhile, using part of the grant money from Southern Consumers, the Bee had bought a 1965 Ford van. A new promotional brochure by Elizabeth Walter boosted mail orders. A dozen commercial sewing machines were at work on some of the quilt piecing and construction of smaller items. And, at long last, the quilting bee got a telephone.

With each new order, each new meeting of the board of directors, each new ring of the phone, and each new paycheck, the Bee was becoming a real business, capable of survival. Stanley Selengut knew it would click and he recognized that it would be long-lasting. Says he:

I also knew they would never become a major industry. But once the people learned how to develop skills to produce and market a product, there would always be people who would buy it. The product may not be in the same shape as back then, but they're a viable selling concern now.

I think the quilters were shown that if a bunch of very simple, good-willed people desire to go into a small business, they can, and they have the ability to develop and market products and run a business. It takes a lot of courage. Usually, people from a poverty area have very little confidence in their own abilities. They never think of themselves as "business people."

I used to go to those board of directors meetings and they were very interesting. These heavy-set black ladies in their fifties and sixties were sitting around a board of directors table, discussing their business. It was profound because it could have been the same kind of meeting at the Exxon Corporation, the same kinds of discussions, problems, and efforts to work through those problems.

If anything, what I owe to them is that I worked out a lot of my prejudices through the Freedom Quilting Bee. I came from a middle-class home where we had black maids. In my growing up, seen as normal in my background, the black lady was a servant who took care of me. She was a second-class citizen who didn't eat with me at the table. In our neighborhood, there weren't any black people except servants.

We grow up with inherent prejudices. We think of black people as less skilled, dumber, unambitious. But I worked through a lot of that with the Freedom Quilting Bee. They're bright, ambitious, in some

ways even profound and in some ways they have a
wisdom beyond some of our own voracious instincts.
In their business decisions, the products they chose
to make and how they wanted to price their products,
they showed a lot of sensitivity, a lot of their own
goals and needs.

In December 1969 the Freedom Quilting Bee exhibited its wares at Stillman College, a black, Presbyterian institution in Tuscaloosa. One of the
quilts was bought by Doris Leapard, a local businesswoman. She kept it on
her bed for more than a decade. In 1981 she sold it to Dr. Robert Cargo, on
the faculty of The University of Alabama and a collector of Alabama quilts.
The quilt is a magnificent Lone Star, mostly of red-and-tan-hued paisleys set
on black background. It probably was made in 1968; its creator is unknown.
Now titled Star of Bethlehem, the masterpiece typifies what a New York
kingpin of native crafts was able to prove way down South: that "simple,
goodwilled people of poverty" could blend courage with desire and breed
success.

In 1982 Dr. Cargo's quilts were exhibited at the Birmingham Museum of
Art, where the Star of Bethlehem made its second public appearance. Then
his collection went to the Montgomery Museum of Fine Arts, where the
Wilcox treasure was shown once more. Unknowingly, in the descriptive
material Dr. Cargo prepared for the exhibit, he linked this quilt to a time in
the world when art and business came together under highly improbable
conditions: "Rich fabrics, probably from Liberty of London; juxtaposed
against the black background frequently used by Freedom Quilting Bee, the
exotic star seems to float in a void of space."

And so it was with the Freedom Quilting Bee itself—that last heartbeat
of hope in an otherwise decadent place of existence—an exotic star floating
in a void of space.

7 *A Factory Comes to the Cornfield*

"Dear friend, Tis with Fingers of love that I pause here to request the honor of your present, at the ground breaking of the sewing center." So begins the handwritten letter from Route One, Box 72, Alberta, Alabama, dated February 10, 1969, that was duplicated and mailed countrywide to friends and associates of the quilting bee. "It will take place, March 8–1969 at 10 A.M. We are so greatful and Thankful to the Lord that he have answered our prayers and ables us to by a piece of land, throught the help of our meny Friends. We are now ready to build a beautiful sewing center better than we ever dreamed we would ever have. We are looking to see you on that date." Noting "Dinner will be served," the invitation was signed by Mrs. Eugene Witherspoon, manager; and Mrs. Eddie Young, president.

How the Freedom Quilting Bee acquired a sewing center is the story of an uphill battle. First, the all-black co-op needed to purchase land. Almost all the area was owned by whites, so the chance of a sale was slim. Then members had to raise money for materials to erect the center. And they had to build it themselves with a work crew that included only one skilled laborer.

The spark plug who set it in motion was Stanley Selengut. This red-haired cosmopolite soon discovered the quilters were hardly close knit. Members' home communities were spaced across the Black Belt. Even half a year after he had settled in, five groups were still working in three counties. Before his coming, major units were in Possum Bend, Gee's Bend, and Alberta, and many individuals were working in the lonely confines of their homes. An early spotlight was the Gee's Bend residence of Bee treasurer Mattie Ross. Then the activity was centered at the home of a Gee's Bend minister.

By April 1966 Roman Pettway, who owned a mercantile establishment at Gee's Bend, let the women work there. As a result, the co-op had a mailing address to receive scraps of cloth as well as a place to pack and ship. Minder

Coleman used her profits to buy a sewing machine for the women working there. And, best of all, the Pettway store had electricity.

Finally, cooperative headquarters came to Route One, Alberta, and a small, unpainted house that until recently had been occupied by Eugene and Estelle Witherspoon who, partially through her management of the quilters, had been able to move up the road to a more comfortable dwelling.

Known locally as "the quilt house," the place had two rooms, each fourteen by fourteen feet square. Francis Walter had once described it as "an 80 year old dogtrot tenant shack." When the Witherspoons lived there, one room was a quilting workshop, especially for members in Alberta, as well as an office. In fact, it was the first office of the Freedom Quilting Bee. When the Witherspoons moved, the entire shanty became a sewing center. In one room, Mrs. Witherspoon supervised the office work, surrounded by a cutting table, fabric bolts, and finished quilts. The other room housed a table, a quilting frame, and space for half a dozen quilters.

The rickety shack was the edifice from which Stanley Selengut was to produce and market native quilts, but he found communication from there with the total membership next to impossible. So was dissemination of fabric as well as efforts to coordinate color schemes and ensure quality control. Also, there was no telephone. Even if there had been one, calls could not have been placed to most members because they did not have telephones either. "So even in dealing with the early orders," Selengut states, "it became apparent we needed our own building."

The Co-op Buys Land

Because of the unusual leadership and vision of Mrs. Witherspoon, it was essential that a permanent sewing center be located at her home base of Route One, Alberta, rather than ten miles down Highway 29 at Gee's Bend. But an immediate problem was finding suitable land blacks could buy from whites. After anxious months, a humble white farmer from Alberta named Lee Rose agreed to sell the quilters an acre on the Alberta route, along the road toward Gee's Bend. He and his wife had been well acquainted with the Witherspoons for years. Rose became only the second neighboring white to break tradition and sell to blacks.

"The high point of the whole sewing center process was when we actually had been able to buy the property," Francis Walter contends. "That was the accomplishment, because we didn't know whether we could do it. It would have been so easy for some of the ruling-class whites down there, such as they were, to have pressured Mr. Rose not to sell. If they had, he wouldn't have sold. We were afraid that would happen, or he would think it might happen."

In this eighty-year-old dogtrot, vacated by Estelle and Eugene Witherspoon, Stanley Selengut began marketing the Freedom quilts nationwide. (Courtesy, Reverend Francis X. Walter)

The cooperative bought the acre, planned a groundbreaking, and sent out invitations. Selengut engaged one of his New York friends, Martin Stein, the architect and husband of Sara Stein, to draw blueprints for the building, a 4500-square-foot masonry structure that would cost more than $20,000. Then money was raised to pay for the building from philanthropic foundations. As Father Walter says, "The small foundations were willing to venture a little

Estelle Witherspoon attends to paperwork in the 1960s in the co-op's first office: the kitchen of her former home. (Photo by Nancy Redpath; courtesy, Reverend Francis X. Walter)

money on us and we used that money well. In those days, the civil rights movement was something everybody who was liberal still approved of. So we asked the foundations for enough to build our sewing center." Solicitation yielded $34,000; later, an additional $7,500 was received to complete construction.

Two weeks before the groundbreaking, Selengut, relying on his background as a civil engineer, began to stake out the acre, pulling up cornstalks that hampered his effort. "It's a long way from having a Park Avenue office to finding yourself laying out a building in an Alberta cornfield and pulling up cornstalks to make room for the building," he reflects. "But it's a learning experience. It brings you into focus." In the midst of it all, Lee Rose made another offer to Estelle Witherspoon: he would sell the co-op a house, a well, and twenty-three acres of land. The house was a relic redone to include plumbing and a kitchen. His proposal sounded as though he was asking for $10,000 in addition to what he had received for sale of the first acre.

A week later, Mrs. Witherspoon presented the facts to the members of the co-op board. Father Walter assured them of an interest-free, $10,000 loan from the American Friends Service Committee, in Atlanta. They voted to buy. After dinner, the Witherspoons took a $500 check to Rose to see if he could accept it as down payment for the $10,000. He did, instantly. The next morning, Father Walter made the arrangement known to the co-op's Birmingham lawyer, Erskine Smith, and the American Friends. Smith prepared a contract, and the group from Atlanta furnished $9,500.

The Witherspoons and the Roses drove to the county courthouse in Camden, where the Roses signed the deed over to the Freedom Quilting Bee. That evening, unable to find an envelope, Mrs. Witherspoon wrapped the check for $9,500 in a Christmas-party napkin, and she and her husband delivered the check to Rose.

Father Walter explains the transaction:

> Mr. Rose knew he was doing us a big favor to sell
> land to black people. So he said it was twenty-three
> acres and it turned out to be about seventeen. As a
> result, we paid far more per acre than it actually would
> have been worth, but everybody was "satisfied." I
> mean we knew it was going to be extremely difficult
> if not impossible to buy land from a white person.
> The blacks didn't own much land and not at all where
> we wanted to buy.
>
> Mr. Rose's pride was involved because he was selling
> to and taking money from black people. It was a sen-
> sitive transaction, what the Witherspoons do best, and
> they pulled it off. I didn't go; I never talked to Mr.
> Rose myself.

Only days before the groundbreaking, Selengut stayed in the cornfield while the Freedom Quilting Bee bought a house, a well, and twenty-three acres of land—more or less—for $10,000.

Freedom Celebrates a Groundbreaking

A pageant unlike any other in these parts, the groundbreaking attracted more than five hundred people, including writer Calvin Trillin, who reported the event on March 22, 1969, in *The New Yorker*, enabling hundreds of thousands more to learn about the Bee.

"We tried to make it very elaborate and wanted it to last all day," declares Father Walter, who with Mrs. Witherspoon produced the undertaking. He had planned the groundbreaking as a fivefold allegory. First, celebrants convened across the road from the building site—on the one acre the quilting bee had first bought from Lee Rose. On that land was a shack occupied by a mentally retarded black man. "It was symbolic of the poverty from whence we had come."

The program began with freedom and folk songs rendered by black folk singer Bernice Reagon, of Atlanta, wearing west African attire. Although ecumenical, the groundbreaking featured the pomp and theater of the Episcopal church; an American flag, the Alabama state flag, and a processional cross were displayed. Father Walter was dressed in the full adornments of a priest of his denomination, including a cope and alb borrowed from a high-church parish in Birmingham.

In phase two, he wanted the participants to relive the civil rights movement, so they took to the middle of the highway, marching from the shack to the building site and singing "We Gonna Do What the Spirit Say Do." The music was led by Mattie Ross, who danced and frolicked along the way.

"The third location, the groundbreaking, symbolized what we had achieved after we had gone through the re-enactment of the civil rights struggle. We had achieved this building." The future home of the Bee was staked out with string and a cross was formed in the center. The SIP director dedicated the site and blessed the corners as well as the center, using a ceremony adapted from Episcopal ritual. The proposed building was officially named the Martin Luther King, Jr., Memorial Sewing Center as a testament to the quilters' love for the slain civil rights leader and his cause, in which they so actively participated. Then each woman on the board took a spade and removed one shovelful of earth.

Quilting Bee president Callie Young and her husband, Ed, led the procession to the road, where everyone got in automobiles and went to Gee's Bend, or Boykin, for the fourth whirl of activities at Pleasant Grove Baptist Church. This agenda included remarks by co-op officers, local black leaders, Stanley

Selengut, and foundation officers; prayers, choir music, and poetry readings. "We received tributes from friends in the movement and friends at the foundations. Then we paid tributes back to them, recognizing that none of this could have happened without outside help."

Next, dinner was served at the Boykin school cafeteria, eaten on school building porches and the grounds outside. Another round of music followed. Then the well-wishers were invited to the school's home demonstration building for more speaking and a chance to observe a showing of quilts and other co-op items.

"Stay as long as you like," said the printed program as it ushered guests into the concluding segment of the ceremony. "As you return to highway #5 you will see, halfway up the road from Gee's Bend, an old quilt hanging on the left side of the road. PLEASE STOP at the gate there and drive or walk

Reverend Walter, right, officiates at the co-op groundbreaking in 1969. (Courtesy, Stanley Selengut)

down the dirt road. We want you to see for yourself the shack we use for an office. Then you will share with us even more our happiness at building a beautiful new sewing center."

A melting pot of people, half of them black and half white, were on hand: members of the co-op, many of them dressed in colorful, self-made dashikis; local residents; officials from the Federation of Southern Cooperatives; faculty from The University of Alabama; foundation executives who were helping to pay for the building; Tom Screven, from the New York quilt auctions; an associate from Life's Treasures; Preston Schwarz, a New York textile importer who had let the quilters buy on credit the dashiki panels he imported from a factory in Holland; many of Francis Walter's Christian friends who were church activists in civil rights; the manager of a Wilcox County cooperative that provided Brickcrete, a sort of concrete brick, to build the sewing center; and Jody Bradshaw.

As Calvin Trillin told his readers: "Lee Rose and his wife watched from the driveway. Rose told a visitor that he and his wife had been wanting to move closer to their children and had been happy to help out the colored folks by selling them the land."

Tom Screven's memories of that day are special:

The weather was still with a little chill in the air.
Even before we went down, Francis was telling me
about the vestments he was going to wear and the
flags he had borrowed from the church. I was wondering how it would go.

So we went down. Francis was in his Episcopal
regalia with the flags. Bernice Reagon was in her African regalia, a beautiful head turban and long dress.
She had at least one child with her, an angelic little
boy, very light-skinned with curly brown hair who
looked as though he had stepped out of a Renaissance
painting, and so clinging to her long dress. That was a
moving scene. The little boy was awed by all this
strangeness. Francis awed everybody with his brocades
and gold embroidery on his garment.

It was an amazing procession from the site where
we began to the hillside where the center would be.
One of my strong memories is of the hillside. An old,
dead tree was behind the singer, the speakers, and
others in the ceremony.

Then it was to the church. I hadn't been in a real
country black church before. Ms. Reagon played a
couple of African percussion instruments to which
there was much foot-thumping and keeping time. The
church had a wooden floor, a very thumpable floor.
Everybody was in finery and the food was unbelievable. It was the Wilcox County version of high French
cuisine.

I hadn't been that close to country black folks ever
and have not since then, but I've had a different view
of poor people since that day. I began to realize then
that people who don't have a lot of formal education
have a lot to impart to those who do.

Days after the groundbreaking, Father Walter received a long-distance call from a young researcher with *The New Yorker:*

Calvin Trillin had turned in his story and she was
checking for possible mistakes. She said, "He has a list
down here of all the things that were served at this
dinner. I would like to go through these foods and you

tell me whether you remember if they were really served. Fried chicken, barbecued pork, collard greens, black-eyed peas, and sweet-potato pie."

I verified her list, but then I said, "Oh, that's not all." So I named a few others: turnip greens, potato salad, biscuits, cornbread, egg pie, lemon cake, and great big tea cakes. I said, "You're a checker, aren't you?" She said, "Well, that's what I do." I said, "In other words, you really didn't believe we had that much to eat." She said, "Well, I just wanted to be sure." I understand why she felt the need to call.

The Sewing Center Is Constructed

Now that the groundbreaking was behind them, the quilters had much work yet to do: putting together a sewing center. "It was wonderful to watch the way that thing got built," Selengut remembers, "because the ladies were mixing cement and the old men were running block. Of all the people working on it, they only had one skilled craftsman. He was the supervisor."

First, though, came the blueprints, compliments of Martin Stein. When the Steins visited Alberta/Gee's Bend, he was vice-president of Urbahn Associates, Inc., a prestigious New York City firm offering worldwide architectural, planning, management, and construction services. He had designed the Launch Control Center for the National Aeronautics and Space Administration's Apollo Project at the Kennedy Space Center, in Cape Canaveral, Florida. He had also planned hospitals, universities and the most sophisticated of scientific research facilities.

In 1968 this same man found himself in the confines of an isolated horseshoe in the Alabama Black Belt teaching uneducated men to brace benches while his wife taught their wives to make marketable quilts. Hearing of the sewing center in its dreaming stage, Stein offered to design it, free. But he needed to remember a couple of things:

It had to be a building *they* could build. The job couldn't be very complex. It had to be a simple wood-and-masonry construction that the people who were not trained as construction workers could build themselves. That was the primary goal. And they had to work with inexpensive, easy-to-use, local materials.

Secondly, it had to meet their functional needs. It had to be big enough to serve as a workplace and a community place because the quilting bee was an income-producing endeavor *and* a social entity.

Sara Stein adds:

On a higher level was going to be a board of directors meeting room. On the main level, plans called for a big, open space where they hopefully were going to have several commercial sewing machines. They would sew there instead of in their homes, especially in making the smaller items to produce more income than from making quilts.

To enable the women to work, they wanted to be able to do some of their chores there, particularly washing, because that was time-consuming for anybody taking care of children. If they could wash there, they could have more time to work, and life could be better for the whole community because nobody had machines. They were washing in tubs with water they had to haul and heat on the stove.

They also needed good bathrooms, a shower-bath, because they didn't have them in their homes. They needed a kitchen because they cooked a full meal in the middle of the day. And I think they desperately wanted a soda machine. They just loved soda. They drank more soda than I'd ever seen anybody drink in my life. I couldn't understand in a place with no money how they could spend so much on soda. It was consumed by the case.

Guided by the architect who had designed the Apollo space facilities from lift-off to splashdown, one skilled laborer, and a community of inexperienced, hardscrabble workers, mostly husbands of co-op members, the Martin Luther King, Jr., Memorial Sewing Center came into being. It was constructed of Brickcrete, a patented, bricklike concrete block made by another new black-owned and -operated cooperative in Wilcox County. The building was erected with a low budget—and with love.

"I figured I'd be a help-out for them," Allen Richardson, Jr., the job foreman, told a *New York Times* reporter who came down to do a piece on the quilters while construction was in progress on the one-and-a-half-story building. The newspaper's April 18 piece revealed that he did not receive overtime for his work or pay for rainy days and accepted only about a third of the $6-an-hour pay he usually drew on similar jobs.

Co-op president Callie Young and Eugene Witherspoon oversaw the work and administered the $35,000 building fund. According to Martin Stein, now president and chief executive officer of Urbahn Associates, if the $20,000 structure had been built at that time in a Northern urban area by trade-union labor, it would have cost from $70,000 to $90,000. Completed, the center had sewing and storage rooms, two bathrooms, a kitchen and laundry equipped with $15,000 in appliances, and a soft-drink machine.

Stein had wanted the building painted white. Some of the board members objected, saying his intentions were discriminatory. They wanted a darker color. But he thought white would be seen easily by travelers along Highway 29, would contrast attractively with the adjacent green countryside, and would reflect the heat. So white it was, but a black, Martin Stein-designed FQB logo was affixed to the right of the front door.

"We didn't want it to look like anything else on the road," Francis Walter declares. Until it received a newly built, dark-red roof, a mustard-yellow paint job, and other changes in the summer of 1985, the Martin Luther King, Jr., Memorial Sewing Center was the most unusual piece of architecture in Wilcox County. To some, the ultramodern facade even conjured thoughts of a giant spaceship from another galaxy that landed accidentally on a sparse stretch of Alabama cornfield and made itself at home.

Pictures of four former public leaders were hung from the walls inside, peering down on the quilters and their workaday labors as poignant reminders of a century of history: Abraham Lincoln, who freed the slaves; John Kennedy and his brother Robert, who paved the way for major laws affecting the civil rights of black people; and, of course, Martin Luther King.

By the summer of 1969, the co-op had moved in. Many finishing touches were missing because the money had run out. In fact, the center was never completed in the manner Martin Stein intended. The top floor was too hot for board meetings. Because the building was impractical to heat, the exposed beams on the ceiling, objects of beauty, needed to be covered with a lower ceiling. A different heating system had to be installed. Also, the grounds were never landscaped. But, still, the step forward from a dogtrot shack to a factory in only three years was almost unbelievable.

The Co-op Hosts a Wedding

On July 19, 1969, the Martin Luther King, Jr., Memorial Sewing Center was the scene of the community's most grandiose gathering yet: the wedding of Jody Bradshaw and Stanley Selengut.

When Ms. Bradshaw decided to work with the quilters, she came with Selengut and they stayed with the Witherspoons. As Selengut explains:

One night there was a beautiful moon. We were
walking around Alberta, I proposed to her and she
accepted. When we came back to the house, we asked
Mr. and Mrs. Witherspoon if we could get married
in their new factory building because, as a labor of

love, it was going up more like a church than any
church I had seen in the whole community.

They thought that would be terrific so we planned
our wedding to happen at the Freedom Quilting Bee.
We asked Francis Walter if he would marry us. He said
he would come, of course, but he felt it would be
more appropriate to ask one of the local black ministers. It was really interesting. I'm Jewish. My wife was

Sign at the entrance to
the Martin Luther King,
Jr., Memorial Sewing
Center. (Photo by Nancy
Callahan)

From "a cornfield so wet
we was bogging down"
sprang the new building
for the Bee in the summer
of 1969. (Photo by Nancy
Callahan)

Protestant and we were going to be married by a black
minister in Alberta, Alabama.

My sister, her husband and my wife's best girlfriend
came along and we were expecting a very simple wedding but we came down to a whole bustle of activity.
It seems the Freedom Quilting Bee had invited everybody who had ever bought a quilt plus every neighbor
within fifty miles, black and white.

They are relatively poor people and to feed everybody they had to slaughter all their cows, chickens,
and pigs. But they made a wedding Amy Vanderbilt
would have been proud of. They had rushed the new
building so it would be finished in time. They decorated tree branches, built an altar, and covered it with a
Double Wedding Ring quilt. They dressed a bunch of
little black kids in hand-sewn, white-lace costumes
and got them to be bridesmaids. And they had a rock
'n roll band, a jazz band, and a bunch of the older
ladies singing traditional church songs.

It was a hot summer day, and several hundred people
crowded into that factory. They had an old rinky-dink
piano used to play "Here Comes the Bride." The guy
who was to give away the bride was the one skilled
black carpenter who helped build the factory. My wife
was wearing a white lace pantsuit, all these little
bridesmaids were behind her and my best man was

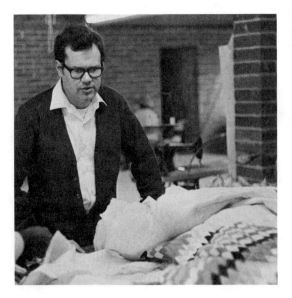

Reverend Walter exam-
ines quilts in 1969 inside
the building that resulted
from his "clothesline"
vision three and a half
years earlier. (Photo by
Nancy Redpath; courtesy,
Reverend Francis X.
Walter)

Mr. Witherspoon. He was crippled. So here I was at
the altar, holding the hand of this crippled black guy.

It was a delicate situation but the minister did a
marvelous job. He didn't put too much of Christ in it
to offend my being Jewish, he put enough in to make
Jody happy and enough of a sermon to please the local
people. After he pronounced us "man and wife" I
kissed Jody, and a couple of people started singing "We
Shall Overcome." Then the whole several hundred
joined in.

We slept our first wedding night in Mr. and Mrs.
Witherspoon's bedroom. They gave up their bedroom
for us. The wedding was a self-sacrifice to thank me
for giving them all that help. They couldn't pay me
physically but they paid me back tenfold. It was a
profoundly generous, unselfish, and interesting thing
they did.

Ms. Bradshaw says:

We really fell in love over the Freedom Quilting
Bee. After we decided to get married, I suggested we
get married there because I felt it would epitomize our
life together. And for the length of time we were together it really did.

But what was most unbelievable was the style with
which they served dinner to several hundred. It was as
though it was something they did every day of their
lives. And from their standpoint they were a black
community faced with a Jew and a Christian, both of
whom had been divorced. The poor preacher never
had performed a wedding before but Lonnie Brown
did a beautiful ceremony.

Selengut took special care to give his best man an appropriate gift, for Mr.
Witherspoon experienced much difficulty walking because he had fallen from
a tree during childhood while going after a coon or possum:

One of the presents I wanted to get him was a mule.
I spoke to his brother about the kind to buy, learned
what a good mule would cost and was going to buy
the animal for him to ride. His brother found a handsome white horse he felt Eugene would like even better
than the mule. So he bought this handsome white
horse.

When I got down for my wedding, I was shown

this horse I was to give my best man. The horse looked
a bit mangy so we took colorful ribbons and cloth
swatches from the Bee's inventory and braided his
mane and tail. We got that horse looking pretty terrific,
like a patchwork horse in a way.

When we presented Mr. Witherspoon with his wedding gift, it took us a couple of minutes to convince
him this was his gift, that now he owns this horse and
can ride it. He was so pleased, he looked at me and
said, "You know what I'm going to call this horse? I'm
going to call it Stanley."

Selengut was industrial consultant to the Freedom Quilting Bee for more
than two years. Early on, his expense money from Southern Consumers was
exhausted. Thus, he put much of his own money into the enterprise. From
day one, all the time he applied to the project was volunteer. "There was
nothing wrong with that," he reflects. "It was fun. The only regret I have is
that it would have been nice to have stayed with it a little longer."

Selengut has maintained abiding friendships with Estelle Witherspoon,
who visits him when she is on business in New York, and with Francis
Walter. And, after more than seventeen years, a filing cabinet in his east-side
apartment brims with sweet memories of his days in an Alabama cornfield:
financial statements, store orders, letters, publicity, and the picture of a
handsome white horse named Stanley.

8
Church Groups
Aid the
Quilting Bee

In 1970 two dissimilar but significant events occurred at the co-op that symbolized the long-in-coming power of its black women members. Many black families in the area desperately needed plots on which to live. In most cases, white land owners would not sell to blacks. But, by 1970, the Freedom Quilting Bee was the owner of twenty-three acres of land, more or less. So the group sold eight frontage lots to black families, who subsequently put up homes.

Also in that year the Freedom Quilting Bee Day Care Center was created to meet the needs of children whose mothers were making quilts. Housed in rooms behind the quilting work place, the center is available now to any area child—ages two to six—whose mother works away from home. It was established despite the strong opposition of the Alabama Department of Pensions and Security.

Then, after the quilters had moved into their new building and the Stanley Selengut times were winding down, the co-op received help with the daily running of its business from volunteers belonging to two Christian denominations: the Catholics and the Mennonites.

Sister Catherine Tightens Office Procedures

Catherine Martin, a white Catholic nun, became one of the best friends Freedom has ever had. She is a petite, genteel figure with short, white hair who is a member of the Sisters of St. Joseph of Rochester, a religious order of about 580 members, most of whom live in New York state. Born and educated in Rochester, Sister Catherine was a teacher for thirty years; she directed the guidance program for St. Joseph's Hospital in Elmira, New York, and trained young sisters of her order. Then, in 1969, she was sent to

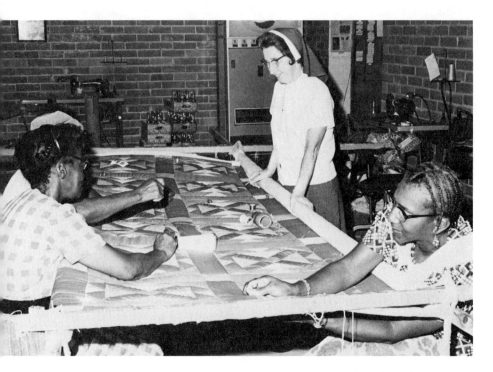

Sister Catherine Martin, who helped with office duties at the Bee in the early 1970s, watches the quilters at work in 1972 on a T square. (Photo by Reverend Arthur Rivard; courtesy, Fathers of St. Edmund, Selma, Alabama)

Selma to work for the Fathers of St. Edmund, a Catholic order that sponsored the city's Good Samaritan Hospital.

Sister Catherine was to work at the hospital, but, not long after she arrived, Father John Crowley, Southern regional director for the Edmundites and president of the hospital, was approached by Francis Walter about problems with the co-op. "They recently had moved into a very nice building," Sister Catherine explains. "They had good machines, the building was well-lighted, and they had an outlet for the goods. But nobody could do the office work. The business part was badly in need of professional help. He said to Father Crowley, 'Do you know of anyone who could help them?' "

The Edmundite priest thought of Sister Catherine, who was trained in business and well acquainted with office work. She visited the place and knew instantly she could help. So Father Crowley procured an old typewriter and typing table from the mission storeroom, and Sister Catherine transported them to the sewing center. Enjoying the hearty approval of the Edmundites, she began a twice-a-week trip to the quilting bee that lasted for years. "When I first went there the women were very poor and getting so little. There were no guaranteed wages. Sometimes, the bank balance would get so low that Mrs. Witherspoon couldn't even pay them that week. She would always say, 'Maybe we'll get a check in the mail. Then I'll pay you next week. The Lord will take care of us. We'll get that check.' And sure enough, a check would come. It would always come."

From the quilters' perspective, Sister Catherine was a godsend. She made time-cost studies and performed bookkeeping and secretarial work. She handled correspondence and interpreted orders.

Previously, a quilt sale had been marked in a notebook and the amount of the sale indicated. When the bill was paid, it would be crossed out. Sister Catherine recalls:

> If you're working just in a notebook it can be very
> difficult. Mrs. Witherspoon had a fantastic memory so
> she would look at the invoice or the quilt order and
> say most of the time, "This quilt was paid for," or
> "This one was not." We went through checks to give
> us definite information about the payments. So it wasn't
> all memory. But if we had no check and Mrs. Wither-
> spoon said they had paid, usually they had. If she said
> they hadn't paid, usually they had not. But then, there
> was a pile in between of invoices we really didn't know
> about.
> So I had to write letters to all those people and ex-
> plain, "We were just a new, grassroots organization
> and our bookkeeping wasn't of the best. Please forgive
> us but we are not sure whether this quilt had been
> paid for." I tried to word it so I wouldn't hurt anyone's
> feelings.
> Well, the letters came back, from California, Chi-
> cago and New York City. A number said they did pay.
> Some put copies of the checks in the letters. Others
> said, "No, we're sorry; we forgot all about it." Still
> others said, "We forgot. We're sorry but we can only
> pay $10 a month."
> At least we knew who owed us, and we took their
> word. Then I made a card for each one to keep track
> of what was owed us. That was a step forward.

In 1972 the quilting bee was awarded a contract with Sears, Roebuck to manufacture corduroy pillow shams. The company sent officials to the Bee who set up a separate bookkeeping system for the pillow covers and provided training to inaugurate the system. But the co-op needed to do a cost study to help Sears determine what to pay the quilters and what to charge customers for the shams. As part of the study, Sister Catherine helped the Bee devise a piecework system.

"It's not a factory," she describes Freedom's work place. "It's an informal set-up and they like to chat, which is fine. They like to work at their own pace. Sometimes they want to sing, which is perfectly all right. Sometimes I would be doing my work and this beautiful voice would sound forth with a Negro spiritual or some other beautiful song. Mostly, one would sing and the rest would listen."

Although they enjoyed working at their own pace, they were being paid by the hour. Sister Catherine says that triggered some dissension:

> That caused a little dissatisfaction because the fast
> workers didn't get any more than those who liked
> to amble along, get up and walk around a little bit if
> they got tired of sitting, which was perfectly all right.
> They were allowed to do that but the ones who were
> all business and worked really fast didn't like that too
> well. So we put in a piecework system and had to
> make cost studies on each phase.
> To make the pillow cases we had to find out how
> long it took to put in a zipper, to sew a case, to fold
> and put a case in a plastic cover. We did quilts the same
> way. At that point, we could give a hundred cut-out
> pillow covers to the person who sewed around them
> and tell her, "You will get so much for doing these."
> The people who loved to sew on the machine could
> really do fast work. They made more money than
> they had been making and were delighted. The others
> were delighted because even though they didn't earn
> very much, what they earned was enough. They were
> enjoying sewing at the Bee and chatting. Maybe some
> were elderly and didn't feel they could go at a feverish
> pace but they wanted to be there. At their own pace
> their check would be less but it was all right because
> they knew they had done a certain number of things
> and had been paid for what they had done. That was
> one of the major advances we managed.

When Sister Catherine first knew the quilters, they were earning 45 to 60 cents an hour. At 60 cents, their wages were $3.60 a day, based on a six-hour workday, or $18 a week. "But to them, this was wonderful. Some had never before earned in their lives. They had lived very simply. From the time the quilting bee started and throughout the years, those women have definitely improved their standard of living. Their homes are better. Their children were better clothed and fed, and I think the women even learned from working together." From that 45- to 60-cent wage scale, the group gradually raised salaries to minimum wage several years after the sister's arrival.

As the Bee grew, so did her responsibilities. Help came in 1970, when Freedom became qualified to accept couples from the Mennonite faith— conscientious objectors—who would spend a year or two with the co-op rather than with the armed services. Two of the Mennonite women aided mightily with the office work. Not all were businesswomen, however, so Sister Catherine began to train young women in the area who gradually took charge. By 1974, when the co-op was on a sound business footing, she began to come only once a week. Then she trained a twenty-one-year-old local black woman, Julia Pettway, who eventually took her role—with pay:

> So I would go only once in a while. During my last
> few years in Selma if anything went wrong or if she
> thought it was, I'd get an SOS, go down, we'd find the
> trouble and straighten it out. But at the time I left
> Selma, I hadn't been called in quite a while.
> Now and then I called Mrs. Witherspoon to see
> how things were going. When I got down there she
> liked to take me into a corner, talk a little bit or ask me
> something. Julia felt good if I went down and she had
> a question, but for the business work I was not needed
> anymore. But this was our aim. If we could train an
> area person to do the work, that was the idea.

During those years, Sister Catherine learned and changed:

> I acquired a new respect for those country people.
> In talking to them I came to realize how really close to
> God they live. Right from the beginning I admired
> their pride and self esteem. But they were very humble
> and had a deep faith. Their wisdom and their faith
> impressed me.
> People don't realize what the faith of those quilters
> means to them, and how brave they were to keep this
> thing going, earning so little and even going home
> at the end of the week, not getting anything until next
> week—hopefully. Yet they stayed with it when it was
> very difficult. I know that because I could see they had
> just nothing extra.

After spending the remainder of her work in Selma with the Edmundite fundraising office, Sister Catherine retired in July 1983 and now lives in

Rochester. In wintertime her bed at the St. Joseph motherhouse is covered with a random patchwork quilt whose swatches are fifteen inches square. It was cut from the "largest quilt in the world." When she looks at her copy of *Du Pont Magazine* and the picture of that monstrous creation, she likes to point to her portion—on the bottom at the extreme right. The quilt is one of her few material possessions. It is a tangible reflection of her kinship with the Freedom quilters of Wilcox County. And it reminds her of an age when a grateful Estelle Witherspoon knew firsthand the high value of a $10 bill.

The Mennonites Foster Agriculture

When the Mennonites entered the life of the Freedom Quilting Bee, they too boosted the business side of the co-op—but with hogs and cattle.

It is an article of the Mennonite faith not to kill people. Most draft boards were understanding of this position so conscientious objectors of this faith had the option of working in hospitals and with charities rather than with the armed services. From 1970 until 1981, the Freedom Quilting Bee was one place of "alternative service" for the Mennonites.

Through an agreement transacted by the Eastern Mennonite Board of Missions and Charities, in Salunga, Pennsylvania, the Selma Inter-religious Project, and the co-op, a number of Mennonite individuals and couples left the comfort and security of their up-North homes for a strange, desolate slice of earth.

All were white. Most were young. Many were college graduates. One retired couple believed life with the quilters would be rewarding. Numerous single, short-term voluntary service workers, or "VSers," came for a summer. Even a college professor stayed for a spell. Despite their differences, all were versed by tradition in agriculture, which was ideal for the Freedom Quilting Bee because the Mennonites could convert all that land behind the sewing center into a productive farm.

First, the quilters entered the hog business, thanks to a Mennonite couple who cleared two acres and constructed a farrowing house to hold six sows. When the price of pigs was high, the co-op would sell one, then pay its overhead.

In 1978, though, the situation changed because the price of hogs fell below the cost of raising them. So the pig project gave way to the cattle business. The Bee started with three cows, gradually adding a few more. They now have nine, slightly more than the co-op's fifteen acres of pasture and woodland can support. According to Ralph Reinford, the most recent Mennonite to work with the Bee, "The cattle have been somewhat of a banking account because whenever they need some cash or extra money, they usually sell off a cow or two."

Ralph Reinford, a Mennonite who did agricultural work for the co-op, owns an early quilt made from swatches of silk and corduroy donated by New York fabric showrooms. (Photo by Nancy Callahan)

Born on a dairy farm near Philadelphia, Reinford earned a degree in agriculture and sociology from Eastern Mennonite College, in Harrisonburg, Virginia. While there he met his wife-to-be, Barbara, who became a registered nurse. The twosome arrived in Wilcox County on July 30, 1978, remained through church auspices for almost three years, and then elected to stay a couple of years more as county residents. Unlike the other Mennonite women who worked with the Bee, Barbara Reinford, as a registered nurse, made house calls under the authority of a doctor.

The church allocated stipends to the Reinfords and the other volunteers for housing, food, utilities, and other bare essentials. The couple lived at the quilting bee's "guest quarters," the five-room dwelling next door to the sewing center that was acquired during the Lee Rose land deal. In addition, each received from the church $15 to $20 monthly for personal use.

Reinford's major task was to manage the cattle. Because there were more cows than natural acres of feed, they had to be fed with hay and grain. So the Mennonites furnished Reinford a tractor, and he broke ground for planting, raised the crops, and fed them to the cattle.

The college-educated Reinford's perspective on agriculture was quite different from that of the quilters, especially in sales management and administration. He felt a deep difference existed in the way his administrative role was perceived by the quilters and by himself. As an example, when he thought it was time to sell a cow, rather than do so, he was required to make a proposal to the co-op board of directors: "Even when one cow was to be sold it made for discussion. Opinions differed among the quilters and it had to go through all the board members."

The board also voted on how many acres Reinford would plant, or whether he should plant at all: "With the increased cost of seed and fertilizer, it didn't pay to plant such a small acreage. When buying grain would make us come out better, I would recommend it to the board. That was the kind of thing I would recommend."

Because the Bee's cattle herd produces four or five calves per year, the project hardly loses money. "They usually break even," states Reinford, "or they come out a little bit ahead. Because of the number of cows, the calves are always there, always."

Much credit for the cattle population at the Bee and in the community goes to Reinford. One of his first actions was to seek help from the Heifer Project International, of Little Rock, Arkansas, which gave the quilters a purebred, quality-stock bull. When the people of the community now have cows they want to breed, they take them to the Freedom bull.

Ralph, Barbara, and other Mennonites spent endless hours in the guest quarters searching for ways to make more jobs for the local people. "There were more people involved in what we were doing than just the volunteers," he contends. "We felt we had the backing and the resources of the Mennonite

Church. Often, we brought in businessmen to evaluate what was happening at the quilting bee, and to give our program direction. We were not aliens or there all alone, because we had the backing of our church. And we felt we had very adequate resources in technical skills and finances."

Despite this support from the Mennonite Church, however, from a job perspective the Freedom Quilting Bee is still the largest industry around. As Reinford explains, "The quilting bee is the only job-creating impact in the community."

In August 1983 the Reinfords left the Black Belt for the Mennonite clusters of the North. The Freedom Quilting Bee does not plan to request the aid of other Mennonites because remarkable progress was made by the co-op from the days of the feeder-pig project to the time when Reinford kept the cattle. The cows are now in the capable hands of Nettie Young, Freedom's comanager, who has been with the co-op since its genesis. From the time those first pigs were brought in, she was given the task of supervising the farm endeavors. She is naturally equipped for the task because she and her children had run their own farm for years while her husband would be gone for months at a time, working in a New York factory.

According to Mrs. Young, "We don't have no real good pasture so we don't keep but a very few [cattle]. Fast as we have calves we'll sell the old cow and keep a heifer calf. We don't keep more than about four or five brood cows— the cows that are going to grow the calves for us. We have mens to take 'em to the stockyards to sell 'em. Sometime we have good luck, sometime we have a little down luck. We sold one cow and got high as $300 for it."

Mrs. Young believes the co-op will always be in the cattle business: "You know, if you own a field and sell a couple of cows and that bill got to come up right now, well, you could get some money. Don't never drop cows. You want to get the money and pay that bill."

Since the departure of the Mennonites, Mrs. Young has assigned various men to assist her with the more laborious aspects of her duties: "We'll have to take 'em to the stockyard if it has to be me 'cause I'm holding cows. I feeds 'em. I see to 'em being fed and see to keeping the pastures up and see to everything going right with 'em."

Some people think Mrs. Young carries a large burden because she already has responsibility as Freedom's comanager. "But it ain't bad," the way she sees it. "I got a man to do the bumming."

9   *Freedom's Bread and Butter: The Sears Contract*

In 1972 the Freedom Quilting Bee made a long-lasting arrangement with Sears, Roebuck and Company to produce corduroy pillow shams. Because civil rights is no longer the new, fever-pitched issue it was in the 1960s and because the patchwork look has been superseded by other styles and trends, the co-op has relied on its pillow sham business until even now for its very survival.

The catalyst for the link between Sears and Freedom was a New York City couple, Bob and Joyce Menschel, who became among the most enterprising and tenacious supporters of the co-op. Joyce had been born and brought up in Norfolk, Virginia, and was working on Wall Street as a security analyst when she became engaged to Robert B. Menschel, city-raised and a partner in the investment banking firm of Goldman, Sachs and Company.

Menschel heard about the Freedom Quilting Bee in a Wall Street taxi pool from Jay Pack, a partner in a small stock brokerage firm. Pack had learned of the Bee during the latter part of 1968 from Stanley Selengut. As Pack remembers:

Oddly enough, Mr. Selengut owned an old New York brownstone on East End Avenue. It happened to be next to an apartment house to which my wife and I had just moved. I called him because he ran an ad in the paper about investing in real estate and gave this East End address. I had lunch with him and thought he was a nice guy. I had no interest in his real estate but he did tell me about the Freedom Quilting Bee and that started my interest in it.

Stanley was then the only selling agent, and he sold the quilts when and where he could. There was a time when he got an order from Bloomingdale's for an enormous number of quilts. Bloomingdale's was under the impression the quilts were going to march in as factory-manufactured items, but when delivered, they were handcrafted, not factory-made, so they simply returned them all.

At which point, according to Stanley, the quilting bee was ready to go bankrupt or close to it. So he had these large cases of quilts. Even I took one of the boxes to my apartment and proceeded to peddle the quilts as best I could. The large double ones were $150. Many of the single- or twin-bed sizes were from $75 to $100. I bought a lot, used them for gifts and sold them to all my friends.

Pack sent the proceeds to Wilcox County, along with personal donations. "I told Bob Menschel I was in touch with the quilting bee and it seemed like a very worthwhile cause. In the late sixties, we were all concerned with civil rights in Alabama and Mississippi." Pack also told Menschel some of the co-op members could not see well enough to quilt properly. A move was afoot to buy them prescription eyeglasses as a substitute for the dime-store variety. Respecting Pack and his zealous intentions, Menschel wrote a check for $125,

Pressures of commercialization forced the Bee to discontinue production of several whimsical but labor-intensive patterns, such as this Indiana Turn-Around, which is black on yellow ochre. (Photo by Nancy Callahan; quilt owned by Michael and Nathan Goodson and Willita Zoellner, Tuscaloosa, Alabama)

which his friend sent down to Dixie. Menschel thought this would be his only contact with the faraway Freedom Quilting Bee. But not so.

Months later, in the spring of 1969, Pack asked Menschel for another donation. The quilters were moving into their building and direly needed new sewing equipment. So Menschel supplied a second check, for $200. Pack knew this fellow taxi pooler was to be married soon, so he suggested that Menschel ask his fiancée to come by the Pack home, look at quilts he and his wife had bought from the co-op, and select one in return for Menschel's generosity.

Joyce Menschel "expected to pick up a rag." But "Bob said, 'Just go and be nice, Joyce. Pick out a quilt and we'll write them a thank-you note.' But when I got there I was amazed. The quilts were extremely beautiful. I asked what the problem was and was told the buyer at Bloomingdale's had changed, the quilters had filled a big order and the new buyer didn't want the quilts."

Thus, fifty of the co-op's quilts had been rejected by Bloomingdale's, many of which were at the New York residence of Jay and Sheila Pack. Mrs. Menschel, newly married and no longer on Wall Street, found the quilts very salable and of excellent craftsmanship; after all, they had been created for Bloomingdale's. She told the Packs, "I'll sell the fifty quilts and you all go on about your business."

But, at that time, her husband saw no room in their small apartment for fifty quilts. "Bob made me call them back and say, 'I'll take a dozen.' He wouldn't let me have fifty." Later in the year, the twosome returned from a trip and discovered massive, floor-to-ceiling boxes of quilts at their front door.

"So I took my first dozen," Joyce says, and by January 1970 she had sent a $240 check to the quilters.

> Some of the sizing wasn't as regular as it could have been but everything about them was beautiful. They were sold in a week. I called ten people and said, "I'm showing quilts on Thursday. Do you want to buy them?" Every couple of Thursdays, Sheila Pack would come over and we would have quilt day. When the quilts were gone I would send for more, under the impression that after I sold fifty, the Freedom Quilting Bee would go about its business. But the fifty never stopped.
>
> After the quilts kept coming I could see more problems than met the eye. The sizes were irregular. They didn't invoice properly. I could tell Bloomingdale's had designed and styled the original group very well. But when I got farther past those originals I saw a much cruder quilt. Some were absolutely beautiful. In some, one wrong fabric ruined the whole quilt.

1. This Star of Bethlehem, circa 1968, used printed cotton fabrics from Liberty of London, obtained for the Bee through the assistance of Stanley Selengut. (Photo by Nancy Callahan; quilt owned by Helen and Robert Cargo, Tuscaloosa, Alabama)

2 and 3. These 1967 quilts are characteristic of those produced by black women of Wilcox County before the birth of the Bee. *Left:* An all-wool crazy quilt made for the co-op by Minsie Lee Pettway. *Right:* A star pattern created by Freedom's comanager, Nettie Young. (Photos by Nancy Callahan; quilts owned by Charles J. and Mary McCarthy, Gloucester, Massachusetts)

4. Lucy Marie Mingo did the appliqué stitchwork for this 1966 Chestnut Bud, one of the co-op's first productions. (Photo by Nancy Callahan; quilt owned by longtime *Vogue* editor Diana Vreeland, New York City)

5. Du Pont corporation commissioned the Bee to produce "the largest quilt in the world" for a 1966 American folkways promotion at Sakowitz department store in Houston, Texas. (Courtesy, E. I. du Pont de Nemours & Co., Inc.)

6. The Coat of Many Colors, also called Joseph's Coat, was a popular item in the baby size in New York department stores during the 1970s. This 1981 version is currently sold by the Bee. (Photo by Nancy Callahan)

7. To raise funds for Freedom's day-care center, mothers of Bee members made and sold this star-design quilt, circa 1970. (Photo by Nancy Callahan; quilt owned by Rose Gladney, Tuscaloosa, Alabama)

8. China Grove Myles's Pine Burr quilts made her a
legend in Wilcox County. She is shown here with one
of the last quilts she made before her death in 1976.
(Photo by Rhodes Johnston, Jr.)

Joyce Menschel Becomes Freedom's Broker

After Stanley Selengut became engaged in other matters, Joyce Menschel became the prime marketing agent for the Freedom Quilting Bee, selling quilts and sending the money to Alabama. "I was never officially anything," she states. "I was just helping out." Regardless, from the latter half of 1969 until the mid-1970s, Mrs. Menschel sold quilts from her apartment and arranged for co-op sales to two New York department stores, Bonwit Teller and Saks Fifth Avenue. She was also the chief communicator between the quilters and those stores. "What Joyce arranged for Bonwit's," her husband declares, "was from 80 to 90 percent of the quilters' business, maybe more. Other than the few drop-ins they got in Alberta, for a number of years this was it."

But Mrs. Menschel encountered a problem: "In the early days the quilters really didn't know how to invoice properly. I would send letters trying to explain every step. Finally we had the boxes shipped to us." When she received the quilts, she would make sure they were prepared professionally to be taken to the stores:

I interviewed at Bloomingdale's and other places to
find out what the problems were. When I talked to the
man at Bloomingdale's, he brought out the quilt boxes.
They were so dilapidated and falling apart that the
merchandise could have been dirty. It was embarrassing
for the store. They would ship the quilts in an old
toilet tissue box or whatever they could find locally.
We got them boxes and asked them to wrap each
quilt in a plastic bag, which they might have been
doing already during those first shipments.

Because the quilts were irregular-sized craft and were not meant for mass production, Mrs. Menschel thought Freedom should produce a standard, easily duplicative item for Bonwit Teller and Saks Fifth Avenue. That product blossomed as the baby quilt, useful on beds or as wall hangings, small tablecloths, and picnic blankets. Ironically, the baby quilt was more lucrative for the quilters than the larger sizes because it took less time to produce.

Sized thirty-eight by fifty inches, the quilt pattern used was Coat of Many Colors, which many people felt resembled a cathedral window. It had been fashioned for almost a century and a half by black Wilcox quilters in memory of the biblical Joseph, who had been given a multihued robe, for which he was cast into Egypt and conquered trials as hard as their own.

At both stores, Coat of Many Colors sold steadily. "We would have the orders shipped to our home," Joyce explains. "Then I would ask a friend to come over with a pair of scissors, needle and thread. We would resew all their problems because they had no quality control." "For years," Bob Menschel points out, "I would come home and see Joyce and her friend on their hands and knees, trying to make the things salable."

During those times, the quilters encountered serious difficulties in acquiring quality material for their quilts. Their major source in Selma no longer carried what they needed. As Mrs. Menschel says:

> We found out there wasn't enough available in the South. Then we started talking to a man in Montgomery who would try to keep their yellow material. Saks had wanted the quilt with bright yellow background instead of white muslin. The quilters couldn't get that yellow so we tried to track it down around the country.
>
> "I found a man in New York who would sell them the fabric but he wanted to know if they had a Dun and Bradstreet rating. Of course they didn't so I said if something happened and they didn't pay, I would personally pay. But that wasn't good enough for him because I was a lady. Finally, Bob had to call him. He took a man's okay right away and a man's personal guarantee that if the bill wasn't paid, we would pay it.

Locating suitable fabric always seemed a challenge to Mrs. Menschel, especially for the co-op's dashiki business. The quilters had been obtaining that fabric from Atlanta, but at one point their source ran out. An order needed to be filled, and no fabric was available with which to fill it. Mrs. Menschel declares, "It was always to fill an order. In those years they never thought of saying, 'We'll get an order of dashiki fabric.' They were living so hand-to-mouth that when they got an order, they realized they needed fabric and they needed it *then*. Very often, they couldn't get it."

As a dashiki source, Mrs. Menschel was able to buy the cloth from a New York agent whose supply house was in Holland. She also found a Dacron pillow form source on New York's lower east side to aid the co-op's quilted pillow business: "They used to stuff the pillow by hand and that had to stop because of mixed wads. I mean, one doesn't stuff a pillow by hand in today's world. I used to order pillows and have them shipped to Alabama so they could make the covers and ship them out. It was a more professional way."

In attempting to enhance the market value of the quilts, Mrs. Menschel prepared fabric cards so the workers could more easily reorder colors. She also made signs bearing helpful quality-control hints that were placed in the sewing center. "Have labels been sewn on quilts?" said one sign. "Have all loose threads been removed?" said another.

Mrs. Menschel reduced the number of patterns used by the co-op: "The patterns were much more varied than they are today. They were doing

Wedding Rings and May Apples and all sorts of designs. We suggested on the basis of what they seemed to be selling that they limit their patterns to four or five. That way, they could repeat them in different colors."

Mrs. Menschel also set up pattern color charts:

When I started, the quilts had been designed by
Sara Stein and Stanley Selengut and they were very
beautiful. It wasn't hard to figure out why their designs
worked, then say, "You couldn't get this fabric but you
could get that one as a substitute." I could tell color
coordination and see what the design was based on.

The problem was that you never could substitute
one fabric. You had to substitute four or five. But you
could hold fairly well to what they had in mind.

A couple of times, Joyce Menschel talked to Sara Stein. In the beginning, though, Sheila Pack photographed the quilts so the pair could learn the color combinations and patterns. According to Joyce, "When we became involved, we couldn't keep straight the name of the quilt, the color, or what we had sold. We wanted to be able to say, 'Can we have another one of these?' Finally, we got a different system."

Trying to teach members how to invoice, size, and measure, Mrs. Menschel sent down pages of step-by-step instructions. After a quilt was completed, she encouraged the women to label it with the correct size and name. She cautioned them to maintain proper fabric inventory. She advised that, when future Bloomingdale's orders came in, certain materials should be used for those orders *only.*

Joyce took the problem leftovers to a businessman on Long Island, where the Menschels had a summer home. During the summers, he would sell the quilts on consignment.

In the newness of Mrs. Menschel's volunteer work, a mound of correspondence was mailed back and forth. She soon learned, though, that the written word was not necessarily the most effective way to communicate: "At first I was trying to write them long letters but then I realized so few of the people could read, and even if they could read, they couldn't very well understand what I meant in letters. Bob's firm had a WATS line so I would call in to the operator of his firm and she would connect me to Alabama. I could spend as much time as I wanted to discuss what was going on."

Mrs. Menschel contends the major contribution she and her husband made in their first stages of work with the Bee was in stimulating the members to perform more professionally. But did they want to be more professional?

"They had to be," she declares. "They didn't have a choice if they wanted to sell, stay in business, and deal with big stores."

Freedom Begins to Produce Smaller Items

Mrs. Menschel also prompted co-op entry into the potholder market: "Bob finally convinced me that even though quiltmaking was a wonderful craft, they were not going to put food on the table solely by making quilts. They had to have an alternative. There would be certain ladies who would always quilt and the others would be the money-earners." Her husband adds: "Quilts are not something of which very many are sold. If a lot were sold, this group would have a factory of 10,000 employees." Thus, the Menschels started thinking about potholders.

"Bob kept saying, 'Give me a smaller item, something not labor intensive.' It's easier to sell a small item than a large one to begin with. If it's not labor intensive you can make and sell a lot very quickly."

Mrs. Menschel found potholders could be produced with little effort and low material cost. She was also drawn to any small crafted item. So she paid a visit to Artisans Cooperative, an international craft group based in Chadds Ford, Pennsylvania, to study contemporary crafts it sold. While there, she talked founder Deirdre Bonifaz into selling potholders for Freedom. Thus began a long, lucrative potholder business from one more outlet in the East.

An early 1980s Freedom brochure listed the potholders at $3 each. Given that figure, the price of five potholders now equals the $15 the co-op was charging for baby quilts when the group began those shipments to the Menschels' New York apartment in 1970. The difference is that five potholders can be made in a matter of minutes, but a 1970 baby quilt took twenty-three hours.

While this New York homemaker was marketing the products of the down South quilting bee, her husband frequently advised the women on business issues. In July 1974, for instance, he received a shipment of "very crude country brooms," handmade from palmettos growing in the wilds of Wilcox County. The quilters were thinking of going into the broom business and wondered what he thought. He discouraged the idea on the premise that they needed to concentrate on a product of which every household needed at least one. And every household, in his judgment, did not need a palmetto broom.

Once when the co-op's low bank balance precluded payment of bills, the Menschels loaned the group enough money to relieve the debts, but he points out the danger involved in such action:

We used to worry about their bank balance. Any time it would fall below $1,000, we would turn a bit panicky. We always tried to keep at arm's length because we figured once we got into giving or lending them a meaningful sum—even if we could have done it—that would have changed the whole relationship.

The Freedom Quilting Bee would have become a
charity. The beauty of the group is that it never was a
charity. It stood on its own two feet. That's why they've
made it.

The Menschels had already been introduced to Mrs. Witherspoon on her
trips eastward, but in the early 1970s the couple paid a weekend visit to the
Freedom Quilting Bee. They wanted to see firsthand the human side of
the co-op as well as how the women worked and how it could maintain
its integrity as a quilting industry. As Menschel says:

We were trying to find a balance between that which
started them out in the mid-1960s but never would
have lasted, and paying them *more* than fifty cents or a
dollar or whatever it was at that point. It was this
finely tuned balance we were thinking about, and
Estelle understood. Estelle wanted them to make more
money and at the same time keep the integrity of the
Bee. I felt that as long as someone like Estelle was
around, the Freedom Quilting Bee would last.
Whether it would last as a place where two or five
women worked once a week, or whether thirty or
forty would work five days a week depended on
whether they continued to make some of the right
moves.

Menschel was convinced that under Mrs. Witherspoon's management the
co-op would clearly make those moves:

Born thirty or forty years later, Estelle would probably have been a member of Congress, not only from
Alabama but from any state. She has brilliant instincts.
She's a saleswoman, an organizer. You have to imagine
the politics and petty friction that must exist in a group
of this type. Estelle has always been able to roll with
the punches. Whether you meet her at Merrill Lynch
in New York or wherever, she's someone you have to
admire. It's something you don't get with books, but
Estelle has it.

So the Menschels came to the Bee, pored over records, talked with the
women of the difficulties they had only been able to relate before by telephone
or letter, and gleaned a more accurate view of the organization's down-the-
road needs. Menschel came to realize the co-op could not survive long or
hire more than a few women unless it made a more businesslike product and

was oriented more toward production. Contrary to his earlier perception of quiltmaking in romantic, aesthetic terms, he watched the reality of four or five women sitting around a frame, engaging in a long, detailed, even monotonous endeavor. "Visiting there, one could quickly see labor is what it's all about."

Many of the patterns required from fifty-four to sixty-nine hours from start to finish, but Mrs. Menschel had first sold the quilts for $55, hardly a dollar an hour for the cost of labor and much less than that when the cost of fabric is figured in. As her husband says:

They wanted to find a way to become a drop more
efficient, to make money. The women not only enjoyed
making quilts but they desperately needed money.
These were people living in the second poorest county
in America.
Everybody can talk about it as "quilts" and "a work
of art," but a work of art was eating and taking care of
their children, and doing it in the community; and
employing older women who probably couldn't get
jobs in factories, giving them a chance to sit around in
a community-style manner, chat with their friends—
but make some money, because if you really get down to
it, most of them were basically unemployable.

Based on the couple's on-site observations, they pondered what the quilters could make to ensure financial stability. As Francis Walter recalls their involvement: "Bob understood about making money. His work with the group was not to satisfy people's souls with beautiful artwork and handicraft. He realized that was important to get them on the map, but he was interested in the women making money, as much as they possibly could."

Menschel had believed from the start that Freedom's future depended on some sort of small item. "It had to have some of their talents but it had to be something they could mass produce in great volume so they could get their money. The one goal was to get the women to make money."

The couple made phone calls and sent letters as well as sample wares to department store chains and other retail buyers in a search for work the women could do. All was to no avail, which left the quilters for the most part with their orders for Bonwit Teller and Saks Fifth Avenue.

But Bob and Joyce Menschel never gave up. They admired crafts; thought the work of the Bee was majestic; and believed strongly in what the workers were trying to accomplish for themselves, their families, and the community. As he says:

You had to take your hat off to these women because
at the same time this was going on, you had the

Sharon Rockefeller group (Mountain Artisans) in West
Virginia. Hundreds of thousands of dollars was put
into the Rockefeller operation. Government money,
private foundation money, everything under the sun
went to the Rockefeller operation and it was getting all
the socialite attention. But unfortunately, it never
worked because it was not grounded on any business
basis.

We were taken with this one because it had lower
visibility, at least after the 1968 cycle, and it was doing
something by sheer effort. It was not subsidized. After
they got started, the women had a great product without anybody's help. It was selling not out of charity
but because it was beautiful. And Joyce and I felt it
deserved to live.

Foundations in New York did give them $1,000 or
so but it all ended. Those contributions were a product
of the march, the '65 to '69 period. Then it was no
longer stylish to help them and they were on their
own.

This was one more reason why the Menschels felt such passion for the
Bee.

Freedom Wins Sears Contract

Sears, Roebuck was a client of Menschel's investment firm, Goldman,
Sachs. He had many connections at the Sears Chicago headquarters and was
keenly aware of its program to aid minorities. In 1940 the company first
purchased from a minority source. Since then, it has tailored a multi-million-
dollar minority development enterprise.

Bob Menschel knew that if any business in the country was qualified for
this program, it was the Freedom Quilting Bee. So, even before his trip to
the co-op, in the autumn of 1970 he began a mission to link the Deep South
artisans with one of the nation's largest department store chains. "Acquiring
the Sears contract was sheer persistence," he says. "It started with a breakfast
here in New York. I told them they had to listen to the story and see some
of the products. I wrote a few of the people but it was a large company and
took a long time for them to react. I was constantly calling Chicago and
Atlanta to see if they were interested."

Menschel wrote letters and attached to them brochures and New York
publicity about the plucky, laborious bunch of women. He shipped to Chicago's Sears Tower an assortment of Freedom's work. He dined with representatives of the company, and time after time he seemed to achieve nothing.

As he now laments, "You were dealing with a group here that was doing things in a real country manner. Department stores couldn't understand it and mail order houses doing billions of dollars of business understood it even less. So it was not easy to open the door."

The standard reaction, he says, was:

"Yes, we like it! Gee, I've never heard of 'em. Can they supply us? Will they deliver? Can they send it to six different stores? Will they be perfect? And will the labels be on?" Those people really didn't understand it. I think they wanted to be very careful in terms of quality and it took them a long while to believe this group could deliver something they could use. A group of people turning out a one-of-a-kind craft was not the kind Sears was looking for. They were willing to pursue it because I kept after them and Francis Walter was helpful as well.

Father Walter explains his part: "One of the roles I played was what in psychological terms would be called 'reality testing' by people such as Bob Menschel. The cultural differences between Bob and Estelle were so great." Father Walter was a line of communication between the two.

Bob Menschel persevered. Finally, in 1971, Kevin Clary, a buyer of decorative pillows and accessories, thought Freedom's pillows might be a potential Sears supply source. He flew from Chicago to the Montgomery airport, rented a car, and drove west to Alberta, though he encountered problems locating the way. He found Mrs. Witherspoon to be a "wonderful character, the resident chaplain and everything else. It's the funniest thing. When I get there I first get hit for a contribution to her church, and with Mrs. Witherspoon you don't say no. I mean when you walk in there, that's the first thing you do, or we don't talk."

Upon his arrival, Clary found the sewing center quite small and only twelve women were in the building. Yet their products were magnetic in appeal. The pillows were immensely attractive to Clary—from cotton, square-patch designs to those with one large star spread across velvet. But they were of higher quality and price than those then offered by Sears.

Clary believed that, if Sears was to establish a contract for such an item, "We would be placating them but not achieving what they wanted to achieve." He flew back to Chicago and talked to a couple of manufacturers who were making a product for Sears known as the corduroy pillow sham:

It was a bed pillow cover, a day bed or decorative pillow sold by Sears at that time for between $3.98 and $4.98. I'm sure it's in the catalog today. It's been there

for fifty years or more. And the thing I liked about
it was its very stable level of demand. It would not
peak and valley.

   With furs, for instance, or anything professional,
suddenly there's a runaway and you can't get enough.
Then all of a sudden you have more than you can use
in three years.

   Sears's corduroy pillow sham was on a much lower price scale than the
Freedom Quilting Bee pillows, which sold in a range from $6.50 to $12. "It
was a commodity pillow, not a fashion pillow," Clary declares, "and it was
way down from the Freedom Quilting Bee's gorgeous decorative pillow, but

Annie Williams, one of
the Bee's younger mem-
bers, works on a Grand-
mother's Dream. (Photo
by Nancy Callahan)

QUALITY IS THE LIFE-BLOOD OF SALES!

Customers today expect - and usually DEMAND - greater value and better service. It will take careful and exact work by each person here to satisfy these requirements.

Everyone must help to insure Sales for added growth and security.

This sign inside the co-op building demonstrates its commercial thrust since the peak of nation-wide publicity. (Photo by Nancy Callahan)

I wanted to give them something that was easy to sew and package, and would have a demand for which they would continue to get orders."

So in 1972 the Bee agreed to produce corduroy pillow shams for Sears. No pillow would be involved at all—just the sham. They would be sold to consumers who would stuff the shams with their own pillows. Sears would give technical advice to the co-op, which would be in complete control of the account.

At that time, two sources were manufacturing the sham retailed by Sears: Spectrafoam and Company, in Los Angeles, and Fashion Pillows, Inc., in Jackson, Georgia. From an economic vantage, Sears could not take on a third sham supplier, so Clary asked Fashion Pillows' president, Walter Jones, if he would be willing to drop his $70,000-per-year contract with Sears in deference to the quilters. It would not involve a severe financial loss for Fashion Pillows because the company had a yearly Sears contract for $2 million. Clary calls it a "moral issue":

You don't penalize someone who's doing a good job. He was more than cooperative. I got his permission to do it and he sent down his engineers to help them with their selling.

Then I went back to Mrs. Witherspoon, gave an-other donation to the church, and started training. We made sure they understood how to read a Sears order, how to fill out a vendor report, order goods, and read the invoice.

By that time Mrs. Witherspoon had received sample yardage and the quilters had made some initial samples which we had to approve as good quality. Was the packaging right? Was it something Sears, Roebuck would be very proud to sell? And, what was most

important, would it stay sold? Then we gave what I
lovingly referred to as "Marty's [Dr. King's] Place" its
first initial contract to service the catalog.

Sears had thirteen catalog distribution centers. From Alberta, Alabama,
the Freedom Quilting Bee began in mid-September 1972 to produce shams
for seven of those centers: Boston, Philadelphia, Atlanta, Memphis, Chicago,
Minneapolis, and Kansas City.

Meantime, the co-op had been turning out dashikis by the hundreds. In
August 1971 the Washington-based National Cooperative Business Associ-
ation, which had been founded in 1916 as the Cooperative League of the
USA, became a lucrative friend to the rural Alabama troop of women. Its
Cooperative League Fund received a grant from the New York Foundation
to provide Freedom with technical, management, and marketing help.

Through the Cooperative League Fund, the quilters were busy with orders
for the quickly made dashikis and small craft items from Greenbelt/Scan
stores, in the Washington/Maryland area, from Hyde Park/Forum stores, in
Chicago, and from the Berkeley Co-op, in California—retail co-op stores
that marketed Freedom's products and gave the group practical advice on a
complimentary basis.

The simple manufacture of red, gold, green, and brown pillow shams of
close-woven pinwale corduroy for Sears, Roebuck and Company was a far
cry from the aesthetic demands of the quilts Joyce Menschel was selling to
the fashionable markets of the East and of the newer orders she had picked
up from Taylor and Ng, the San Francisco department store. It was the
ultimate metamorphosis for a scattering of poor, isolated women who, six
years earlier, had convened to pool the talents and energies of their fingers,
eyes, and artistic senses. But it was the first step in Bob Menschel's goal for
the group: to make some money.

Sears retailed the pillow sham for $3.98. Of that amount, Freedom received
from $1.90 to $2.20 for each finished package.

Clary enjoyed his experience with the Bee: "From an emotional sense, to
serve those people down there was one of the most rewarding things I've
ever done with Sears. It was a lot of fun and, importantly, Sears was doing
a very quiet, positive thing. There is still a lot of respect for the people. I love
them."

Roy Kristofferson, the Sears representative to the co-op from 1976 to 1980,
notes the comparative significance of the quilting bee as a Sears supplier,
which he discovered on a trip from Chicago to Alberta's rural route: "I drove
by the place because I didn't realize it was a manufacturing facility. It's out
on a dirt road practically and it looks more like a little schoolhouse than a
manufacturing facility." Kristofferson was astonished to learn of the small
physical size of the out-of-the-way sewing center that for years had been
supplying Sears with pillow shams:

As a general rule you wouldn't be the size the Freedom Quilting Bee was and still be a Sears source. Any
source that does business with a major company such
as Sears or J. C. Penney is usually bigger. I thought
they were doing things for others but by the time
I got down there they were basically making just our
pillow shams. It was kind of a shock to go in there
and find twelve to fifteen people. In one of my folders
were articles about them that were written in New
York. When you start seeing articles about a company
in trade magazines, you start assuming they're bigger
than twelve to fifteen people in a small building. Sears
has quite a few minority sources but this was probably
one of the smaller ones.

During Kristofferson's affiliation with the co-op, the women typically
produced 30,000 "units," or shams, within a six-month period: 5,000 units a
month, 1,000-plus per week, 200 in a day's time.

Since late 1972, the making of that commodity has not only fed, clothed,
and sheltered many members of the co-op, but it has also educated their
children and kept the Bee alive. Estelle Witherspoon as much as says so. A
Christian mystic, she also believes the co-op's work with Sears has been
divinely inspired: "It has meant everything to us. If it had not been for the
Sears, Roebuck contract and the Artisans Co-op orders, no doubt we would
probably have had to close the door. But the Lord's just been so good and so
kind, letting the peoples and their orders in for us to keep us working."

Mrs. Witherspoon is ever mindful of the numerous craft co-ops that have
closed their doors, even with government funding: "I've got faith in the Lord
because I ask the Lord for his blessings. What way those blessings is coming
I don't know, but when Sears sends these orders, that's another one of His
blessings. I've just got that kind of faith in the Lord."

For well over a decade, the women of the Freedom Quilting Bee have
produced more than 100,000 corduroy pillow shams—from fern green, fiesta
red, royal navy, and federal gold, to goldenrod, cherry red, cocoa brown,
and avocado leaf. Among the current colors are old rose, Indian copper, and
barley.

Paid by the piece, the sham makers perform three processes: some cut the
material, others attach the zippers, and still others do the side-seaming.
According to the co-op manager, "They enjoy making them and they make
more money doing that than they would just sitting out there quilting.
Quilting is very slow but they can make these covers real fast."

Using commercial sewing machines, Mrs. Witherspoon's side-seamers can
turn out as many as 300 shams daily. When that happens, the zipper women
are capable of attaching zippers to those 300 shams in the same amount of

time. Using a cutting machine, women attendants are capable of cutting material for 1,000 or more pillows in an equal period of work. Because, as with quiltmaking, each woman follows her own pace, some are faster and more productive. "We've got some pretty fast sewers, and if those machines don't give 'em any trouble, they can really do it. Those big commercial machines, they'll do it fast."

Sears now pays the co-op $4.15 per sham and sells it for more than $6. "And with that," according to Mrs. Witherspoon, "we just do come out. We don't make a penny off of it. But still, it keeps me able to have those ladies to come in with work and pay some bills."

Sears has long accounted for the majority of the Bee's annual sales. The turning point was 1974, when quilt orders dropped drastically. "Quilts no longer were as chic," the Menschels contend. "Prices got higher and quilts no longer were $50 but at least $150. No longer was it a bargain but a specialty."

Since that time, the Bee's financial health has been dependent on Sears, Roebuck. In September 1980, for example, the Bee did $7,500 in business. Of that figure, $5,100 came from Sears. The most graphic case in point thus far is 1982, when the co-op's business amounted to $200,000, most of which was provided by Sears, enabling members to receive wages totaling a record $120,000.

Bob Menschel states, "The beauty of what's happened down there is that 80 percent of their business is something from which they can make money, which can then pay for the continuation of a very wonderful craft. If it hadn't been Sears, I or someone else hopefully would have been smart enough to get another group involved. But I am almost certain that without Sears, the Freedom Quilting Bee would not be around."

The Balance of Craft and Business

By 1975 Joyce Menschel was no longer marketing the co-op's quilted items because of the birth of her second child as well as lack of time and space. But she continued for a couple of years to send down fabric on request, which she selected from the stockroom of her contact on the lower east side. She also arranged for sales representatives of Eastern fabric companies to call on the Freedom Quilting Bee during their Southern travels. And, when members were on marketing trips in New York, the Menschels facilitated their visits to textile factories, where they observed firsthand production-line operation. The couple also set in motion similar trips to plants closer to Wilcox County. Menschel encouraged such ventures so the co-op's upper echelon could understand more fully how to preserve Freedom's craft uniqueness and at the same time survive—two accomplishments he correlates with the derring-do of a tightrope walker: "Very few of them are able to achieve it. I think one would be hard-pressed to find any other craft group with a twenty-year history."

From his longtime study of American craft organizations, Menschel believes such groups are never able to balance craft and business:

> They either become all business—which I don't
> think is what they should do—and then they become
> another factory; or they become all crafts and go out
> of business after a year or two because they can't suc-
> ceed. The answer is down the middle, and in finding
> wider distribution. Somehow, in their native sense,
> that's what the Freedom Quilting Bee was able to
> come up with.
> In all our years following craft groups, I don't think
> we've seen anything like this one that has succeeded
> without that grant of fifty to a hundred thousand dol-
> lars from the government. There are half a dozen
> groups from Maine to Atlanta. I see their goods still.
> Their products are very nice but most of the groups,
> once you begin to learn about them, are subsidized.
> The Freedom Quilting Bee had some early subsidy
> but along the way, regardless of what anyone might
> say, there's no question that it has existed as a business.

Menschel contends that a "viable" crafts organization cannot exist any other way. "I mean, if the Rockefellers couldn't make it work, nobody could make it work," he exclaims about the collapse of the government-subsidized Mountain Artisans.

The Menschels' last tangible assistance to the Bee was in 1977, until 1985, when he was instrumental in obtaining $25,000 in grant money to make improvements in the co-op's sewing center. For well over a decade, he has been a recipient of Freedom's monthly financial statements:

> I try to give Estelle a ring every two or three months.
> I say, "Estelle, is the money coming in? Are you build-
> ing up?"
> But if we were to see something in a monthly report
> that looked as though they were in trouble or if the
> Sears business were falling off dramatically, I would
> call Estelle immediately and make sure we did our best
> to put it back on track. As long as we're around we
> will always do our best to make sure they survive.
> At this point they don't really need us. Estelle would
> be the first to call if they had any problems, knowing
> Estelle. She's not bashful.

10   *Freedom*
Leads the
Co-op Movement

After two decades, the Freedom Quilting Bee is
the oldest handcraft co-op still in existence that originated with the civil
rights movement. But, more importantly, because of its one-member/one-
vote concept of decision making, it has flowered during those years as a
leader and role model among other co-ops—in Alabama, the South, and
countrywide.

Federation of Southern Cooperatives

The Bee's first regional involvement occurred in 1967, only a year after its
founding, when Estelle Witherspoon attended a meeting in Atlanta and
signed her co-op as one of twenty-two charter members of the Federation of
Southern Cooperatives, an organization that seeks to uplift the living stand-
ards of many rural people in the South. It now provides technical help, raises
funds, and addresses state and national policy issues for more than a hundred
rural co-ops and credit unions. Since it started, this nonprofit, tax-exempt
association has given a watchful eye and guiding hand to the Freedom
Quilting Bee in planning, managing, and marketing.

A close observer of that relationship is John Zippert, director of program
operations for the federation's Rural Training and Research Center, near Epes,
a community in Sumter County. A white man, whose face is covered with
a curly black beard and dark-rimmed glasses, he was born in 1945 in New
York City, where he was raised and educated. From the time he was nineteen,
he has worked either in civil rights or in the cooperative movement. He
joined the Southern Federation in 1971.

Zippert says that, in addition to mobilizing resources through democratic
control with benefits equal to participation, a key advantage to co-op mem-

bership in his federation is education. "Even if one of the cooperatives we work with fails," he reasons, "we hope the members learned certain skills in how to organize, get information, talk to the movers and levers of power, so that when they want to do something else, they would retain that knowledge and skill and be able to move and deal with the next situation."

Using the Freedom Quilting Bee as an example, Zippert thinks the college-trained resource persons sent by the federation to the Alberta sewing center have been role models and incentives from the outside world. "I don't think Mrs. Witherspoon's daughter, for instance, would have gone on to college had the cooperative not been there. The local people could say, 'Here's an accountant, or an agricultural specialist, a potential role model for me to look at and follow.' "

The federation has provided the quilting bee with an unending wellspring of aid—from travel money for craft shows, to a $5,000 grant for construction of the sewing center, to board of directors' training sessions and airplane tickets for out-of-state consultants. The federation operates a small craft store in the Atlanta Omni that provides a market for the quilters and other member co-ops. And, upon the advent of the Sears account, the federation helped Freedom with its more complicated tangle of accounting, billing, inventory, and pricing.

Even though the co-op has provided lasting employment for its members, federation officials and Freedom members know too well that lack of jobs is a major Wilcox County problem. Federation statistics reveal that in the 1970s the per capita income in Wilcox was more than $2,000 lower than for the United States as a whole; more than 40 percent of family incomes were below the poverty level. The statistics also show that the Freedom Quilting Bee's entire membership falls within the level of poverty.

To lessen job problems, Freedom has long dreamed of increasing the number on its payroll, which could result from broader market opportunities. But for years lack of sufficient working capital was a drawback. In 1981, however, long-term financing became available when the Freedom Quilting Bee, aided by technical help from the Federation of Southern Cooperatives, won approval for a $26,000 loan from the National Consumer Cooperative Bank in Washington, D.C., created by Congress in 1978 to provide credit and technical help to cooperative activities across the country. To be paid back monthly within five years at 8 percent interest, the loan money was mostly used to increase the Bee's inventory.

All too often, Freedom had been losing valuable orders from Sears, Artisans Cooperatives, and others because lack of money prevented the group from having the inventory to fill specific orders, sometimes even on an emergency basis, by a certain deadline. Quilting bee leaders believed that the loan would also provide two additional benefits. First, the co-op would be able to purchase more effectively by buying in larger bulk quantities. As it was, the quilters were often forced to buy in small quantities, thus losing bulk discounts; and they were buying from mills whose delivery times were shorter but whose prices were higher. They thought purchase of large quantities would enable the co-op to offset partially the effect of continually rising material prices.

Secondly, because of the Bee's small working capital, it had been unable to sell on consignment. Yet many craft shops carry items on consignment only. Thus, officers contended that such a loan would allow them to pursue new, untapped markets more aggressively than ever before. Upon receipt of the loan, the Freedom Quilting Bee was a regional pioneer, the first and only co-op within the federation to receive money from the National Consumer Cooperative Bank.

Alabama Cooperative Association

Under the loan, the quilting bee was required to obtain $5,000 in technical assistance to enhance the quality of its operation. So the quilters made a contract through the bank with the Federation of Southern Cooperatives, from which they received leadership training through the spring of 1983. The co-op is eventually required to repay half the $5,000 to the bank. But, meanwhile, the federation appointed the head of its Alabama unit, Ezra Cunningham, to provide leadership training to Freedom's board of directors.

A black man in his sixties from Monroe County, a southern neighbor of Wilcox, whose name became synonymous locally with civil rights, Cunningham was no newcomer to the Freedom quilters. A regional co-op man since 1967, the former farmer, teacher, insurance salesman, and black organizer has been the Alabama coordinator, heading the Alabama Cooperative Association, for the Federation of Southern Cooperatives since the late 1970s. He observes the activities of thirteen co-ops affecting 20,000 people.

Working mostly from his Monroe County home in Beatrice, the fiery and feisty Cunningham made sure that Freedom's board met on a regular basis and board meetings were grounded on sufficient dialogue. As he tells it:

When they were first meeting, they didn't know
how to conduct a board meeting. One or two people
would do the talking and all their hostilities would just
build up.
See, poor people are just hostile to themselves. And
when you get poor people in a meeting, the hostility is
not necessarily directed at the person trying to conduct
the business. The hostility is that "I feel so incompetent
and so poor, I just can't speak in a meeting because
I might break a verb." And you sit there and get mad.

So the hardest part in working with them was to
draw hostility out and get people to say what they
feel. A lot of progress shows now. If you'd been there
ten years ago, you'd be happy to say you had a part
in developing what they are. A lot have grown to
express their feelings and help make some decisions.
They can conduct a meeting.

Over time, Cunningham taught the board how to take meeting minutes
and how to devise an agenda. He points out that the Bee's only other exposure
to parliamentary procedure was the church. Thus, the first membership
meetings were based on the church business meeting within the black Wilcox
culture. In fact, board meetings today typically begin with prayer and hymn
singing. In church business, he notes, members would make decisions, but
they would be carried out by the pastor, clerk, and deacons. "That was the
way they first tried to operate the Freedom Quilting Bee, but now they
operate pretty well like a little business."

Because of the technical assistance provision of the 1981 bank loan, Cunningham, who frequently quotes Bible stories, merely continued all his past
work with Freedom's board: refreshing members' concept of the cooperative
process and teaching them more about decision making. He also helped
improve their reading skills. "We found out some of the people couldn't read
too well. That was some of our hold-up."

Cunningham, whose warm manner and sheepish grin belie his down-
home reputation as a "radical," attended each monthly board meeting of the
co-op for much more than a decade. As a volunteer now, he participates every
few months, bringing to gradual conclusion his longtime work with the
women. He has formed major judgments about the organization. First, it is
the only cooperative in its stratum, he explains, which, despite having acquired land, buildings, bills, financial aid, and much outside direction, is free
of debt.

Cunningham points out too, that though the original Bee membership
had the lowest formal education of any co-op in the Alabama Cooperative
Association, Freedom has blossomed more than any other:

I think I've been more help to the Freedom Quilting
Bee. The others set up resistance that is hard to overcome because they feel they have all the know-how.
The others have that education and don't want you to
say "I'm wrong."
The Freedom Quilting Bee is doing people a lot of
good. When $10 was about as high as they had ever
seen, now they are going home sometimes with $160 a
week they can call their own.

One of the first financial goals of the Bee, says John Zippert, was for the workers to make prevailing minimum wage their hourly salary. Today, they earn at least that. Some make even more. He contends that, because of the cost of material, shipping, overhead, and management, even if today's quilt were to sell at $200, members would not receive much more than $1 or $1.50 an hour for the actual work. So the Sears pillow shams and the small quilted items financially enable them to continue their quiltmaking. But Zippert believes the amount made by co-op workers and what is earned for an individual quilt should be viewed in context:

> We're talking about Wilcox County, where if there
> were no quilting bee, people would not be working,
> period. I have always viewed the Freedom Quilting
> Bee as an income supplement. In 1970, the median
> family income for black people in Wilcox County was
> around $2,000. So we're talking about a program that
> provides between $2,000 and $3,000 of supplementary
> income to women in Wilcox County. If you can add
> to a person's income what amounts to double the family
> income—and in many cases the quilting bee is making
> that kind of input—that's significant.

Zippert also notes that, while Freedom incomes serve as large complements to smaller than average salaries, those incomes make possible a substantial additional benefit: Social Security: "They get access to the government retirement system to which they would otherwise not have access." He points to one more advantage to cooperative life at the quilting center: "I doubt there are many sewing factories in America that have pictures of Martin Luther King, Abraham Lincoln, Bobby Kennedy, and John Kennedy in their place of work. That's important and sometimes overlooked. It may mean nothing. On the other hand it may mean something to the people there, that they are working in a place where they can put pictures on the wall of people they think are important, as opposed to working where they can't do that."

Zippert holds that the co-op has grown and matured because of its alliance with the federation. He singles out Nettie Young, the Bee's comanager, as someone from the community who has grown along with the co-op, learning about business as well as working with and managing people. Day care center director Mary Robinson is another whose maturity has become obvious, he says, along with some of the younger ones working in the office. "You can see the effect of our training. People have grown as the quilting bee has developed, even some who have worked there and left."

Zippert cites the example of Alberta-born Minnie McMillian Williams, who until 1971 was on the staff as an assistant to Estelle Witherspoon. "Some of the skills she got there she went on and used elsewhere." Without money or resources, she assisted black students and their parents in a strike against the Wilcox County school system in September 1971. The following year, she worked under grant money with the Selma Inter-religious Project as a legal paraprofessional in Wilcox County's struggle for decent, desegregated schools. "The Freedom Quilting Bee was a catalyst for Minnie," Ezra Cunningham says. "It was a kick-off for her to get some feeling of being somebody, going on and doing something."

In 1979 the Freedom Quilting Bee began to have surplus money at year's end. In view of the gross sales of $200,000 in 1982, Zippert hopes the co-op will move into the million-dollar sales bracket during the 1980s:

> It is one of the leading handcraft cooperatives of which I'm aware, in the quality and artistry of what they produce, in the benefits they're providing members, and in their willingness to take leadership in extending the whole cooperative movement to other people. Some co-ops might do that well in providing wages to their members but are not active in promoting cooperatives for other people the way the Freedom Quilting Bee is. I hope we can help them add $100,000 in sales a year, and people commensurate with that.

Freedom Joins Artisans Cooperative

In 1972 Deirdre Bonifaz founded and became president of an organization called Artisans Cooperative. She based it in Chadds Ford, a small, rural town in Pennsylvania, thirty miles from Philadelphia. During the same year, the Freedom Quilting Bee became a member; this provided an entrée to the Pennsylvania/New England craft markets. Since 1976, when Artisans established a board of directors, Estelle Witherspoon has served on the board— for a time as chairman—providing a voice at the national cooperative level for her sisters back home.

Deirdre Bonifaz was born in New York City and raised in rural New England. She was surrounded during childhood with artists who were forced to do other things to survive. "I had an understanding," she reflects, "of how hard it was to be a creative person in this society and make a living at the same time." One summer she went to Ecuador and saw a cooperative of Indians doing handwork. "But they were in a very remote village and had no link to the marketplace. I saw the need for that link to be established. Then with my own art background and my concern about people having opportunities when they aren't able to have them on their own, Artisans Cooperative took form."

Once a consultant to the Cooperative League of the USA, Mrs. Bonifaz seeks to link people in rural areas such as Wilcox County all over America, where they are struggling to operate some kind of business within the community, where work alternatives are nonexistent, and where they need to reach an affluent market far from home.

When Mrs. Bonifaz began her venture, her only associates were three groups from Appalachia, the Ecuadorian chain, and the Freedom Quilting Bee. Later, Artisans received technical assistance and grants, including support from the Ford Foundation. Today, its Chadds Ford headquarters embraces a store, gallery of American folk art, mail-order business, and technical assistance program. Other sales outlets are on Nantucket Island, Massachusetts; at Faneuil Hall, in Boston; in Philadelphia's New Market; and in the Philadelphia suburb of Ardmore. Now, more than a hundred American cooperatives and partnerships are encompassed by the organization; the crafts include pottery, jewelry, baskets, glass, handwoven rugs, and metal sculpture.

Through training programs and consultant visits to the Bee, Artisans has strongly influenced the product line Freedom markets through the Chadds Ford cooperative, including small items such as pot holders, place mats, napkins, chair seats, aprons, buffet runners, and bibs, in addition to the quilts. According to Mrs. Bonifaz:

> We do a lot of product development and product
> design with our members. Freedom is one of the most
> responsive members in that sense because the women
> all work in one place. A lot of our members have peo-
> ple working from their homes. That's not nearly as
> effective in their really being able to know the market.
> When people are all working together and get the
> training classes together, new products are designed to
> be put into production more easily than when people
> are scattered around the countryside as they are in
> many rural communities.

Most of the quilting bee's current products have been designed by Artisans Cooperative, but are also being sold to outlets other than those conceived by Deirdre Bonifaz. "We select the fabric so we're sure the quality and colors are what we know to sell in this part of the country. Then we are able to specify what goes into what quilt." Artisans also sets the price for each item it markets. In quilt prices, for instance, the crib/wall hanging size is $115, more than ten times the price Francis Walter first paid the women on Highway 5 for a regular quilt. The single is $395, the double $450, the queen $575, and the king $675.

Artisans catalogs, frequently featuring colorful Freedom quilts on their covers, are sent to 300,000 people the nation over. These promote the wares and deeds of the Bee in places and to people in ways of life far beyond the most fantastic notions of those who first began to seek their livelihood and economic independence from the Martin Luther King, Jr., Memorial Sewing Center.

Mrs. Bonifaz sells three of the Bee's quilt patterns: Bear's Paw, Grandmother's Dream, and Coat of Many Colors. She says Grandmother's Dream, whose blue, cream, and rose colors are selected by Artisans, is a quilt to which the crafts buyer readily responds. But, she says, "there's the Coat of Many Colors, which is *theirs*. They have always done it that way and we've never changed that. It is a very brilliant, almost stained glass kind of print. If it's done in solids it looks contemporary. If it's done in prints it looks traditional. At different times they're all popular. We have been carrying all those quilts since 1972, although we keep on varying colors as they tend to be popular. The Bear's Paw is the most classic."

Although Freedom's quilts are most popular in the sense of being beautiful, dramatic, and expensive, Mrs. Bonifaz encourages the Bee to produce that which is profitable for its members, such as the small, machine-made items that do not require much handwork. "That's important to us," she explains, "because their business is a livelihood for many women."

In 1972 the Bee made $200 from the sale of quilted products to Artisans. A few years later, annual sales averaged $1,500. In 1982 Freedom received from the group the sum of $35,000; more recent figures are running higher. "We try to have orders projected every month so the people can plan," Mrs. Bonifaz points out. "But it's their stable market. What Freedom needed was something that stayed with them through the years. That's what Artisans Cooperative stands for. It's not a fad that makes a good story or is fashionable at that moment. It's part of every month of the year."

Estelle Witherspoon will forever be grateful for the quilters' relationship with Artisans. "It has meant everything to us," she declares with feeling. "Mrs. Bonifaz always tells me, 'If you don't have anything to do, just let me know. I'll be sending some work down there, and if I can help out financially, I will be glad to do that.'" Mrs. Witherspoon cites an incident from the summer of 1983: "One week I was fixing to shut the door because I didn't have nothing to do, nothing to work and nothing to pay the people. She called and wired me $3,000."

Still on the Artisans board of directors, co-op manager Estelle Witherspoon was chairman from October 1981 until October 1983. Attending the meetings in Chadds Ford four times a year, she has missed only one or two sessions since 1976. "Sometimes I'm going to be kept from going because of my mother being sick. So I just have to keep my fingers crossed and pray that I will get there to help out."

According to Artisans leader Mrs. Bonifaz, Mrs. Witherspoon has gone beyond her traditional duties as board chairman to encourage those from other co-ops to believe a group such as Artisans can work:

She has been a source of inspiration and hope for
the board because of what she has done in Wilcox
County. In the last ten years I have worked with many
women's groups, particularly in Appalachia, of people
trying to carve something for themselves in rural
America. Freedom Quilting Bee is by far the most
successful one, simply because of the way they work
and the commitment of the people who are at the
helm.

That is to the credit of Estelle Witherspoon and
Nettie Young and people who have surrounded them,
who have seen that by doing certain things a little
differently, they can increase their own market.

Sometimes people have such a fierce pride, they
think you're interfering if you tell them that in Boston
you can sell this color but you can't sell another. That
kind of market feedback is what makes a big difference
for groups that succeed and others that just want to
go their own way.

Through the Freedom Quilting Bee, women from Gee's Bend, the two
Albertas, and beyond have made friends from their own county whom they
never knew before. For them, the co-op and its mission were and are an
ironclad, common bond. Through the Federation of Southern Cooperatives,
they have locked arms with cooperatives across the South to build a better
life for thousands whose poverty-rooted backgrounds are not so dissimilar
to their own.

Through Artisans Cooperative, the quilters have embraced a kinship with
creative forces abloom in secluded, low-income places, both here and abroad.
Once when the Bee was encountering bookkeeping problems, Deirdre Bonifaz summoned a representative from a co-op in India to come to Wilcox
County. "Aside from getting money to people every month for goods and
keeping some stability in their own economy, the wider priority in this group
is to form networks among people who are poor and struggling everywhere,"
says the Artisans founder. "They all share the same kinds of problems. They
can strengthen one another by being aware of what's going on in another
area."

As an example, Mrs. Bonifaz points out that quilts are being made in Haiti
that contain the same prints used by the Freedom Quilting Bee as well as
other American quiltmakers and are sold at a store in New York City. "They
are being made in Haiti for a fraction of the cost American quilters are
making them. What that does is pit poor people against one another, because
the women in Haiti are desperately poor and working for very little money.
They're being exploited by being made to copy things with which poor

American women are trying to make some money. It's that kind of thing we would like to stop."

According to Mrs. Bonifaz, one of the membership qualifications of the Artisans is that the producers in a member group exert control over the group, a phenomenon that does not always exist. She declares, "It's hard to make that happen. That's why I point to the Freedom Quilting Bee as the most successful. I'm not saying there aren't problems; there are many. But they have succeeded in holding together in that spirit. They are a beautiful symbol of what a cooperative can be when people are working together."

The Women
of the
Freedom
Quilting Bee

Today, more than two decades since its founding, from eight in the morning until three in the afternoon, it's life as usual at the Freedom Quilting Bee. In season, watermelons rest on either side of the front door, waiting to be cut at lunchtime and served to those inside. On a Monday morning, more often than not, Mrs. Witherspoon keeps in her office desk drawer portions of her famous egg pie, made for church doings the day before. Sensing the need for a worker to take a break, she will call the woman into her office and give her a piece. At times her door is closed, when she is counseling a quilter about personal troubles.

Not many people come to Alberta unless they live there. So the women mostly look at the concrete, or "Brickcrete," walls; bolts of material; sewing machines; frames of outstretched patchwork fabric; and each other. But Hazel McCloud, who lives next door, pops in several times daily with offers to do the "bumming." Although he is a man, he is on the quilting bee board of directors. The mailman is an everyday figure from outside. So is the United Parcel Service man, who comes often. When visitors travel to Alberta, it is usually because of the Bee, and they come from all sorts of places. When the telephone rings, the call could be from anywhere in the world.

Some of the women have rollers in their hair. Others wear colorful bandannas. There are no strict dress codes because the atmosphere is informal. They do their work, sing, drink soft drinks, and share secrets. Most of all, they care about each other. It is as though history has melded them into a single soul, the Freedom soul, whose energy permeates their physical building.

Each of these women has her personal story, her contribution to the whole. So it was with her sisters from the past, whose gift to these contemporary black women was the opportunity for them to make it on their own.

There was Ora McDaniels of Possum Bend, who had fearfully run from

Francis Walter because his skin was white. Her home became a repository for quilts on the Camden side of the Alabama River, to be collected by Father Walter and others. She made it possible for women on her side of the river to participate.

Someone else was Lucy Mooney, an elderly woman from Boykin. She had lost an arm several years before the coming of the Bee but still was able to make quilts for it. One of her blue-denim productions went to folk musician Pete Seeger, who proudly displayed it on his living room couch.

Another was Maggie McMillian, the Hoot Owl pot holder originator. She once went to Gastonburg and taught a group how to make that pot holder. In so doing, she put valuable spending money into the pockets of several.

Lizzie Willis, of Selma, initiated the Selma chapter of the quilting bee, which for a time produced many fine quilts. A civil rights worker since 1953, she was a "citizen teacher" in Dallas County. During the Selma movement, she and her sister housed four visitors from New York—three ministers and a reporter with the *New York Daily News*—along with Senator Edward M. Kennedy, of Massachusetts. When she learned of the quilting bee through a news article, she quickly prodded her quilting friends into action. One of her works, a Grandmother's Choice, was purchased by Henry Geldzahler. Another she sold to the co-op was a Lone Star resting on a yellow background and framed with a sky-blue border. The star probably contained a thousand pieces, each no longer than a finger tip. The Lizzie Willis Star was the talk of the town at Gee's Bend, where the quilting legend was challenged to higher plateaus.

The names of the quilters and their struggles through life are etched forever on the formative years of the Bee. Each was unique in the artisan roll call. But, one by one, like stellar lights who landed together, they found themselves on this planet in one place and at one time, sharing the most basic of ties with their workaday family.

They were all rooted in the depths of poverty and in rural isolation. They had a fierce faith in God, who resided at the center of their souls. With a few exceptions, their formal education was minimal. Their resolve to improve their lot in life was unceasing. Granddaughters of slaves, they had worked for their civil rights as feverishly as they had chopped cornstalks. And because of their new right to vote, by the time the white man came along with his wad of $10 bills, they had been full-fledged American citizens for even less than a year.

Meet the women of the Freedom Quilting Bee, typified by a few from the original cast. They are cheerful, positive creatures who would rather talk about the good times than the bad. Given a choice, they would rather laugh than cry—any day of the week.

Minder
Pettway
Coleman

It is a sunny, springtime afternoon at Route One, Alberta. One mile from the start of Gee's Bend, Minder Coleman is dressed in her Sunday best, her head topped with a salmon-hued turban. She is sitting on the front porch swing of her government-built house, peering downward on acres of vegetation: a rainbow of greens, in which occasional trees and tree stumps appear only as dark splotches from her hilltop haven. From her porch, the view ahead is like a valley footing a Chinese mountain, an Irish riverplain landscape, or a French Impressionist painting.

The setting, though, is Wilcox County, where Mrs. Coleman is airing a few of her quilts. Hanging on a fence to one side of her home is an Eggplant version, constructed with sixteen blocks, each containing two eggplant shapes joined at the bottom of one and the top of the other. Every eggplant consists of four swatches of cloth. Between the blocks are long, thin rows of dark material, now and then printed with chains of circles looking like flower clumps from the first painting of a child. It is a many-colored work, the scheme and pattern of which Mrs. Coleman devised. She is proud of her invention.

Sprawling from the porch among boxes of show-and-tell cloth bits are several other quilts, including a Double Wedding Ring and a Dresden Plate. Made of sacks for flour and fertilizer, they manifest a primitive elegance. Their personalities echo those that went to New York two decades earlier to be bought at auction by connoisseurs, then thoughtfully placed across the city.

"I always loved the best material," she says as she fingers an eggplant. She came by the "best material" easier than most, for she worked for years at a cloth factory in Linden. While there, she collected carloads of thrown-away pieces, dozens of which are still stored in boxes at her home.

In her hands are the history of her life, for Mrs. Coleman has made her

Minder Coleman, one of
Freedom's founding
members, had also been a
key figure in the Roose-
velt-era agricultural co-op
established at Gee's Bend.
(Photo by Nancy
Callahan)

life with her hands. "I tell you now, my hands've done did so much. I done plowed, I done hoed and I done weaved."

Weaving looms were much in evidence during the Gee's Bend of the 1930s, and Mrs. Coleman was one of many who learned the art. She, Mattie Ross, and Patsy Mosely even wove some draperies for Franklin D. Roosevelt's White House. Mrs. Coleman still remembers that they were 76 inches wide by 250 inches long. "And we had a great big hem on 'em and fixed 'em where a rod would go through. They went to all those windows up there to the White House."

She also helped to weave fabric, thirty-nine inches wide, for a blue-and-white striped suit for the president. "I don't know who made it for him, but me and those women weaved it on a loom. Mattie's got a piece of her dress in the smokehouse if she ain't burned it up. I wore mine out, I loved it so. It was checked." As Mrs. Coleman tells it, the president was so pleased with the suit that he sent her a thank-you note, now stored away among her things. "He wrote me and told me he liked it. He died. You know he's dead, don't you? He died after he wrote us and said, 'Dear Ladies,' just like that. He said, 'Dear Ladies, I enjoyed the material 'cause I'm wearing my suit, and when I die, I hope they'll put it on me.'"

Born in the Bend on October 11, 1903, on the site of Pleasant Grove Baptist Church, Minder learned to quilt as a child and soon realized her talent:

> My mother learnt me before she died. Little children
> come in and want to do something. She put me to
> sewing. That's how we started. I never did have a book
> or pattern or nothing. She just drew her own pattern.
> She made those old-fashioned quilts.
>
> After I started to school, I just went on and took up
> sewing to make those things that a teacher would
> have us make. "What you want to do, young 'un?" I'd
> say, "I'm gon' help piece up a quilt or make a pair of
> pajamas or a dress." But quilting was my choice.

Mrs. Coleman is a woman of enormous industry. In the New Deal days of the Gee's Bend Farms, Inc., she was the co-op's president. A lifelong farmer, in later years she also worked at the Linden cloth factory, then in Catherine at an okra factory, and finally in Uniontown at another okra factory. "When we finished cutting okra down yonder at Catherine, they was sending from Uniontown. Didn't have enough women."

Mrs. Coleman owned a truck because, though she worked for others, she grew her own okra, peas, and tomatoes, as well as cotton and raised goats and hogs. So she trucked women to Uniontown to spend their days in a factory while their husbands stayed home to work the fields. Then she bought a station wagon, still parked to the side of her home, also useful to transport working women.

By the time Francis Walter came on the scene, Mrs. Coleman was into her sixties, well beyond the age at which one usually begins a new career. But her work with Gee's Bend Farms had taught her what women could do if they combined their abilities. She was not working anywhere then but at home. "I was sewing," she recalls, in self-assured tones. "I was making quilts but I didn't even know I was making 'em for the Freedom Quilting Bee. I was making 'em just for myself. And he come."

When Father Walter told her about his idea for a co-op, she gave it a ringing endorsement and began to serve informally as its head. She donated her Linden cloth scraps, spread the word among her neighbors, and thus the operation began.

When the Freedom Quilting Bee was incorporated in the spring of 1966, Mrs. Coleman signed on as vice-president. And, while it was still an infant endeavor, she trained the women in her area. She also served as a contact for Father Walter, who frequently collected the finished products at her home. Estelle Witherspoon says that at times the quilt boxes were so overstuffed they could not be closed for sealing and shipment. "It was Mrs. Coleman who would sit on the box tops till they could be taped for proper mailing."

One of her first assignments may have been her most unusual. In February 1966 Father Walter received a letter from Valena McCants, of Mobile, whose father had died in January. Learning of the quilting group through a priest working in Mobile's freedom movement, she sent the Bee the funeral ribbons that had interlaced the flowers on her father's grave and requested that they be made into a quilt. Mrs. Coleman and one of her friends produced two twin-sized Liberty Tree quilts, one in pink, red, and gold; the other in pink, green, and orchid. Stitched onto domestic lining, they are now folded on the ends of the owner's beds, and Mrs. McCants plans to pass them on as family treasures.

"Reverend Walter went to selling those quilts to the New York peoples," Mrs. Coleman continues with great delight. That her handwork would go to a place such as New York makes her feel "delicious." In the quilting arena, her call to fame is the Double Wedding Ring. "Reverend Walter would get that order, come to me and say, 'Minder, I want some Wedding Rings pieced up. Get your group of peoples and make so many.'" Mrs. Coleman looks at the Wedding Ring resting on her porch and notes that she persuaded the first quilting bee members to make theirs by the same pattern she had used to craft that one.

"Those dark pieces are nothing but flour sacks and fertilizer sacks. They don't put 'em in sacks no more now since they found out the folks like me went to making dresses out of 'em—or quilts. They went to putting it in paper bags. I reckon they say, 'Y'all quilting bee folks and y'all on minimum wage.' "

Unlike most of the original members, Mrs. Coleman did not accept money for her varied contributions. The money she would have received was placed in the Bee's bank account and used to build the sewing center. "I tell you what he did. He put that money in the bank and when we got enough, I said, 'Build a factory.' That was my suggestion. 'Have a house, a business office.' And I told Reverend Walter to build it up here. He said, 'Mrs. Coleman, we ain't got enough money to buy no lumber.' I said, 'We gon' make enough quilts and buy the factory.' "

Mrs. Coleman claims she wanted the center in Alberta because the Gee's Bend men were not as supportive of the project as were those from Alberta:

The men down here didn't want their wives to work
in a factory like that, and they wouldn't sign the paper.
But Eugene Witherspoon and the rest of the mens up
there did come down here to our meetings. We had a
meeting kind of like mass meeting to practice on what
we wanted to do and how we wanted to do it. So
that's how the men got with us and worked with us.
And these down here wouldn't. They were jealous
of the wives.
    This time of year they was plowing mules. Had a
wagon. When they came out of the field at noon, we'd
have a dinner eating. If we worked here, we would
cook dinner here. Our husbands and our friends was
gon' be here with us to eat. That's the way we did.
And if we worked down at Aolar's, we had specialty
cooks. They was gon' cook and fix the table and then
we was gon' eat and go back to work on our quilts.
That's the way we handled it.
    And then we worked up and worked up round and
about. Eugene and Stella sometimes would sit up all
night near about with me and my husband, Willie. He
was in the rolling chair, sitting down. Eugene was
helping us take the boxes up.

All the while, Mrs. Coleman received no pay for her labors. "I'll tell you about me," she offers the reason. "I worked a mule and worked and made my money off my farm. And then we canned a lot. We had all that food. That's the way I got mine. So I just took mines and told 'em I wanted a factory. After then, we just went to selling quilts and paying for the thing." She worked full time at the Freedom Quilting Bee until 1978, the year her husband Willie, a farmer, became ill. He died later that year.

Mrs. Coleman believes the Bee is a community asset not only because the women enjoy working together, but also because it is a way to qualify for Social Security: "They get paid by the hour and are working on their security now. The card. I just wouldn't even give 'em my Social Security 'cause I wasn't working there, and why I got my security, I worked at a big factory."

Sadly, Mrs. Coleman's personal quilting efforts also ceased in 1978 because she was bitten on the hand by a hog, which caused irreparable damage. "You know, I had ninety head of hogs and I had 'em in that pasture there." She looks through the brightness of the sun to the land on her left. "The water runs in there and that's where I fed 'em. I went to feed that hog and it was a great big old male hog. He jumped up there and grabbed my hand. Dr. Blackburn said, 'I never got to see anything like that.' Terrible. He said it deadened the nerves. Cut all them nerves. But I ain't gon' let nothing get me down. I do my work."

If Minder Coleman were less of the soul she is, she would have much more to complain about than that encounter with the hog. In the late 1960s the lock and dam down the river from Gee's Bend were activated. When the new lake was formed, a third of the Bend was submerged, and the land owned by the Colemans disappeared. They were forced to sell. Gee's Bend land prices were not high to begin with, and because of the new flood tracts, the typical going price plummeted to $150 per acre. "That throwed Gee's Bend to have to sell the land when they didn't want to sell it, because the water had covered it."

And, when the road was built in front of her house, she had to give up a huge parcel of what had been a turnip green patch in the section running down from her home. "So he took all that land and if he gave me a dime, you give me one."

After Mrs. Coleman was bitten by the hog, she became nervous and lost much of her hair. "You know what?" She questions as she removes her turban to show the close-cropped snatches still intact. "My hair used to be all down here." She gestures to the nape of her neck and her shoulders. "Since that hog bit me, if I talk a lot I get nervous. See how it rises up. All my nerves. That's what the hog did. Bit all the nerves. You know, every finger got nerves. That where your nerves at."

Mrs. Coleman is an expert of sorts on things that can go wrong with the human body, for she once took a nursing course given in her own home. A nurse came with medical books and was helpful in teaching her how to deal with "crippled peoples," including Mr. Coleman. Tragedy struck when he was taken ill and had to go to a Veterans Hospital. After their son gave his approval, a doctor there amputated Willie's feet without her permission. She says the amputation was unnecessary. Eventually, she sued the doctor, he left town, moved to California, and died of a heart attack on the day of his West Coast arrival.

Mrs. Coleman could never claim a penny. It happened not long after her hand was torn apart. She could not care for her husband until it healed, so he went to the Veterans Hospital. When her condition improved, she made arrangements to bring him home. "I said, 'I'm gon' take my husband home at 4:30 because I didn't sign for his feets to be off.' I said I wanted him to be home with me the fourth day of July. Dr. ——— said, 'Okay. You can take him. You can dress him?' I said, 'Yeah, here are my card.' I showed him my card what I had taken up. And after then I had taken him back up there. They cut 'em off right along here."

Mrs. Coleman carried her husband home and nursed his leg stumps back to health. Letters came from the hospital urging her to bring her husband back:

I say, "This is my husband. I'm keeping him as long as I want." When the men brought him in, they said, "Minder, how you heal this foots?" I say, "You a doctor. You ought to know." He say, "Minder, who give you the training?" I say, "I went to nursing school. I went to school every day in Alberta. Here my card." He looked on my card. That man got in that car and left and they didn't know where he was. He got to California. He called me. He said, "Don't tell nobody where I at." And he dead. Fell with a heart attack. Got there that day and fell with a heart attack that night. They sued him for so many thousand dollars. I ain't got nare penny. They yet send me $117.48 a month. I get that from the government.

After his feets didn't never get well good, I sued 'em after I brought him home. I healed him. You couldn't tell it had been cut. I looked in the book, went to the drug store over here and got every kind of medicine what you should get. I bathed him in purple. I done forget but it was a purple powder. I got some antiseptic healing oil, clorox and some rocks-eye. I poured it in my bathtub. I got a deep bathtub. And Epsom salt. I bathes him in that.

Then I sued 'em. And then another doctor worked on him and say he didn't have no need to cut his feets off. I was so mad I just cried. Water just run all over that place.

But for Minder Coleman—farmer, weaver, seamstress, quilter, factory worker, nurse, depression-day co-op leader, and keystone in the genesis of the Freedom Quilting Bee—tears dry quickly: "I'm just so happy, I don't worry about nothing."

Aolar
Carson
Mosely

On April 18, 1969, *The New York Times* ran a story about the Freedom Quilting Bee and its new sewing center as it began operation on an Alberta cornfield. Pictured in the article was Mrs. Wisdom Mosely with her little namesake granddaughter Aolar (pronounced *a-O-lur*). She was standing over her new wringer washing machine, which the newspaper reported she had purchased with earnings from her quilting.

She typically had fourteen mouths to feed, the story explained. "But Aolar Mosely still manages to make improvements with her earnings." First was the washing machine, then the bathroom fixtures that had yet to be hooked to the plumbing. The newspaper noted that she later hoped to buy a food freezer. She did buy the freezer and also purchased two beds from a furniture company in Camden—all with money she earned from the Bee.

A small, humorous woman with penetrating eyes, she had not realized even a decade later that she had made *The New York Times*—not that knowing about it would have affected her in any way. For, after all, New York is far away from her neat little plot at Gee's Bend. Just the trek to Camden is a major accomplishment.

Now in her seventies, Aolar Mosely has been called a mystic by those from worlds away from her own: someone who would be just as comfortable carrying on with a bunch of monks in a French monastery as she would be entertaining family and friends in the Gee's Bend house built for her by President Roosevelt. For sure, her thoughts, her talk, and her actions are based on a theology honed and polished over the course of a lifetime: ever onward, ever upward till the day when her house that Roosevelt built is exchanged for a heavenly home. "I want to go to that place up yonder where every day is Sunday," she states emphatically. "That's what I work for."

"I've never before heard the name 'Aolar,' " a visitor comments.

"Tell the truth!"

Aolar Mosely and her
quilt top of pink **Z**s, her
first patchwork effort
since a house fire de-
stroyed her longtime
collection in 1984. (Photo
by Nancy Callahan)

"Is it a common name around here?"

"Well, I don't know but one around here named Aolar and that was my granddaughter. Named after me."

"Who were you named for?"

"I don't know. My Mama didn't tell me."

"How was your husband given the name 'Wisdom'?"

"The Bible said that. They got it out of the Bible. Wisdom."

Born to Simcer and Elizabeth Carson on May 12, 1912, in a part of the Bend then called Carson, Aolar grew up on stories her father told about how all the blacks would spend their days working in the fields. "It was like a squad, you know. The white men would have 'em all in the field working together."

Mrs. Mosely is much a part of local heritage. Her father came from somewhere across the river and was brought to the Bend as a child. Her mother was at least a second-generation resident whose family's fingers had worked the soil deep in the 1800s. That line may have come from North Carolina with the Gees. "As far as I know, all of 'em was here 'cause I knowed her uncle and he was here. He was an old man. They called him 'Big Uncle.' "

Although her parents were representative of the original Gee's Bend, Aolar Mosely is symbolic of twentieth-century life in this backwater—from field-work as a child, to participation in federal assistance programs of the Great Depression, to involvement during the sixties in the black quest for civil rights.

As a youngster, Aolar worked the fields for a white man called "Blood Young," who paid her fifty cents a day: "They started me out in the field when I was a school girl still. I didn't go to school. Mama was picking cotton. We had to pick cotton, too. They didn't pick cotton like they do now. Cotton don't open now like it did then. We started picking cotton in September and had to pick all of September. If I weren't picking cotton down in my Daddy's field, I had to go to your field and help you pick yours. I didn't went to school. I didn't get no further than the fifth grade."

When she did attend school, it was held in a little church, taught mostly by her uncle and her older brother, who had received enough education to qualify to pass it on to others. The poorly structured classes met whenever enough children could get together. For payment, her father would give the teachers corn, meal, and syrup. When not teaching, the educators would pick cotton, tend hogs, and engage in other agricultural endeavors.

"The first teacher I remember—oh, Lord, I forgot her name. But I had stopped going to school when she come." Mrs. Mosely still thinks about having to learn her alphabet and the manner whereby her family encouraged her education: "They wouldn't let me go to bed until I said my ABCs. They would help me to read when I went to bed. I'd sit down, they'd bring that book and I'd be so sleepy."

Mrs. Mosely was eleven when she made her first dress:

My mother cut out a dress and told my sister she
wanted her to make it for me tomorrow. Then she
went on to help the lady quilt. So I got 'em all to bed
that night and I made my own dress. Nobody told me
nothing.
Mama and them was going to sit up with the sick.
You know, they used to sit up with sick people. So
that next night she said, "Virginia, go in there and get
it on the dresser and make it."
I said, "Mama, it done be made." She said, "I won't
let you mess it up." I ain't said no more. My sister went
and got it. She said, "Mama, Aolar made this dress."
Mama said, "I cut all the pieces for messing it up."
Then she got up and looked at it. She didn't say another
word to me.
Ooooh. Not a soul learned me how to sew. I always
was sewing since I was a little bitty girl. That's just
my gift, I reckon.

On that occasion, as she has done ever since, she used a sewing machine. "I ain't never learned how to sew with my hand. Most everything I make with a machine. My Papa bought the machine. It was $40. A brand new one. They was cheap then. Mama would sell chickens and pay on it. Or quilt quilts for an old lady that wasn't able to quilt. Sometimes they just gave her some meat, some lard, some eggs or a chicken."

As a child, Aolar first observed the phenomenon of the quilting bee. Her mother would move from one house to another to join groups of quilters. "Oooooh boy, did they do some quilting. They didn't have something to buy a blanket. They *had* to quilt to cover up."

The girl helped to supply her mother with quilting frames by going with the others into the woods where they would find four long poles, trim them, and let them dry. Her father would bore holes in the ends of the poles and attach them together with nails. For quilting, her mother used balls of thread priced from 10 to 20 cents per ball. One ball would be enough to quilt a quilt. "Oh, she was a good quilter," says Mrs. Mosely of her mother. "But I ain't a good quilter."

Her own debut in that discipline came when she was twelve. "I'm going to tell you the truth," she affirms. "We couldn't get cloth back then like I can now. When an old shirt would wear out, we'd tear them up and sew 'em on.

I'd just tear up the shirts and the overalls and make me a quilt. I sewed just as much as I could get me some rags. I really loved to sew."

Still, Aolar Mosely does not admit to the talents of a quilter, even though she was one of the founding Freedom Quilting Bee members and worked at the co-op for years. She believes her main abilities were supervising, managing, and teaching the others:

When I was working to the quilting bee, I mostly
went around, told this one to do this and if they didn't
do it then I'd fix it right. I'd put up the quilt and I'd
stretch it. I cut the pieces for them to sew with. I fixed
the machine if it needed fixing. I could sit down there
and show them how. "Now, you quilt it just like this."
Anything they needed done, I was just free to do it.

When we first started working there, we weren't
getting nothing. We were so praising, so thankful it
was a way to make some sometime. We didn't get any
money. You see, we were doing that trying to get to
somewhere. We'd just get that two dollars and fifty
cents. Oh, we were thankful for it 'cause it was just
ladies. That's all. Just womens doing work.

Before the time the quilters moved into their permanent facility, Mrs. Mosely was an effective organizer and behind-the-scenes contributor. When the nucleus of activity was Estelle Witherspoon's home, she would go there at night and cut out pieces of material for the next day's labor. "When they get there, they ain't got nothing to do but go to sewing. They won't have to wait on 'em."

On quilting days, Aolar would go home in the evening, cook her husband's supper, and return to the Witherspoon home to quilt more. In those times, she also supervised small groups from her own home. When she received the money to divide with her members, she likely would give more to them and keep less for herself. "If I'd come out behind, it'd be okay. I wanted them to feel better." When the women would adjourn from her home to eat supper, she would continue to work, putting the quilt in the frame or performing other mundane chores to facilitate a speedy session when they reconvened.

Mrs. Mosely worked at the sewing center until 1981, giving the group her full flow of energy. Then she began to go there mostly as a volunteer. "I was working for to get paid from up yonder one day," she explains as she points toward heaven. "I just love to help peoples. That's all I was doing. I just love to help 'em. I did all I could to help 'em till they got to somewhere." And when they got to "somewhere," Aolar Mosely lessened her responsibilities and gave others opportunities to foster skills parallel to her own.

After she married Wisdom Mosely in 1929, she lived through Gee's Bend's depression and subsequent help from federal resettlement, when she and her husband paid $3,500 to the government for a house and 116 acres of land. "Wasn't that cheap?," she is asked. "What do you say. Wasn't it a blessing! But you know, the better the land was, the higher it was." She explains that in Gee's Bend there are varying shades of land quality. Some is level, some hilly, and some wooded. The Mosely purchase, though a godsend, was not of the highest caliber.

Even so, she had been raised in a pole house. When she married, her father-in-law had given the couple a plank house. And now the government had provided them an even better plank house. "When they built this little house here and I moved in it, I thought I was somewhere! Yes, ma'am. The government built all these houses, built everybody a house."

Mrs. Mosely was in her early twenties half a century ago when the government moved in. She remembers the canning centers, where she would put up tomatoes, sweet potatoes, and English peas. She recalls a store, a ginhouse, a school, and a medical clinic—all compliments of Uncle Sam. She thinks back with amusement to the clinic, for it was a place her family went often, not for healing but to visit and mix with the other people.

Her memories turn also to the Red Cross, the agency that replaced a summer's community diet of wild plums with more nourishing staples. "The men used to go over there and they'd give 'em something to eat such as meat and lard. I thought that was nice by my not having nothing. But you know, I was blessed. Ever since I've been married I ain't had to suffer a thing but Jesus. And I could have got Him if I weren't too lazy." Mrs. Mosely erupts into long and loud laughter. Then she is asked for an explanation. "Don't have time to tell you. See, it takes time to go to Him, and a mind and a desire."

Married at seventeen, Aolar Mosely is the mother of seventeen children, thirteen of whom survived early childhood and are scattered from Gee's Bend to Mobile to New York. Her husband, a farmer, died in 1977. She is convinced she will live at least to the age of eighty-four because she once had a dream that told her as much: "One night in my sleep a white man came to the door. He was great big and he sat right there," she nods to a chair in her living room. "He had a book and he did mark. I got up and stood over him. When he marked I counted. He marked 84, he shut the book up and went on away. That told me how long I would live. Any time he marked, I counted 'em, and when he got through, he shut the book up and he ain't said a word to me. He went right back out the door. Never said a word."

Mrs. Mosely would like to have had a chance to complete the twelfth grade. But, despite her fifth-grade education, the Freedom Quilting Bee has been a stage from which she could advance her favorite activities:

I told you I already liked to sew. And I really like to
be nice to peoples 'cause God loves us all. I never
thought I was no more than anybody else. I just always
loved to piece them quilts and loved to sew:
    You know, none of my sisters was interested in
sewing like I was. My husband used to quarrel with
me. I just loved to go out to the quilting bee. At that
time we were just making a dollar and a half a week.
And he said, "Aolar," and I said, "Uh-huh." He said,
"You stay home with me and I'll *give* you a dollar and
a half a week if that's all you got to get."

She laughs some more. "But I told him, 'No. I want to help the other
peoples.' Wasn't nothing but womens, you know. We didn't have no strong
backers to back us up. Reverend Walter did what he could. He was so sweet
to us." At one point, she began to earn five dollars a week, a feat that impressed
her husband. "He told me it was real nice that I was getting some money.
When I got five dollars a week that was good. That was some money 'cause
things were cheap then. It ain't like it is now."
    Although the Gee's Bend men had to buy gasoline for their wives to make
the trip to Route One, Alberta, Mrs. Mosely reports that some did not mind
at all when their wives began to make money. "They'd be glad I got money,
you know, lazy as a man was." She glories in her statement and continues.
"When they first started, we worked for nothing till it got to something.
When we began to work by the hour then we got to something. The quilting
bee has done something for Gee's Bend in a lot of ways. It's done brought us
a long way."
    Two of Aolar Mosely's daughters worked there at one time, but later found
higher-paying positions in Selma. "Nowadays you don't make as much to
the quilting bee as you do to a Selma factory. But if you work in Selma, you
got to spend gas and you got to waste up your sleep. You got to get up and
be there at seven o'clock. At the quilting bee it won't take as much gas to go
there as it would to Selma. And then when you got to be there at eight
o'clock, you ain't got to waste up your sleep. I think that's the best job to
have—with the quilting bee. It's real nice."
    Mrs. Mosely also believes the communion among those who work at the
Bee is an added incentive for employment there. "I want to tell you those
girls aren't spoiled. They work nice together."
    It is four o'clock in the afternoon. Road sounds from a school bus float
through the Mosely home. Moments later, her granddaughter walks in with
books. She is Aolar Diane, the one from *The New York Times*. Now seventeen,
Diane is a junior at the high school in faraway Pine Hill. She catches the bus
at seven each morning for the fifty-mile ride to school, and is bused back

home for fifty more miles in the afternoon. "She says she don't want to do it but she got to do it," Mrs. Mosely explains.

Because it was not racially integrated, Boykin High School, down the road, was closed years earlier by the federal courts. Diane was born during the Selma to Montgomery march. In fact, her birth prevented Mrs. Mosely from marching. The lifelong seamstress had become a civil rights enthusiast as a member of Pleasant Grove Baptist Church, where Martin Luther King, Jr., had held a series of mass meetings.

"Did you ever meet Dr. King?," Aolar is asked. "Yes, Lord. I was in that movement. When they were going to Montgomery walking, this girl wasn't born then and I was going with 'em. My husband said, 'You ain't going nowhere 'cause while you're gone, that girl might have that baby. I just hollered 'cause I couldn't go with 'em. And she was born before he come back."

Despite her physical absence, Mrs. Mosely was there in spirit. "I was saying, 'Go on, Jesus. Go on, Jesus.' Ooooh. It was real nice. I was a hundred percent with it." She was in most all of the marches in Camden. "When I couldn't be there, I'd be hollering. I didn't have sense enough to think they would kill me."

But Aolar Mosely is not a fearful woman to begin with, for fear is counter to her Christian faith. As an example, she says if she plans to go to her son's home a few houses away and the timing is off, the devil likely will tell her, "Go on, go on, go on." The she will say to herself, "Well, I reckon I'll sit down and go tomorrow." The way she believes, Jesus is the one who has told her not to go because Jesus is first in her mind. Likewise, if she is cooking, walks away from the kitchen and forgets what she is doing, she says Jesus reminds her to go back to the stove. "He told me to get it. That be Jesus."

Such is the faith she readily shares with others, and the opportunities are frequent, for Mrs. Mosely is called on for advice whenever there is trouble. "I often teach peoples, tell 'em what the Lord said, and when they get into it, they call me and talk with me. I was talking to my son. I told him, 'Jesus said he died because he loved the world. He told 'em love rounded 'em all up,' and I said, 'If you love, you'll feel it come back in.' "

In November 1984 Aolar Mosely's home burned to the ground in a fire that destroyed almost everything she possessed, including her longtime collection of quilts. Within months, her grandsons, some of whom she had sent to school to study brick masonry and other trades, built her a new brick home on the site of her original, New Deal purchase as a testament of love for their grandmother.

Mattie
Clark
Ross

"I never thought I'd live to get old." That's Mattie Ross responding to a question about the most unexpected event in her life. And what a life it has been for an octogenarian whose silky-smooth facial features suggest a much younger woman. She is a quiltmaker; retired farmer; member of the choir at Oak Grove Baptist Church; former civil rights activist; and original treasurer of the Freedom Quilting Bee, a position she continues to hold, though she is no longer an active co-op worker.

A visit with Mrs. Ross is a pleasant and rewarding occasion. As one passes the end of Alberta, the calendar leaps backward to another plane, where the only car on the road keeps to a snail's pace to make way for the chicken biddies, a mother cow and her calf, and a large family of goats. Heavy traffic is foreign to these parts, so jaywalking is in their genes. Nine miles past the Freedom Quilting Bee on a knoll a few yards off Pettway Road is a small, government house. It is neatly groomed, wire-fenced, and beautified by flowers that edge the property front.

"I'm Mattie Clark Ross," beams a hale and hearty woman in polyester as she extends a firm right hand.

The hostess and her guest proceed immediately to a bedroom closet filled with her quilts. For photographs, they take the folded creations from storage and spread them over two beds, the living room sofa, the front porch swing, and the clothesline on the side of the front yard. Although it is a cloudy, rain-spitting afternoon, within minutes the woman's home is aglow with color, a showcase for the fruits of an artist and a glimpse into the heart of her soul. As stars, stripes, squares, zigzags and triangles, the material bits have been welded in the patterns of her upbringing as well as in modes filtered in from the aesthetic world outside.

One of Mattie's works is a Double T in yellow and black. Another is the Missouri Star. Its background is light blue; the long strips separating the blocks and the stars are worn-out blue jeans. The Sun Star, perhaps the most elegant offering, features twelve many-shaded eight-point stars, each of which contains another eight-point star. A velvet Star of Bethlehem block, colored in pink, baby blue, and white, decorates the living room fireplace. A Mixed Star, also multicolored but involving strong use of red and black, is planted on the sofa.

Permanently fixed on a bed in Mrs. Ross's best bedroom is a Gentleman's Bow Tie, in red, yellow, black and white, green, blue, and brown. Her Flower Garden, lying on the front porch swing, is an amalgam of flowers inside flowers. Although the pieces are prints rather than solids, the color contrast is so effective that from afar, they appear in optical illusions as bold, solid flower shapes of red, orange, blue, pink, wine, yellow, and green.

Mattie's Strip quilt, hanging on the clothesline, features a scheme of brown

Mattie Ross, whose home was headquarters for the co-op's first Parish-Hadley project, displays her Strip quilt, in which yellow and red are the dominant hues. (Photo by Nancy Callahan)

and black print strips entwined with solid strips of red and yellow. It gives the appearance of an endless succession of red and yellow steps, or a child's puzzle in which contestants must find their way out from inside.

A Trash Can quilt, also on the line, was made from scraps. A different design is on every block: a blue-and-gold Bear's Paw; a multishaded Nine Patch; a Wild Goose Chase, in pink and black; blocks of long strips and small squares in the primary colors; a block of black, white, and brown squares; a dovetail of navy and yellow diagonals three-fourths the length of the quilt; and still others. No two blocks are alike. Most are dissimilar in size.

The Trash Can has a mystical, almost Egyptian flavor, not only because of the zigzags and triangles that run wildly across the quilt, but also because of the lone, central Sun Star block, which peers over the Wilcox landscape like the all-knowing Eye of God. Too bad the piece is not on exhibit at the Smithsonian instead of being stored in a stack of folded quilts in a bedroom at Gee's Bend.

Mattie Clark was born on October 1, 1902, near where she now resides. "Right there behind my house," she exclaims as she points to her birthplace. "You see the big pecan tree out there in the yard? My Mama set that tree out in her garden when I was a little bitty kid. Was on another man's place, you know."

Like Mattie, her mother, a Pettway, was born in Gee's Bend. Her mother's family lived there also, but her father's origins were in North Carolina. Mattie was one of nine children. When she was about six, her mother died. After her father remarried, he and his second wife had several more children. She was raised in the home of her Pettway grandparents, who rented farmland from "Hargrove Pettway," a white man, who was actually Hargrove VandeGraaff, of Tuscaloosa.

Mattie made her first quilt, a Nine-Patch, at age nine. She completed the fifth grade. In 1918, at age sixteen, she married Clint O. Pettway, almost twenty. He died in April 1953. The following December, she wedded Goldsby L. Ross. Although she never had children, she raised a host of those belonging to her brother, sister, other relatives, and a neighbor.

A lifelong resident of Gee's Bend, Mrs. Ross knows its history:

> An old man owned this place. He was named old
> man Gees. And they got a name they put a bend on,
> old man Gees Bend. That's what they named this
> place, Gee's Bend.
> And the Pettway man that come here, he owned a
> lot of land and all the people decided to be named
> Pettway. But they weren't no Pettway. A lot of people
> was something else but they signed their name "Pett-
> way." They liked that fellow's name, I reckon. My

Daddy was a Clark but signed his name "Pettway."
My husband was a Williams but was named "Pettway."

In view of the slave-trading operation run by the Gee brothers between the area and North Carolina, Mrs. Ross supposes her grandparents were slaves. "My Granddaddy and them said their home was in North Carolina. Old man Gees Bend bought 'em and brought 'em in here and kept 'em on." Slave-time tales crept into conversations Mattie heard as a youngster. "White folks used to whup 'em up and do 'em up all kinds of ways so bad."

Mattie's own growing-up years were not easy:

After I got through the fifth grade, we had to go to
the field and knock cotton stalks. On good days we'd
be in the field knocking stalks, and knocking 'em
down on a cold Sunday so they could plow. We'd pick
'em up, burn 'em up and cut bushes off the land. Then
we'd have to take care of the cows. Three or four cows
were milking every day. We'd take 'em, tie 'em out and
water 'em. We did just every kind of task. It was busy.
We never did have no time like children go to play
now. No time for us to go to play. A few minutes on
Sunday.

Mattie married Clint Pettway just before the end of World War I. "See, my husband was in a rush, getting ready to go to war," she explains. "We went down to the place and the war climaxed that day. The news come over the wires. My husband was fixing to get going that day. I was glad he didn't go. He was happy, so happy."

Until the federal government entered Gee's Bend, Mattie and Clint Pettway fought just to exist. "I didn't have nothing," she shouts in a high-pitched voice. "I didn't have good places to sleep, nothing to eat, hardly nowhere to live. Me and my husband were just working hard. We never did come to have nothing till a way a long time."

The twosome spent their years together farming land they rented in the Gee's Bend swamp. When the area was divided and sold, they acquired eighty-two acres for $2,800. "The government came in, decided to give 'em all a home and cut up the land, so many acres to the fat. They was selling it dirt cheap. When we bought ours, they was just giving land away. We had been here all our days. I reckon they decided partly to give us a hand. Been wiping us out all them many years."

When Clint died in 1953, his widow still owed $1,900 for the land, but she loved farming and continued with it. By the end of the year, she had reduced her debt to $1,300. Eventually, she paid the entire sum.

Thanks to the Farm Security Administration, Mrs. Ross has a warm spot in her heart for the federal government. "We got from under that bondage we was under before we could see any light. Looks like we was under bondage, just working, never getting results out of what you working for." Mrs. Ross takes pride in her home and tries to maintain its appearance in the same fashion as when the government built it. She states that, as a matter of honor, it should be maintained in a manner pleasing to the government. "They told me, 'Y'all keep y'all's houses so good, just like Fort Knox.'"

In many ways Mrs. Ross's life has been one of isolation, especially since the ferry service came to an end. She notes that, in days gone by, she would walk three and a half miles from her house to the Alabama River, then board the ferry for a seven-mile ride into Camden. "They had a skiff and a flat. The big thing what they put their wagons on, it's called a flat. They'd put two or three wagons together on there. Sometimes the cows got in. We used to catch the ferry and carry berries and chickens and things we raised, sell them and get us a little something. Go to Camden, do anything you want and—whisp—we'd be back home. Well, the flats went bad. Peoples quit putting flats down there to cross on."

Without the ferry, the trip to the county seat is forty-two miles one way:

It's a good day's journey. We have to go all the way
around through Alberta. It's just so hard. Then if you
don't have no way to go, you got to pay somebody
to take you around there. We used to enjoy going to
Camden, walking and talking and crossing the river.
The ferry wasn't but 10 cents. But as long as you've
got to go all the way around, that ain't no enjoyment
yet to me.
They're talking about a highway, putting a bridge
across the river, but that's just all they done, talk about
it. Hadn't got to it yet.

Mrs. Ross says that, in times past, "leaders" came into her community and worked with groups of women. From county farm agents to home economics teachers, they furnished ideas on cooking, sewing, and other subjects useful in running a home. They were valued links of communication from the outside. "But since our leaders are gone, we don't have nothing in here. Nothing to do but be isolated. We ain't got nothing to look forward to."

If Mrs. Ross could have had her choice as to a desirable setting in which to have grown up, it would not have been Gee's Bend. "I like the spirit of being born here but sometimes I think we could have done better in the world if we could be living somewhere else. I done got this old now so I think I have to settle down. But when I was a little younger, I could have went off in some other place and lived and I wouldn't even want to come back home. I had peoples in Montgomery. I could have went there and lived with my peoples. I had peoples in Mobile. I could have went there."

If she could have completed high school rather than the fifth grade, Mrs. Ross believes her life could have been more fulfilled:

> Oh, how many times I have wished I could have gone to the twelfth grade. There wasn't no good to have wished it. I tell these children, "I wish I had the chance when I was children that they have now. I could have put my time to good use." See, they don't have nothing to do now but go to school. We had to go to school and work.
>
> I would have been a teacher 'cause I really love to fool with children. I would have gone to Montgomery to college. If today we were in my days, I'd got it all. I'd be working with the folks' children, teaching. And I don't want to teach but little children. Second and third grade, like that.

Still, Mrs. Ross had many opportunities to work with children inasmuch as she devoted so much of her life to raising those of others. Out of that role she has formulated definite ideas on the qualities of a good mother:

> I told the children, "When I growed up, I did all right. But y'all here now and look to me like I'm sup-posed to be a Mama for you. I'm gon' do my Mama proud to be the best I can." Everything that I could do for 'em I did. I fed 'em and I clothed 'em and saw to 'em being well-kept and decent. When they go to bed, I go up, kiss 'em good night, cover 'em up, fix 'em up and do for 'em. And need a whuppin', I give 'em a whuppin'.
>
> I taught 'em how to live, how they gon' be when they got grown, got out there in the world. "You gon' need to know this and need to know that." I said, "I'm gon' tell y'all what I know." And I trained 'em to piece quilts, to wash, starch and iron, cook, scrub and patch their own clothes. I'd say, "Hon, get your clothes and go to patching. I may be dead and gone. Get you a needle and thread and patch your own clothes." And they could do. They made pillows. They'd get flour out of sacks. Couldn't get nothing else to make pillows, looks like. I got the flour out and washed out that reading. People write things in flour sacks.
>
> And I got me some print pieces and showed 'em.

"Put this on around the hem." I had a girl right across
the road there sewing on the machine, cooking, doing
everything I was doing. She wasn't all that old, neither.
They would grow up doing so many things.

Didn't have any of my own but I grew up in a big
family where people didn't mind whuppin' and raisin'
and teachin' you to where you was right. If you were
wrong, if they knowed, they'd whup you. I thought
that was the way I would bring them in, like my parents brought to me.

The most progressive, enjoyable part of Mattie Ross's life was during her
active years with the Freedom Quilting Bee. Like so many others, her
membership had been preceded by her work to achieve voting rights for
black people: "We had the march in '65. We didn't march to Montgomery.
We marched to Camden, at the courthouse, for our rights to voting. We had
never started voting. We should a did it before then but we hadn't got our
rights. We couldn't do it without marching, protesting. We American citizen
and it be all these many years and our forebears didn't know nothing about
voting. We wanted to do a lot more than they did. We marched and protested,
registered to vote."

Mrs. Ross remembers clearly the 1965 voting-rights campaign, when
Martin Luther King, Jr., led meetings in the Bend:

I shook hands with him and spoke to him. I asked
him how he getting along. He said, "Doing all right.
How you feeling?" We said, "We doing fine." And he
just say, "Well, let us try to do the best we could in
non-violence. Don't even carry a hair clamp in your
head. Don't carry nothing of any harm. Non-violence."

I don't know how many times we did march in the
cold and the rain and the heat. I didn't go to jail but
I wanted to. They put them others in jail. I wanted to
go, too, but they didn't put me in jail. I don't know
why they didn't take me that time. I sho nuff could've.

Then Mattie Ross won the right to vote. "I felt good," she says as she
offers a broad, bright smile, adorned with an upper gold tooth. "I felt like I
could do something I had never done in my life, like I was good enough to
do something important like that." She believes her first decisions at the polls
may not have been correct—"but I sho felt good about it!"

Then came the Freedom Quilting Bee, which brought even more changes
into her life. "I was helping people make quilts and the Lord sent a man
through here who had a heart for poor peoples. The Lord just sent him
through here with a spirit to try to help the peoples. He was a white man,

Reverend Walter, a good-hearted man whose heart goes out to peoples." Mrs. Ross then relates how the co-op grew from $10 a quilt to $12, $14, $20, and $50 before ascending to its current monetary level.

"Right in this house we made one of the beautifulest quilts you ever want to see." Made by a group who worked in her home to produce quilts for New York, "it was like a tulip bulb." Before the Bee began, she had long worked in group quilting, during which as many as twelve women assisted her at one time to augment her personal collection. Friends would converge on her home for an entire day, go home to cook supper, and return for the evening. For refreshments, Mrs. Ross would serve peanuts and sweet potatoes.

One of her vivid memories from those times is that of herself and her fellow quilters sitting around a frame with a needle and thread in one hand and a sweet potato in the other. Another is the singing at those parties, for most of the quilters with whom she associated were also members of her choir. "We would sing and we would shout." Rejoicing in the recollection of those gospel songs, Mrs. Ross sings an example in a clear and strong voice:

Some glad morning when this life is o'er,
I'll fly away, fly away.
To a land on God's celestial shore,
I'll fly away, fly away.
I'll fly away, oh glory,
I'll fly away, fly away in the morning.
When I die, hallelujah, bye and bye.
I'll fly away.

"I like my voice, braggin' or not. I do have a good voice. I've got the cold. I can't get my voice together now. I used to have a real clear voice. Done got old and done got hoarsed up. I used to be a soprano leader in the choir." In past years, her choir would meet with those from other churches for contests. She learned how to sing, though, from schoolteachers who lived in her home; and to play the accordion as a youth from older members of her family.

Mrs. Ross worked at the sewing center until the summer of 1979, when she was seventy-seven. The experience enabled her to meet people she never would have encountered otherwise, and it taught her how to be friendly with strangers:

I learned peoples I didn't know till I worked there in
the quilting bee. I didn't know anything over there
between here and Alberta, but in the quilting bee a lot
of us gather and have a good time working there together. We laugh and talk and quilt and do. I learned a
lot of good-hearted peoples.

And lot of different peoples come in from way different places, make themselves friendly with us and us
makes ourselves friendly with them. We enjoy that so
much. I wouldn't take nothing for being up there at
the quilting bee. I just *enjoy* up there when I was
working up there.

The ladies sent to be working in the quilting bee
have been able to do a lot of good things for their
homes that they weren't able to do before they started
working up there. You see this here living room suite?
I have a bathroom in there. The quilting bee was the
beginning of that. I got three beds, mattress, spring
and all. That come from the quilting bee, and they
wasn't paying money then like they paying now. But I
just worked every week and saved my money up. I
think along in them times making fifteen and eighteen
dollars a week. They get good now.

And because of the quilting bee we're friendly with
peoples, more always joyed to be with peoples. I was
always afraid of myself with peoples 'cause a lot of
peoples I didn't know. And I realized at the quilting
bee the best thing to do was show 'em they have a
friend. Show yourself friendly, learn and swap talk
with each other if it is nothing but trying to get you
some BC for a headache.

Mrs. Ross respects women working together for a mutual cause. "A woman
will always do her job," she declares. "If she gets a job, she believes in doing
her job. Gon' do it decent, too." From watching television, she is convinced
that men, on the contrary, are not as motivated and industrious as they once
were and are allowing women to take over the planet. Most of the people
who go to church, she contends, are women. Likewise, she notes that women,
more and more, are assuming leadership roles in business. "I see it on TV.
Women just done took over. They have to. Men done lost their candy. Done
dropped their candy."

Mattie Ross holds her head up and releases the hilarity sparked by her
words, then regains her composure to reflect on life beyond eighty. "I tell
you, what I'm proud about my life is this old age 'cause I never thought I'd
live to get old. I'm in my eighties. I'm proud of that. I'm proud of health and
strength the Lord let me have, and I'm proud I got to a place where I can't
work and still can live if I don't work. The Lord blessed the way so that every
month, Jesus-through-the-white-man sends me a check." She refers with
amusement to her Social Security.

Mattie Ross's final dream for this lifetime is to win over to Christ the lost
souls of Gee's Bend, a goal that thus far has dealt her much inner turmoil but

no positive action. As she explains, "There is something about my life that I would like for some people to know about me, but I haven't got struggle enough to get out with it yet. I have a book, a little old catechism I want to read to a bunch of non-Christian peoples."

On Sundays, Mattie says, big clusters of sinners gather on the steps below her front yard. She wants to stand there with them, read from her book, and help them to see their mistakes, for they do not seem to care that they are not saved:

Looks like they just say, "Till tomorrow." That's
how they live. "See you tomorrow." Far-out peoples
like that, I could talk to 'em, but it looks like they ain't
paying no attention. They weak. Got nothing to do
but live and die.

Christ come in the world. Didn't do no sin. He had
a long way to go before he went back to his Father,
but he done all he could to save peoples. He even died
that all men shall have a right to eternal life. He had to
do that for them. He didn't *have* it to do. He did it
'cause he loved the world so.

See, I love to try to gain peoples to do things that
you know is pleasing to the Lord, 'cause we're not
living, we're dying peoples. And once you're dead, you
don't come out here to get straight, to get saved no
more.

Mary
Boykin
Robinson

The visitor to the Freedom Quilting Bee cannot help but notice the facility's side yard: an arrangement of happy-hued playground equipment, situated among shade trees that are partially painted white with occasional strokes of red and blue. On days of sunshine, the scene is often enlivened by a group of preschoolers darting in and about the yard.

This activity seems inappropriate at the address borne by a women's craft cooperative, but inside behind the quilters' area is a series of rooms that house the Freedom Quilting Bee Day Care Center, an institution spawned to take care of youngsters whose mothers make quilts.

Provided with considerable help by the Selma Inter-religious Project, the day-care center opened in mid-1970 and has been in continuous operation since that time. It serves not only those children whose mothers work at the Bee, but also others in the area, aged two through six, whose mothers are employed away from home. The original enrollment was sixteen. Then the center began to care for some children of unemployed welfare recipients: "enrichment children," as they were called. Thus, their number swelled to thirty-four. But 1981 government cutbacks brought that phase of the operation to a halt. So the roster now carries twenty-three.

Since February 1971 the effervescent Mary Boykin Robinson has been director of the day-care center. She is an educator who possesses more than three decades of experience as a teacher. She was born in Camden on December 18, 1925, completed high school in 1945, and was awarded an emergency teaching certificate because of the shortage of educators caused by World War II. She spent the next several years teaching at local schools during the regular terms and attending Alabama State Teachers College, in Montgomery, during summer sessions.

The lack of a college degree eventually forced Mrs. Robinson to abandon her career as a public school teacher, but a wealth of background in the profession paved the way for added opportunities. She worked with an antipoverty program in Wilcox County that was sponsored by the Southern Christian Leadership Conference; she taught adult classes at night and helped with the small day-care program. When that venture was phased out, the idea was embraced by Friends, Inc., another group designed to uplift black people. She worked with that program until funds were no longer available. When the director's vacancy occurred at the Bee day-care center, she was hired.

The staff includes other members of the area's black community: Jeanette Taylor, the head teacher; Jennie Lue Williams, another teacher; Velma Young,

Mary Robinson runs
the day-care center in
the co–op building on a
shoestring budget.
(Photo by Nancy
Callahan)

an aide; and Addie Nicholson, the center's cook, who is now also president of the Bee. Before the cutbacks, three more women were part of the program.

Using physical facilities owned by the Bee, the center has a contract with the Alabama Department of Pensions and Security, which makes available positions for thirteen children whose parents are unable to pay. Parents of the others pay $105 a month per child. Some thirty-four children could be accommodated, but many working parents are not able to afford the monthly fee; thus only twenty-three now attend.

In 1977 the day-care center received a grand-scale breakthrough: a federal grant through congressional appropriations entitled "94–401 funds," awarded largely on the basis of a proposal written by Mrs. Robinson. Included in the grant was $5,100 to purchase a freezer, refrigerator, and playground equipment; and $4,999 for a van to transport the children to and from the center. More than twenty can ride in the vehicle at one time, but some walk to the center and home again because they live nearby. In addition to serving as center director, Mrs. Robinson drives the van, a 1978 Chevrolet sports model.

"I love it! I love it!," the tall, trim, and fashionably dressed director exults as she breaks into a smile. "I don't know of any other job I'd like to do now but this." She begins each day by picking up the children in her own community of Boiling Springs at 7:15 A.M., then those from another, called Catherine, and finally the ones closer to the Freedom Quilting Bee. "It's a lot of fun," Mrs. Robinson beams. "When they hear me blow, boy, oh, they're excited to death. They like to hear that horn!"

Without question, since 1971, the endeavor has stirred her deep-down spirit and commitment. She outlines the early morning schedule: "When the children arrive, they begin by having devotion. We sing a beautiful song and then we pray. Afterward, they wash their hands, come back and sit around the table. When all the food is set, they are ready to have grace. After grace, they proceed in eating their breakfast."

During the course of the eight-to-three sessions, participants engage in "learning experiences":

They are taught very common sense things like the number of hands, feet and eyes they have, cleanliness, colors, pronunciation of words, and how to communicate with one another. As they grow older, just before we release them to regular kindergarten, they learn to recognize numbers one to ten. Some of them, by the time they get here good, can count to a hundred. They don't really know the numbers but they have a little song they sing.

Every year we have a Christmas program with the children just before we leave for the holidays, and invite the parents. Then again, we invite them at the last of the term to the graduation. You should see those little kids with the caps and gowns on. They think that's wonderful!

We can keep them until they get ready to go to school. Some of them go on to kindergarten but most of them stay here until graduation. We're not pinning flowers on ourselves but everybody says that they are really ready when they get there.

Proper nutrition is another high point on Mrs. Robinson's daily agenda, from breakfast to lunch to mid-afternoon snack. "We must maintain a balanced meal. At breakfast, we always have milk and we always have either fruit or fruit juice. We usually give them grits, sometimes toast, bacon, eggs. If we have bacon, we don't have eggs because it's too expensive." After eleven o'clock, the students are served a hearty lunch, play for a while so their food can be digested, then take a nap until two, when they have a snack.

"We must maintain a balanced meal," the educator affirms:

Most times their mothers hardly cook anyway until later on in the evening about the time the older ones are coming. At home they are missing that heavy, mid-day meal. A lot of the parents don't know how important it is to give the children milk. We *must* give these children milk for breakfast and milk for lunch. They must have their milk twice a day.

Some of the parents don't even think about how important nutritional meals are for the children, some of the main things they get here at the center, things that maybe parents, well, some of them, just don't know.

Mary Robinson, herself a mother of seven, is unhappy that children of welfare recipients can no longer participate in the project:

They took them out because they said they didn't have enough funds to keep them going. They say it's a "luxury," [she quotes one of her government contacts] but I say it's not a luxury because those children are the ones who need it worst of all. Some of them have never before seen a flush toilet stool and they have never even gone inside a building equipped like this one, let alone, been in there every day. It's home to them because they are here more than they are in their own homes. So I told the lady, "Well, I don't know why you want to call it a luxury. I would call it the best thing that ever happened to real poor children."

Many of Mrs. Robinson's former pupils are no longer in her structured blend of learning, nutrition, and socializing with their peers: "See, they're going back to where they were, just at home. The parents are not working, and then most of them have more small babies at home to look after. Actually, the parent hasn't got much time to give them for having to tend to the little bitty ones. This was really a great thing for the children, so it's really a sad situation, I'll tell you that."

In view of the economic difficulties historically prevalent among black people in the rural contours of Wilcox County, Mary Robinson always faces an uphill fight to keep her center alive. Although the state pays the fees for thirteen children, some working parents pay for day care for their children, but in many cases, with difficulty. As Mrs. Robinson explains:

It's hard to get eligible children now. Lots of parents are working, but if you're making just a little above minimum wages, then you're making too much to qualify for your child to be paid from Pensions and Security. They are not really able to pay the $105 because they'd have to be making pretty good money to pay $105 a month.

If I could get them to set the eligibility scale a little higher, allow the parents to make a little more, that would help a lot.

It takes dedication to try to keep things going because so many times money is so scarce that I find myself spending my money, too, trying to make ends meet. Really and truly, I tell you, it's rough right now. It really is. But by the grace of God we plan to keep on, continue.

Meanwhile, it is early afternoon and a hush has settled over the day-care center. Twenty-three children are stretched out on floor mats. Most are sound asleep, some open-eyed in silent reflection. Each is covered with a baby-sized quilt fashioned by their neighbors, the quilters. Amidst the blocks and books and cut-out numbers and letters of the alphabet and aquarium fish and all the other resources that foster early learning, day care is still a first-generation phenomenon undreamed of a century ago or even two decades back by the forebears of these children of the Freedom Quilting Bee. As with its mother institution, day care is an entity Mary Robinson and its other supporters hope will survive somehow.

China
Grove
Myles

In October 1975 the *National Geographic* included a story about the state of Alabama: "Dixie to a Different Tune" it was called. The featured personalities ranged from the owner of a paper mill in Tuscaloosa, to a Birmingham heart surgeon, to a maker of quilts from Gee's Bend. She was China Grove Myles, a maiden lady in her eighties who still quilted the finest of stitches.

As the article pointed out, "Miss China Grove" was the only one left in Gee's Bend who could sew the Pine Burr quilt, a pattern involving hundreds of tedious swatches that unfold before the eye in a breathtaking, three-dimensional effect. The reference to her Pine Burr was only one sentence long; her photograph was nowhere in sight; and her unique quilt could be seen only in the imagination of the readers. But interest was phenomenal.

People from all over the country wrote the *National Geographic* asking how they might purchase a Pine Burr quilt by China Grove Myles. The requests were sent on to Miss Myles, who was befriended by a young white man, Rhodes Johnston, Jr., who, along with one family, composed at that time the entire white population of Gee's Bend. He answered all the letters and specified a price of $500. A West Coast woman was one who placed an order, and she received what was surely one of the most incredible quilts ever executed in Wilcox County.

In March 1976, upon its completion, Johnston photographed the quilt and its maker before the shipment was sent out West. Miss Myles, tall, small-framed, and with dark moles on her face, wore a blue, shirt-styled dress, covered by a flannel, street-length outfit in plaids of green, blue, black, and tan. On her head was a dark blue cloth hat. Her shoes were white lace-ups.

In one photograph, a couple of her friends, Ethel Young and Eva Mae Coleman, posed with Miss Myles and the Pine Burr, for they had assisted in the producton, along with a niece-by-marriage, Lucy Marie Mingo, who

China Grove Myles, a
few months before her
death in 1976. (Photo by
Rhodes Johnston, Jr.)

was at work when the photos were snapped. By the time this quilt was in progress, Miss Myles was in poor health—she would die before the end of the year—so she had summoned her quilting partners to aid in the task.

More than anything else, the quilt depicted the adjectives most used to describe her own personality; warm and cheerful. It was dominated by pastels of blue and pink, but every other conceivable color was occasionally used. The three-dimensional appearance created the effect of circles inside of circles inside even more circles. As in a highly detailed Oriental rug, it was a design in which the beholder could discover additional spots of creative life upon each new inspection.

When China Grove Myles died on October 15, 1976, in a medical facility in Mobile, she left behind a lasting and memorable reputation as a quiltmaker as well as a human being. Born in Gee's Bend eighty-eight years earlier, on May 5, 1888, she was known for many things: her organizational skills, her life in the Oak Grove Baptist Church, her deep spiritual faith, her sunny disposition, her tasty cakes, her compassion, her living alone, her small, spotless house, her swept yard, her hard work, and the tremendous joy she exuded in her gift as a maker of quilts.

Befitting of her life-style, "China Grove" is no ordinary name. She once told Francis Walter that she was named for someone's favorite church, the China Grove Baptist Church. Its whereabouts are unknown, but it could have been most anywhere in the rural South, for in the late nineteenth century, when Miss Myles's life began, stands of chinaberry trees were commonly planted at newly established churches. They would grow rapidly to provide dense and attractive shade. No one in Gee's Bend can verify the story. Sadly enough, all her peers are dead, and she never told later generations how her name came about.

Speaking of his days in Wilcox County, Father Walter says:

When I visited in the homes of some of the older women, I often experienced "the feminine mystique," or maybe I should say "the maternal," in an over-powering intensity. China Grove Myles was one of those women. She was totally integrated and adjusted to her environment. She was aware and really proud of her superior quilting skills. Very few would show a visitor an example of good workmanship. In fact, very few would show a quilt at all. But she would. She would show the Pine Burr. As I would smell a pie baking in the oven, she quietly would show off her work with a total sense of her mastery of the art of quilting. She was a real source of inspiration to the Boykin women.

By profession, Miss Myles was a farmer, whose stamina and outdoor acumen earned her immense respect among many of the other women of the community, who relied on their husbands to perform heavy agricultural chores. She owned a farm with her sister, her brother-in-law, her nieces, and her nephews. They farmed their parts and she farmed hers—all by herself. Her spare time was spent in quilting and in raising her sister's children—the real joys of her life.

One was Emma Lee Mingo, of Mobile, who has worked as a maid for twenty years at the Dauphin Way United Methodist Church. She was raised by her aunt China Grove from the time she was a youngster. "She was one of the best quiltmakers in Gee's Bend," declares Miss Mingo, whose last name is Indian. "She made real good stitches. Small stitches. Her stitches were so small, you would think they were done on a machine. I could not tell the difference. You could hardly see them. And when she would patch something, I could not tell whether it had been done by hand or machine. You could hardly tell they were patched. They looked like they had been done on a machine."

After Miss Mingo moved to Mobile, her aunt would visit her there, bring along a quilting project, work at her craft, and stock up on supplies for herself and her friends. "She would go to a dime store on Government Street where you could buy material real cheap. She would buy forty or fifty yards of material at a time and take it back to the different ones. She would sell it to them. Every time she came down here, she would bring her little bag and quilt the whole time she was here."

Miss Mingo never bothered to keep a clean house while her aunt was there, for the equipment of a quiltmaker would be strewn everywhere, including patterns she had cut from newspapers. When the visit would end, Miss Myles would leave with ten or fifteen blocks as souvenirs of her stay. Typically, those blocks would appear in Star quilts or in Cuckle Burrs, to grace the homes of a wide array of quilt enthusiasts. Miss Mingo says her aunt invented the Cuckle Burr pattern. "It had little all-colored pieces, with folds the size of your thumb." Cuckle Burr could have been another name for the Pine Burr, or perhaps a pattern variation.

Eva Mae Coleman was about twelve when she first knew China Grove Myles. "All of us lived right around here in the neighborhood, right around here together." As she grew up and became a quilter herself, Mrs. Coleman observed with great curiosity the quilts made by her much older neighbor, especially the Monkey Wrenches, Pine Burrs, and Lazy Banks. "The Lazy Bank looked like a set of steps, but it was real beautiful. And I remember another she made that was a stocking quilt. She made it out of stockings. It was the craziest thing I ever seen, but it was pretty."

After Miss Myles agreed to make Pine Burrs for sale by Rhodes Johnston, she became sick and asked for help from Mrs. Coleman, Ethel Young, and

Mrs. Young's daughter, Lucy Marie Mingo, whose husband David was Miss Myles's nephew. Mrs. Coleman says:

> She told me, "Come on up to the house." I looked at
> the quilt. I said, "I can't hardly make that." She said,
> "Yes, you can. You just sit here and watch me." She
> made one round and I took it from there. When I
> finished that block she said, "I can't hardly tell your
> block from mine." And she laughed. She taught all of
> us how to make that Pine Burr.
> You couldn't hardly see her stitches. And that's the
> way we had to make 'em. If we made big stitches,
> she'd say, "I'm gon' pull that one out. That's too large."
> She would go over all three of us's blocks. If they
> weren't made right, she'd tell us, "Take that bug out,
> fold it over and put it in there good. It's not holding
> good." She'd check those stitches. If they were long,
> we had to pull them out. We had to do it right when
> we worked with her.
> She was the best so far as I know. A lot of girls
> called her and wanted to work with her but she told
> 'em she had enough girls. She was the best quiltmaker
> I know.

From Miss Myles, Ethel Young learned how to make the Pine Burr and the Double Wedding Ring as well as a sunbonnet. "That was one good woman," she exclaims. "Me and her got along together just like two fingers on one hand."

Not long after the Freedom Quilting Bee had begun, Father Walter visited Miss Myles. She went to a chest and pulled out a sunbonnet she had made years earlier—so old, it reflected a style reminiscent of the nineteenth century. It became the prototype for bonnets made by the quilting bee in its first few years as a co-op.

According to Mrs. Young, who worked at the Bee "when President Kennedy's brother got killed," China Grove Myles and Estelle Witherspoon's mother, "Mama Willie" Abrams, were the only two at the Bee who could make those bonnets. "Miss Chiney learnt me how to do it."

Most original members of the Freedom Quilting Bee worked at first in small groups, then at Mrs. Witherspoon's house, and finally at the sewing center. China Grove Myles visited the quilting clusters at their various locations and was a member of the organization, but she chose to work mostly at home. She and Ethel Young once made a Double Wedding Ring, for instance, and sold it to the Bee. On another occasion, she assisted Lucy Marie Mingo in producing two black-and-white Chestnut Buds, which the co-op sold in New York to Diana Vreeland. The Bee once made fifteen dollars on one of her Star quilts, marketed by 1960s activist Abbie Hoffman through a Mississippi poor people's craft chain in New York City. She was always ready with information when the Bee needed her advice.

In October 1966 the Mobile Council on Human Relations invited the Freedom Quilting Bee to take part in an arts festival at Municipal Park. Miss Myles made the trip and was an eager participant. She accompanied Estelle Witherspoon; her daughter, Louise; her mother, "Mama Willie" Abrams; co-op secretary Addie Nicholson; Doris O'Donnell, down from New York; and Francis Walter. The event brought $120 home to Wilcox County, and later that month, one of Miss Myles's Pine Burr quilts was displayed at the Mobile Art Gallery.

But Miss Myles was not a member of the Bee to make money or better her economic security, for, after all, she was already seventy-eight when the co-op was founded and was drawing Social Security. "It was just for the love of making quilts," explains Mrs. Young. "She loved to save up what she had. She saved all she could. I know because sometimes I didn't have money and I could go to her and get some any time I got ready." "She did not have much sense of solidarity," Father Walter indicates. "She was not the type who would have been a union leader. She was the kind who wanted to master the best in herself rather than organize others."

But in November 1971 throngs of blacks demonstrated in Camden for higher-quality education for the children of Boykin. It was one in a lengthy series of protests against the Wilcox County Board of Education. Although eighty-three, China Grove Myles was there. And, when a school bus was filled with children and grown-ups who were taken off to jail for having demonstrated, the feisty and emotional Miss Myles banged her pocketbook on the side of the bus, yelling, "Take me, too. I want to go to jail. I need to be with my children." Wilcox officials refused to let her on. "You're too old," they told her. "Go on home."

Emma Lee Mingo and her sister, Adell, saw the event that evening on Mobile television. "They flashed it on the news on TV," Miss Mingo remembers. "The sheriff was there. We saw her and she had sort of fallen off the sidewalk. She hadn't really fallen. She had stumbled and she was getting up. I said, 'Ooooh, there Auntie!' She wanted them to take her. It was exciting!"

The final member of Miss Myles's quilting party was Lucy Marie Mingo, who in the 1950s had married China Grove Myles's nephew. Mrs. Mingo reflects:

A lot of things I learned about sewing, I learned
from her. She would always tell me, "If you make a
quilt and don't make it level, it won't hang right." She
was always saying, "When you make a quilt, be sure

you cut your pieces right. Always try to cut the pieces
the same size."

I'll tell you what Auntie was crazy about. She was
crazy about the Pine Burr, Monkey Wrench, Turkey
Track, Grandmother's Choice, Flower Garden, and
Bear's Paw. The Pine Burr was Auntie's favorite, but I
told her her pieces were too small. That's the only
thing. Each piece should be just about an inch square.

Mrs. Mingo says her husband's aunt first made Pine Burr throw pillows.
Then Stanley Selengut came for a visit, noticed them, and asked if she could
make quilts employing that same technique.

In the months before her death, Miss Myles made possibly seven Pine
Burrs and sent them out-of-state to fill *National Geographic* orders. After her
death, letters from California continued to come to Miss China Grove, asking
for more of the same. But Lucy Marie Mingo was engaged full time as a
county extension worker, and the orders were never filled:

At that time, I told 'em, "Well, I ain't gon' even try,
because Auntie and my mother and Eva Coleman
worked day by day just to work on that."

So many white people met Auntie when they came
here. When she was in the hospital, they left things for
Auntie with me and I would take them to her. She
would say, "You keep it now." Mr. Knight was from
California. He came and brought her a pair of those
scissors that never need sharpening. She had already
passed on so he gave 'em to me.

She just dedicated her whole soul and body to making quilts and going to church. She was an usher in
the church until she was seventy-something-years-old.
And she was just as spry as she could be—until she
had the stroke. When she died, she had bought some
material to make a Pine Burr. She had started on it
and had made twelve blocks.

She was making a Grandmother's Choice, making it
from the bed. She *finished* it that Saturday morning
and even put some little strips around it. Then she had
a stroke and fell out in the back room. It was on the
bed when she fell. I quilted it for her niece in Mobile.
It was pink and blue. I guess she said, "This would
be my last one."

Lucy
Marie
Mingo

Among the names on the Freedom Quilting Bee's articles of incorporation is that of Lucy Marie Mingo. No doubt, it is one of the most poetic names on the roster. When pronounced, it is like a healing balm to the senses, or a whispery wind kissing the trees on the river bank below her home. It would make a good pen name for an author or composer of music.

Lucy Marie is neither. Like China Grove Myles, she never worked by the hour at the Alberta sewing center, but she was in on the ground floor of the movement; and, while holding other jobs, engaged in co-op quilting during her off-hours at home in Gee's Bend.

One of Mrs. Mingo's early efforts for Freedom, a pink-and-blue Texas Star, was placed by promoter Betty Stephens in a Westport, Connecticut, craft shop. "A customer bought it on the spot," Mrs. Stephens reported. Another of her quilts went to Donald McKinney, head of New York's Marlborough Gallery.

Mrs. Mingo also played a major role in the Bee's acquiring work from designer Sister Parish. She was appointed to make two sample quilt blocks of the Chestnut Bud design for the inspection of the eminent interior decorator. One was orange on yellow and the other yellow on white. The project brought Mrs. Mingo five dollars. "If this work is good," Francis Walter wrote on the Parish work order, "we get the contract—Make it good." The work *was* good, thanks to Lucy Marie, so the co-op won the contract.

Tall, slender, poised, and confident, Mrs. Mingo wears blue jeans and a plaid, long-sleeved shirt. She talks freely and appreciatively of her time in the quilting assembly. Now in her fifties, Lucy Marie Young did not learn to quilt until she married David Mingo, but she pieced her first quilt top on the sewing machine at age fourteen:

My mother would say, "You piece your own quilts
so when you get married, you'll have 'em yourself."
My mother learnt me how to do *everything.* Some
days, I felt like she was too hard on us but since I got
grown and got out on my own, I was very proud
because she learned us how to do everything. But there
was one thing I really didn't learn how to do—sew
and make dresses.

   She said, "Baby, you need to learn how to sew, because you don't know who you're gonna marry, and
lots of times, what you have, you have to make it."
I said, "Mama, I ain't gon' learn how to make no dress
because whoever I marry, he's gon' buy what I want."
I regretted that because I had seven daughters.

Lucy Marie Mingo, shown here with her grandson Alph Coleman, continues the Pine Burr tradition of China Grove Myles, her aunt by marriage. This quilt has 23,850 pieces. (Photo by Nancy Callahan)

Lucy Marie Mingo is the mother of ten children. Although her husband has been ill and unable to work since about 1970, each one of her daughters has received some college education. "You know, I've had it," she declares from her living room sofa. "But I wouldn't give up. I just continued to push on. Mrs. Witherspoon was real nice to me. She would always keep some work for me to do. I would work at the school and come home and I would quilt at night. And then she said, 'If you do a good job, you can always have something to do.' So I always had it to do until I just got tired of it. I said, "Well, I'm gon' die anyway. I'm just gon' stop all this.' "

Upon her marriage, Mrs. Mingo began to take her quiltmaking seriously. She would meet and sew with her mother, Ethel Irby Young; her husband's Aunt China Grove; and Eva Coleman, an associate of "Auntie." "There wasn't anything else to do then but make quilts and try to get a little money out of 'em. What made it so interesting was trying to do it very easily and do a good job of it."

At one point, Mrs. Mingo obtained a job at the Boykin school lunchroom, where she worked for eleven years. A high school graduate, she learned from the principal about a special program offered by Spring Hill College, the basically male, Jesuit institution in Mobile. He encouraged her to enroll and she did. It was the Career Opportunities Program, sponsored during the late 1960s by the U.S. Department of Health, Education, and Welfare. The venture was designed to update the math, English, and human-relations skills of disadvantaged persons and to improve their opportunities in the job market.

Mrs. Mingo attended Spring Hill for about three years, had another child, then worked for three years with the sixth grade in Boykin. "After my son came along, I said I didn't want to go back to school because I had gotten up in age. You know, when you get up in age, it's just a hassle to have a family and go back to school. You have to be very strong. So I got in with the extension program."

Since 1973 Mrs. Mingo has been employed by the Auburn University Extension Service. Assigned to thirty-five community families, she helps them to develop a broad range of homemaking skills. "I'm planning to stay with them until the job runs out because when you get in your fifties, it's hard to get a job."

By the time the Freedom Quilting Bee had been established, Mrs. Mingo excelled as a quiltmaker, so she joined it and was called on to teach many of the other members. One of her specialties was the Chestnut Bud. "I was the only person that knew how to make that quilt and I learnt the other ladies how to do it." Before the sewing center was built, she worked with some of the others in the home of Mattie Ross, where they crafted the Chestnut Bud into a quilt, a sofa cover, and window curtains for the William Paleys of New York. In fact, she teamed with Estelle Witherspoon to lead the twelve-woman brigade through that critical challenge.

"But I never did want to quilt," Lucy Marie continues, "because I figured I couldn't make no money there. I was working at the school at the time they were hiring people and didn't have the time because I would come home, go to the field and farm a little bit. There was just too much."

The Chestnut Bud is deep-seated in Wilcox quilting. Mrs. Mingo obtained the pattern from her cousin of an older generation, Pankey Pettway:

> I was always going to cousin Pank's house. She was seventy or eighty years old and had all kinds of quilts. One time I was at her house and she was making this quilt. So I got the pattern from her.
> See, when these people came in, we had all types of pattern blocks and that was the one they picked out. They liked it the best. That pattern is twenty-something years old with me, and cousin Pankey said she had it over twenty years. The pattern had gotten so old, it was wearing out. It's one of the oldest in this area. The oldest quilts the quilting bee is putting out right now are the Grandmother's Choice and the Bear's Paw. My mother made a Bear's Paw for me before I got married and I've been married thirty-three years.

Perhaps more than any other quilter, Mrs. Mingo is a link to China Grove Myles, with whom she shared uncountable quilting hours. Her life is the cultural continuity between that legendary figure from the past and the future of fine craftsmanship in Gee's Bend, as evidenced by her own Pine Burr that she and daughter Willie Dell proudly take outside and exhibit. A masterpiece showing every hue of the rainbow, this regular-sized composition contains 90 blocks. Each block has 265 square pieces. The number of pieces in the entire quilt totals 23,850. "Now, that's a small quilt," she offers. "It's not a king-size. You have to put 110 single blocks in a king-sized quilt. We made the blocks a little large so they could hem 'em down." Reflecting the June sunshine, some of Miss Myles's own blocks and probably a piece of her soul are in this quilt. Other blocks by Mrs. Mingo's mother are there as well.

On one of the beds inside is another Mingo-made quilt, serving as a bedspread. In red, white, blue, and beige, it is a Grandmother's Choice. The material is Sears, Roebuck corduroy that she bought from the Freedom Quilting Bee. A former member of its board of directors who still pays her dues to the organization, she explains that, from the corduroy inventory used by Freedom to produce pillow covers for Sears, the smaller strips are left over and are available for sale. "That's the way I made this quilt on my bed."

Mrs. Mingo says a roll of corduroy is only three dollars; two color combinations are six:

You put both of the rolls together and you can get seven quilts. You know those little strings that I have? They gave me those little strings. I'll take those little strings, put 'em together and make quilts out of them.

The quilting bee is a good help to us because if you were to go down to the store, that cloth would be $2.98 a yard. It's very expensive. I think it's wonderful because if it hadn't been for the quilting bee, where would I have to go to get that material? If it hadn't been for the quilting bee, where would these people have a little job to do something? So they get around and go to the quilting bee. You can go for about three dollars a week and you make a hundred and something dollars.

See, you ride with somebody. Two people go up there with a station wagon and take everybody. So that's where the people work. You make your money and you save it.

There are so many ladies here in Boykin who really didn't have the opportunity and didn't have the skills to go out and get a job. But once they got to the quilting bee, that was something for them. I just didn't only want it for myself. I wanted it for whoever would get able to get them a job there.

A lot of women don't have transportation. They can't drive. They don't have skills. They just sit around the house and do the same thing over and over every day. But the quilting bee is an outlet for 'em. They can do that and make some money. At least they can have something to do. They won't have to sit around the house all the time. So I was very glad when they got it.

Mrs. Mingo now insists on a visit to her mother, a quarter of a mile or so down the way. A front-room bed in Ethel Young's home is covered with at least a dozen quilts she and her friends have made. Many are reminiscent of those that attracted so much attention at the New York auctions in 1966 and are typical of the original Alberta/Gee's Bend variety. Lucy Marie has her eye on one in particular. It is a Monkey Wrench, made of blue-and-gold corduroy bought from the Freedom Quilting Bee.

There is a lot of distance, in more ways than one, between Chicago's Sears Tower and the bed on which Ethel Young's Monkey Wrench is sandwiched between handiworks from an older, less worldly way of life. But the Freedom Quilting Bee brings a bit of the big city to this lonesome bend of the Alabama River with each new roll of corduroy strips.

Nettie
Pettway
Young

"Dear Rev. Walter: I would like to order a cotton quilt, in the twin-bed size, with mostly light pink and white, perhaps also a little light green."—Charlotte A. Schmidt, San Francisco, January 2, 1967.

"Dear Rev. Walter: I am enjoying my quilt very much, and if possible, I wish Mrs. Nettie Young could know that I think she does beautiful work."
                    —Charlotte Schmidt, February 23, 1967.

Stroll through the Martin Luther King, Jr., Memorial Sewing Center on a given day and you'll see a certain set of faces. Come again the next day or the next week and you may see a whole new group, depending on whether it's time to produce the latest Sears order, whip together small items, or make quilts. But one person is always there. She is Nettie Pettway Young, the comanager of the Freedom Quilting Bee and director of its cattle operation. Other than Estelle Witherspoon, Nettie Young is the only woman now working at the Bee who was among its originators. She has been at the sewing center continuously from the start.

As much as any single individual in Wilcox County or elsewhere, Nettie Young typifies the history of the black race in America. She is the daughter and granddaughter of slaves. Although born into freedom herself, she was denied the basic rights of an American citizen for almost the first fifty years of her life because of the color of her skin. In the mid-1960s, she took part in the civil rights movement; and like so many of her black brothers and sisters, spent time in jail. This time was not wasted, though, for, unlike her grandfather and her father, she won the right to vote. She now enjoys the rights common to all Americans, but she has given her life a quantum boost beyond those legal guarantees. For two decades now, she has been an everyday

Comanager Nettie Young checks a sewing machine, part of her duties at the Martin Luther King, Jr., Memorial Sewing Center. (Photo by Nancy Callahan)

crusader in the struggle for the economic independence of women who are black.

The daughter of Thomas Pettway and Eliza Reed Pettway, Nettie was born on June 6, 1917, in Rehobeth, an earlier name for Alberta's Route One. Her maternal grandparents, George and Mary Reed, worked on the Wilkerson Plantation. Her paternal grandfather, of whom she knows little, was Robert Irby. "My grandfather was George Reed and my grandmother was Mary Reed and they was just poor farmer," she states as she sits at a table in the back of the sewing center near the end of a day of work. "Nothing but farming for the white boss of the plantation. George Reed used to chop wood for peoples to make a living on. It was very hard in them days. He did everything with a axe and a hoe and a shovel and a plow."

Her grandfather Reed never talked to Nettie about slavery, but her father did, though rather infrequently. "He said his old masters used to hang him up in a sack and whip him with a trace chain. He didn't tell me how bad he felt about it. He just saying how far back it had been and how hard he had been mistreated. They got out of the really deep part of it before they died, I'm sure, so I don't remember the slave part, the bad part of slavery. I can remember slavery but not the bad part. In fact, I have been in some slavery myself, part of the times I have had." She manages to laugh despite the comment about her own "slavery."

"He was treated bad when he was grewing up," Mrs. Young continues.

"People used to sell people, you know. He was sold to another man. That's why he was a Pettway. He was sold to the master, was a Pettway he was sold to." Eventually, though, Thomas Pettway achieved his freedom. "He lived as free as we are now," exclaims his daughter. "They moved to Mobile from here and they lived in Mobile for years and years. He did public work. That was where he was buried at, Mobile. My mother never worked but in the house. She just nursed children. She just took care of children."

Mrs. Young's father's family, their roots, and their whereabouts are a mystery to her. She does know that when Thomas Pettway married the first time, he had seven children. His second wife bore one child. The third time, he married someone even younger than one of his daughters. By that marriage to Eliza Reed, he sired twelve children, including Nettie. "My father died when he was ninety-six and my mother died when she was seventy. I was growing kids when my mother and father died. I would describe them as the sweetest peoples to me that ever was. They was good peoples. My mother was really a Christian. She believed in God. She worked at churches. She loved the church and she just had good faith in God and growed us up in church. Oak Grove Baptist Church. It was right down the road here."

During Nettie's growing-up years, her parents rented a farm from a white man, Toby Wilkerson. Her father would plant cotton, corn, and a variety of foods for the family to eat:

But the cotton would have to go back to pay their
rent. If he make enough, he may clear enough to get
something out of it.
We lived in a big old log cabin, double with a hall
between them. And they had smokey chimneys. They
would build dirt chimneys when I was growing up.
Sticks and dirt were bracers and the old chimney would
soon break holes through it. When the wind came
through, it would just smoke you out of the house
near about, but still you had to use it.
My Daddy had six of his kids living there and my
mother had nine or ten living there—all together, and
it was just a house full of peoples. In a two-room
house. We had to have bunk beds all around the walls.
We was just as happy as we could be. They was really
just happy.

Mrs. Young pauses to laugh in retrospect at one of the brighter times of her life.

The comanager of the Freedom Quilting Bee believes her mother's Christianity contributed in large measure toward the family's happiness:

She was so lovely to everybody. She was so lovely
till she made us just be lovely. We never was sad. If
it be some days no food, everybody was happy, 'cause
she'll say, "We gonna get something to eat before the
day's over." It won't be nothing so nice or so good but
it'd be food. And we are yet happy. We eat. Sometimes
we get a piece of cornbread or some syrup. Just that
was good.

We never had toys 'cause there was too many. We
would make our wagons. We would saw some blocks
off a little pine tree, big enough for a wheel. We bored
holes through the wheels and fixed to the wheels, put
a bottom on it and we'd have a wagon. We'd just ride
down the hill, cut wood and haul it in the wagon.

We *made* our dolls, a rag doll, and the little clothes
to put on the rag doll, and we was just as happy with
that doll as the children are with their dolls today. We'd
name them after the different girls we'd know. Sometimes you'd want one with hair on the head. We'd go
out in the field and dig up a piece of broom sage. We'd
take that grass and wash the dirt out. That'd be her
hair.

And we'd cut a vine hanging in the tree. We'd have
that for our swings. We'd swing on the vine from
the tree.

We used to play jump-rope with the rope that our
Daddy plowed. We'd get his rope that he plowed the
mules with and we'd throw it and we'd jump it.
We used to have little games we played in a ring. We
all grew round the mulberry bush—and Little Sally
Walker:

> Little Sally Walker, sitting in the saucer.
> Rise, Sally, rise. Wipe your weeping eyes.
> Shake it to the east. Shake it to the west.
> Shake it to the one you love the best.

We was really happy.

For Nettie Pettway, formal education was minimal. It is possible that she
went to school a total of only eight months in her entire life:

My Daddy was never able hardly to pay for us to
go to school. It was so many. We'd go to school, I
reckon, about two months a year. Next, we'd be in the
field, knocking and picking up those stalks, cutting
them bushes, getting ready for the farm. I reckon

I was about eight or nine years old when I first went
to school. I had so fer to go up there that I couldn't go
any smaller. I went to school to Oak Grove but we
lived so fer from Oak Grove, about four or five miles.
We had to walk every day to school and you couldn't
walk that till you were big enough to walk through
the cold and bad weather.

But, even when Nettie was old enough to walk for four or five miles, her
father was not able to send her to school. That was an accepted fact of life:

He be just couldn't afford it. That's all. I knew they
couldn't afford it. I grew up enough to know.
I enjoyed school and wanted to go very bad. My
granddaddy had a book he left here. When I couldn't
go, my mother'd set me down and we'd read in the
book every night. He called it a *Blue West Indian*. It
had math, just all kinds of reading and spelling. I
learned mostly from home. I didn't learn very much at
school 'cause I'm there too quick. Didn't have time.
By the time I'd get used to the children—"

Mrs. Young interrupts herself with laughter, realizing that before she could
ever become firmly established in class, she needed to go back to chopping
cornstalks.

Because she was able to attend school only two months out of the year for
three or four years, Nettie has yearned all her life to learn more—"oh, so
many times"—and continues to spend lots of home time reading. Living in
Alberta/Gee's Bend, what kind of education would or should Nettie Young
have pursued, given the opportunity? "If I just could a completed high school,
that a done good," she laughs. "If I could a finished the twelfth grade, with
a mother which I have, I think that would have been all I needed." If a
profession could have been possible when she was young: "I'd a loved to have
been a nurse, 'cause I love caring for people. And I think that would have
been a good way for me to have gotten around and cared for more people."

Perhaps her religious upbringing steered Mrs. Young into that mold of
thinking. "I used to go to Sunday school every Sunday. Barefeeted." Such a
memory is funny and she chuckles. "A little dress buttoned behind. First
started going to Sunday school with my granddaddy. I loved it. I love Sunday
school today. I still go to Sunday school and church every Sunday. Christianity
means a lot to me 'cause I have had hard ways and a hard time raising all
them children. My mother raised all us to go and I do the same, and I trusts
in Him and I know there's a God."

Mrs. Young can recount even now the day she was baptized and the effect that event had on her life: "A preacher baptized me, by the name of Reverend Robert Brown. He baptized in a pool. We didn't sprinkle or nothing. We baptized in the Baptist style. I thought that was the best-feeling day I ever had in my life, and I didn't get another one of 'em. That was the best-feeling water to me ever been. Don't no water feel like that water. That was good!"

In her early teens, Nettie Pettway met her future husband, Clint Young, who persistently sought her hand in marriage:

He used to come to our house all the time. He got to liking me. He was several years older than I was. He really liked me so I married him at sixteen. Nothing else to do but get married. I couldn't do nothing but sew. I sewed at home. I always did love to sew.

He said, "You know, I likes you, little girl." He was a big boy and I was small. He said, "One day you will be my wife." I never thought about it. Well, he kept on and kept on and sure enough, I got sixteen years old and he asked me would I marry him. I didn't know what to say 'cause I didn't believe him at all. Sixteen-years-old I got married. He was twenty-one. We had a very small porch wedding on the front porch of our house. I was wearing a white dress. My sister-in-law made it for me. And I had a nice veil.

Clint Young provided a house for his bride and himself not far from his mother's home. During a twenty-year span from 1934 to 1954, the couple had eleven children. Mrs. Young adds with pride, "They all finished school." But life was rough. At first, the couple rented twenty acres of farmland for $600 per year. They paid the rent in bales of cotton. When the Farm Security Administration established the Boykin project, they bought a house and farm all their own. Typically, Clint would be away from home months at a time, working, making money, and sending it home, while his wife and children ran the farm. Mrs. Young describes their pattern of life:

I tell you how he did be. He did farm summertime. Wintertime he'd go off on public work. He went first to California. He used to go to Mobile and work the shipyard. He went to work in Wheeler, New York, for eleven years, at Bird's Eye Food Plant.

We had so many children. We had to take care of the children. We had to school the children, and the farm just couldn't do it all. Me and the kids would farm. He would go off and work, but when he came back home, I done harvest the crop. I done paid the bills.

And so he don't have anything to do then. He go
hunting and fish. Every year he come home. In December he be back home. But he'd go back in May.
That a way we worked.

Mrs. Young and her children did all that was necessary in running a farm,
all on their own. "I had to hoe it and see to the boys plowing it. When time
to harvest, I had to grate corn. I had to pick cotton and carry it to the gin. I
had all that to do and did do it."

As a full-time farmer who sent eleven children through school, Nettie
Young possesses grit and managerial ability, which she acknowledges, but in
a modest sort of way. "Yes. I think of myself and I thank God for doing it.
No education. And I think I have done some wonderful things for not no
education. I really do, and I praise God for that."

By the time of the civil rights movement, Mrs. Young was in her late
forties. She was one of the marchers. "My own self," she emphasizes. "Of
course, I went to jail. I went for a purpose. I went not only for me, but for
all those poor, needy peoples, white or black. I had no choice. I was helping
the peoples to help themselves. I was marching for to get a chance to be a
registered voter. Didn't nobody here register to vote before we had the march.
Wasn't allowed to. And thats was my purpose to march."

The site of her original marching was Camden, the county seat, where
she was put in jail. "We was put in jail for marching 'cause they didn't want
us to march none. I was in there for three days." What would a person of
Mrs. Young's quiet, easy-going temperament do for three days behind bars?:

Not anything but sit around and lay down, 'cause
we was locked in, you know. We couldn't do nothing
but sit around and play around. That was all we did.
Mostly we talked. Oooooooooh. Was about forty or
fifty people in one big place. And so we marched and
went to jail and got us out of jail. And then we was up
there at the march to Montgomery. I was in part of it.
I didn't go all the way but the last day I was in it, fer
to get into Montgomery.

After all that was over, something broke that we
could go to register. Everything had cooled down for
us to could do the things that we was marching for
to do. So that's how it helped.

It almost seems destined that Mrs. Young would have been part of the
group who formed the Freedom Quilting Bee. For her, sewing and quiltmaking had been a lifetime pleasure. As she says warmly:

Sewing is almost my heart. I just love to sew and
quilt quilts with my mother. When I was six years old
I started helping her sew. I went on to making quilts
and learned how to make all the different quilts she
knowed how to make: Bricklayers, Monkey Wrenches,
Grandmama's Dream, Grandmother's Choices, Coat
of Many Colors, Broken Stoves, Wild Geese Chases,
Cross Cut Saw, Stars, Sweeps, and Bear's Paws. We
growed up making those quilts. I don't know why
they spell out from but we made 'em through our
own parents. I guess she did learn from her mother
'cause her mother was making quilts and quilting 'em,
too, when I knowed my grandmother.

I growed up sewing. I used to make all my kids'
clothes. I never bought clothes. I made the clothes.

Two of her favorite color combinations are black-and-white and red-and-white. The Bricklayer pattern is a particular favorite.

Mrs. Young no longer makes quilts at the Bee as she once did on account of her responsibilities as comanager. "I help to see to the work being qualified and good before we ship it off," she explains. "I don't make quilts now. I just put a binding around 'em. It's up to me to get 'em hemmed." Mrs. Young—a moderately tall and well-built woman who wears glasses and whose short, gray hair is covered with an African-styled bandanna—views the Freedom Quilting Bee as the crowning glory of her life:

It was one of the best things I've known that ever
come true for the black race. I've never had such a
wonderful opportunity than the quilting bee. And I
think all the womens who work here is proud 'cause it
have made so much for their home out of the quilting
bee.

First money I made, I remember saving that money
for the college for one of my kids, Jerrie Dine. She
went to A and M in Huntsville. And then I bought
washing machines and different things I needed for
my home.

Daughter Jerrie Dine became a home economics teacher, but now manages her own business in New York City. Many of the Young children, all of whom completed the twelfth grade, now live in the North. Several received additional education and career training. The oldest son is Larry, a construction worker. Next was Amos, who died in an automobile accident. The first daughter, Rennie Lee, works in hospital management. Annie Liza is a registered nurse. Clint was employed by the City of Cleveland for years, but is now disabled by a heart condition. Johnnie Lee, another son, works for a pulpwood company. The next son, Lineo Srpero, is a city bus line employee in Connecticut. "He's a foreign name," says Mrs. Young. "One of my friends named him that name. I think it's African or somewhere over in there." The next daughter, Jennettie, is one of Jerrie Dine's business partners. Marie is a licensed practical nurse, and Jackline once worked for Pitney-Bowes in Stamford, Connecticut.

"I couldn't a did what I did without the quilting bee," says Nettie Young, ready to go home from a day of labor far different from the cornstalks and the cotton fields of her past. "It was just a miracle to me that it happened. I just love it. It mean all to me. I love it."

If George and Mary Reed and Thomas and Eliza Pettway could only know, they would rejoice.

Polly Mooney Bennett

On a golden spring day, finding Polly Bennett is no trouble at all. A mile down from Alberta and its small collection of business endeavors, her home is a pleasant, white-framed structure trimmed in what Polly calls Japanese red. Her front porch is the kind on which generations of Southerners have sat and talked and watched the cars go by. Backed by seven acres of farmland, the Bennett front yard is lush with azaleas afire in pink and red. Wind-brushed oaks peer down from high in the sky. Across the road is a thick assortment of woodland—plum bushes, hardwoods, and pines.

What lets you know you're there, however, are the quilts blooming across a clothesline, right out front, splashing in the breeze and pulling in the rays of the sun. Mrs. Bennett's quilts are a highway safety hazard; a driver could become distracted by their bold, arresting beauty and stray from narrow, twisting Highway Five. "Sometimes I hang 'em out there and watch peoples just about run off the road," says Mrs. Bennett. "We did that as children when we were at home. We would quilt a quilt, hem it, and hang it out on the line. That's the way I do all my quilts now—when I finish quilting 'em, I hem 'em and hang 'em out on the line. That's how I advertise a lot of 'em." Highway Five is a widely traveled route between Selma and Mobile. Sometimes strangers stop on the spur of the moment to order a special piece of stitchwork from the poised and charming quiltsmith. Others appear months later at Alberta's business district to ask which house was the one that featured the lovely patchwork parade.

Some of her friends who enjoy making quilts for others are reluctant to bargain with customers who appear without warning, she says. "You know how you can be scared of people if you don't know who is who. Some of 'em'll be kind of scared to let 'em in. Some of 'em, they all right, but you know how the world going now. It's danger, but I just take a chance."

Polly Bennett, one of the
early Freedom family
standouts. (Photo by
Nancy Callahan)

Mrs. Bennett is fortunate that her polyester billboards do not have to hang in Gee's Bend, the place of her birth on the backside of creation and a thousand suns from this dream of a setting for commercial show-and-tell. Her sales approach has produced orders from Fairhope, down on Mobile Bay near the Gulf of Mexico, to Birmingham and beyond, and those who buy spread her name through their network of quilt consumers. "Right now it just seems like a dream, making quilts for people, and my quilts going somewhere I'll never go. They in New York, Detroit, and Texas. Some of those people come driving way back here and pick 'em up."

Several of her Texas quilts were bought by Lois Deslonde Ruth, who shared her professional handicraft knowledge with the Freedom Quilting Bee in the summer of 1966. "Others in the area are just as good," declares Mrs. Ruth, "but she's one of the best. What makes her work outstanding is that the pieces are well sewn together. No threads are showing where they shouldn't be showing. Her quilt would stand many washings without coming apart. It's one you could be proud of and could hand down from generation to generation. She also has a good eye for piecing colors and putting them together. She has a good artistic eye."

Mrs. Ruth owns a couple of Lone Stars and a Wedding Ring done by her twenty-year friend from the Black Belt of Alabama, and has ordered others for gifts faithfully shipped from Alberta to Texas. "I can always depend on Polly Bennett," states Mrs. Ruth. "If you put something in her hands, you're going to get it back. She'll say, 'Well, I have so many quilts I have to get by such and such a time, but I can start on yours in the next three or four months,' or something like that. I can depend on her to complete it in that time or sooner than I expected."

Born in the Bend on September 27, 1922, one of twelve children, Mrs. Bennett is sixty-four now but looks fifty. "Everybody tell me I don't look to be my age. Don't have no secret. Just work hard." When she was six, her parents separated, and Polly went with her mother, Mary Brown Mooney, to "the Hamner place," a plantation at Gastonburg, six miles from Alberta in the direction past her present home. Mary Brown Mooney, a tenant farmer, had to rely on help from her children; by the time Polly was seven or eight, she had begun to carry her share of the load. "I plowed, hoed, picked cotton, dug sweet potatoes, and dug peanuts, just did every little something to be did. The best part I liked about farming was plowing. I don't know why I liked to plow." Unlike so many of her day and circumstance, she holds no resentment toward her childhood of farmwork. "I just loved to farm! Driving on the road now when I see land plowed up, I just wish that I were able to work in the field now. I just love farming."

Polly attended a public school for black children at Boiling Springs, where no tuition was charged, though the pupils had to provide their own books. After six years, her formal education ceased. "I just stopped, just had to work in the field. I felt kind of bad over it, but it wasn't nothing much that I was doing in school, so I didn't feel too bad about it. It was kind of tough during that time. The people were working and weren't getting nothing much for what they did. So we just farmed and made most every little something that there was to make on the farm—cotton, corn, sweet potatoes, and peanuts. We made velvety beans to feed the hogs, the cows, and the chickens. But we didn't raise no rice or 'bacco." She never considered a career that called for education—"My Mama wasn't able to send me to college."—but looking backward, she would like to have been a nurse. "I just like to help peoples who I think are sick. If somebody I know down and need help, I just feel like it's my place to try to help 'em if I can, do what I can for 'em."

Polly was nine or ten when her mother taught her how to make a quilt. "When we were small at home, we would take clothes done got old, tear the best part off, and make quilts. I learned how making the Nine Patch. My mother never did make none of them fancy quilt, just common quilt. I just made Nine Patches. On some I'd just tear a strip and sew different colors together." As a child and on into adulthood, Mrs. Bennett made quilts not for show but for use; she remembers piling as many as eight quilts on one bed when the cabin got cold. "And then we'd get rags and stop them in the cracks. Where we lived was built like a house, but on the inside it wasn't no sealing at all. Just sealed up on the outside, just a plank on the outside. And the floor had cracks in them. Back in them time, the people turned the hogs loose. In the wintertime it would be cold and they would be up under the house. I was always in a kind of devilment, just to have fun. Those hogs would be up under the house. When she wouldn't see, I'd get the drops on my Mama. I'd get me some ashes, pour 'em through the crack on the hogs, and see 'em run fast. To have a little fun, do that and see a head of hog take out and holler."

A tall woman who wears her hair pulled back in tiny plaits, Mrs. Bennett is at home today in blue jeans and a knit top in mostly pale blue stripes. Her voice is like soft, slow music, and her eyes have a pixie-like hold on the one to whom she's talking. She never rushes or retards her conversation. It gracefully flows to the same, steady beat. And she pauses to smile after every point.

Walking in the wind out front and gazing at her four creations as they sing to the folks on the road, Mrs. Bennett in a deep sense is sharing four sides of her own special personality. At the far end of the clothesline is a quilt in myriad shades of beige, salmon, orange, and green. Most of it is in print fabrics rather than solids. Close up, the work shows a combination of two patterns based on circles and stars. From afar, the prints are so dominant that any pattern is lost. It is not the kind of quilt she would have made growing up to keep warm in a shelter sealed with one layer of plank, and not the type that would have gone to New York in 1966, either, to tell the world about the black quilters of Wilcox County. Mrs. Bennett herself does not know its name; she made it from the requirements and the material of a customer unfamiliar with traditional quilting on this spot of earth. A being of keen intelligence, she is someone who can adapt.

Next in line is the quilt top for a Double Wedding Ring. Pieced on a white background are rings of red, green, and blue, the strong, pure, primary colors. This quilt is a fanciful swirl of circles dancing in and out of other circles; seemingly they have no beginning or end; they keep on mixing with one another. That is how Mrs. Bennett sees her own life, an energy of connection and intermingling, especially with those who are down and out, with anyone who needs her help.

Another of her show-offs, set for sale to someone else, is a version of the Log Cabin, ranging through snippets of pink, salmon, and the warm oranges, on light and dark strips of blue. It is a geometric marvel, a magical play on angle and hue. From one vista it is a series of earth-toned swatches welded with the mightier, more dominant jerks of color. It is its creator's concept of earth and sky. As a child she must have picked cotton from fields singed with these same earth colors, then looked up at a sky blended of these same bands of blue. Behold it another way, and an emotion of architecture comes to view—a community of cabins, signifiers of the rich local culture that is now simply a homesick memory in Mrs. Bennett's mind. And when the pieces that look like logs make their radical, light-and-shadow, back-and-forth turns, they become as portions of crosses. Centered on the quilt is the one completed cross; like the faith of its maker, it is whole and easy to depict.

The other quilt on exhibit this day is a Lone Star, done in powerful primary colors on a backdrop of royal blue. Perhaps Polly is more like her Lone Star than any of the others. So often she has stood by herself, independent of thought and action. Back in the days when so many of her black brothers and sisters were marching and being jailed in Selma, Camden, and elsewhere, Mrs. Bennett was silent, inactive. She believed in civil rights and she respected the person of Dr. King, but she failed to appreciate marching and other activist tactics:

> It seems like some of the white didn't like the col-
> ored; some of the colored didn't like white. I never did
> join in that march. You know, the Bible tell you, 'You
> got to love everybody to get to Heaven,' and I don't
> hate nobody. I love everybody, and then I try to treat
> everybody right. And marching—now, they probably
> know what they were doing and seed into it, but I
> just didn't see no sense in it. I never did get in it because
> it just look like to me they was out there just gaining
> enemies. I don't know. You gon' have enemies but I
> ain't gon' try to make none. It's nobody I see that I

hate. I love everybody. It's in the Bible, 'Do unto others
as you would have them do unto you.' Well, I tried to
do that. I live my all by the Bible, and I try to treat
people like I want them to treat me. If you don't treat
me like I treat you, I ain't gon' treat you wrong. I still
ain't gon' treat you bad. And if you come to me for
a favor and ask me to help you, if I could help you I
will do it, but I just didn't believe in that civil right. I
mean, I didn't believe in that marching, and they saying, 'non-violence.' When the peoples out there marching, some of them beat 'em up and they didn't fight
back. If somebody walked up to me and hit me, I
don't know how I would a took that. I had some little
relatives in there but I just can't think of who they was
now. Everybody down in the Bend was in it. You
know, they was kin to me 'cause it's a lot of them people
down there in the Bend that are related to me. I never
did talk with none of 'em about it.

When movement life was much a part of Mrs. Bennett's family and friends,
she was working as a maid for one of the local white women. It was a position
that lasted for thirty-one years, a job she says she enjoyed:

She never did tell me, "Polly, do this," or "Polly, do
that." When I first started to working for her, she
showed me what she wanted me to do. From then on
I just went there and worked just like I would work
at home, just like I wanted. If there was something I
was supposed to do and I didn't do it today, well, I
could do it tomorrow and she wouldn't say nothing. I
just liked to work like that, but one thing I disliked
was cooking. I never liked to cook, even when I was
at home. But that was part of my job, cooking. They
said I was a good cook. Sometime the husband would
tell me they wanted a pie or something. I'd tell him,
"I don't know how to cook that." He called hisself
telling me how to cook it. Well, I'd go ahead on and
cook it. Some day he would risk telling me, "Polly,
you know how to cook to start with." But I done
turned my head and laughed.

During her summer twenty years ago with the Freedom quilters, Lois
Deslonde was a recipient of Mrs. Bennett's gracious, at-home entertaining
and her flair for work in a kitchen. "She makes you feel at home whenever
you go there. She wanted to do something for me before I left the area. She
knew I was from Louisiana, and she knew the kinds of foods Louisiana

people like to eat. She took the time to prepare this delicious meal that was sort of like Louisiana cooking. She and her husband were warm, loving people."

By her own admission, Mrs. Bennett was not a good quiltmaker before the days of the Freedom Quilting Bee. Except for an occasional Star, she was strictly a Nine Patch quilter. More often than not, the dimensions of her quilts were uneven; sometimes one side would be as much as one foot longer than the opposite side. "I didn't much care because I was making it for myself," she recalls. "But Reverend Walter come out and he started buying the quilts. After I started working for the quilting bee, I started doing better."

In the spring of 1966, Mrs. Bennett had been quilting with two friends who had acquired new scraps. They lived across Chilatchee Creek in Dallas County. "Dallas ain't far from here," she explains. "When you cross that bridge, you got in Wilcox. Before you cross the bridge you was in Dallas. We'd just meet up over there, sit down, talk, and piece quilts. So two young mens come by there, a white one and a colored one, and they seed the quilt that we was making on. I don't even know those two, but they said, 'There's a man that will buy them quilts. You won't get nothing much for 'em, couldn't get as much as they worth, but if you get something, it would be better than nothing.' And sure enough, Reverend Walter took down us name. Then it wasn't too long after then we got a letter and had us name on it." That was a list of the original members of the Freedom Quilting Bee and instructions on how the group would work. "He was real nice, and he seemed like he treated all the members the same. God sent him through, 'cause the quilting bee have helped a lot of people."

Mrs. Bennett played a historic role in the early growth of the co-op, quickly earning a singular reputation as an accomplished seamstress far from home. "Please send another quilt made by Polly Bennett," said frequent letters to the organization. Then, when Francis Walter visited Stanley Selengut for the first time, the New York man of business was captivated by two quilts, a Grandmother's Dream and a Snowball, both made by Mrs. Bennett. Of all the confections in Father Walter's arms, Selengut kept those two to show as samples of what the women could do. "They wrote a letter back, picked out two of my quilts and put 'em up for demonstrating," Mrs. Bennett remembers.

Some of them quilts wasn't right, but they picked
mine out and said they was the best. After they did
that, I said, "Well, my quilt's going somewhere I'll
never go," and then I went to doing better, 'cause if I
make something and do something for somebody,
I want to do the best I can. When my quilts sold I felt
good about myself. They still say my quilts is good.
I ain't had none to come back. I don't make too many

but thank God for what I get. And then another thing
that make me feel good is I've never had a customer
had no complaint. Everybody said it was right, and
when they come and ask me about making one, I say,
"Well, I can't make no little stitches." They say, "Your
stitches is all right." They not too tiny. I can't make
'em tiny, but they be's straight.

Unlike the Chestnut Bud, the Bear's Paw and other patterns deeply rooted
in black Wilcox quilting, the Snowball, no longer fashioned, was a happening
simply of chance. Lois Deslonde had been attracted to a rug featuring a
circular design, which would make a nice quilt, she believed. So she scanned
quilt books and found a similar pattern called Snowball. She recalls: "Polly
is creative and she's always willing to accept a challenge to try something
new. I took her the picture of that design and asked her to work it into a quilt
pattern, which she did. And it turned out very beautifully."

The Snowball is a series of circles, or balls, but half of each circle is one
color, the other half a different color. "She made one that was red and blue,
with borders of red and blue," Mrs. Ruth continues. "To make it interesting
she used solid reds and printed reds, and the same thing for the blue. You
wouldn't think of a snowball being half red and half blue. That was just the
name of the pattern."

"I don't think nobody made that Snowball but me," says Mrs. Bennett.
"Lois taught me how. She got down, drawed it off, and cut the paper. Then
I took it and went from there. I loved Lois. She was real kind. She treated
everybody alike."

Mrs. Bennett's front porch also played a key role in the story of the Bee's
success. In the autumn of 1966, officials with a maternity-clothes factory in
Linden agreed to give throw-away scraps of cloth to the quilting bee and sell
the group larger swatches not needed by the mill. The Bee paid a transportation firm to deliver the materials to Polly's easy-to-get-to front porch. From
there the goods were parceled out and the women went to work.

Still a lone star even after the co-op moved into its building, Mrs. Bennett
never worked at the Martin Luther King, Jr., Memorial Sewing Center. "I
think I went down there twice just to help them out and show 'em how to
make on a Star and another quilt. They got together and voted not to give
no more material out. Everybody had to come down there to work. I was
sorry I still couldn't work for the quilting bee but I couldn't go down there
and take no material."

It is not her nature to quilt closely and for long periods of time with other
artisans. "She likes the privacy of her home," says Lois. "Now and then she'll
call friends and neighbors to come over and help her quilt, but many times
she does an entire quilt by herself. She takes great pride in doing the entire

quilt alone. She's particular about the way she likes her quilting done and for that reason she'll do it completely alone."

"I could work in a group," Mrs. Bennett says, "but when I'm working I don't like to do much talking. If we working together, I would like for everybody to be fair, for you to continue to work, not work a little, then get up and go over yonder or stand around, do something, and come back while I'm still working. If I go wrong, I would appreciate it if you straighten me on my work. Then if they go wrong, some people don't want you to tell 'em if they've done something that ain't right. When we working together, I won't say mine's better than nobody else's, but I'm doing pretty good. Then somebody else, they don't do it right and I say, 'Do the thing this way.' Well, some people don't like for you to tell 'em that. So I would just prefer working by myself. I wasn't working *at* the quilting bee; I was working *for* the quilting bee. I did my work at home."

The quilting bee meant extra money for Mrs. Bennett and her husband Mark, who at that time was a tenant farmer. "The most that I did with it was to help put on a room back there, a room for me to quilt in, 'cause I was working in the living room. I would be ashamed for anybody to come in. It's a lot of things that I wouldn't a been able to get if I hadn't been making quilts. I bought this sofa, I bought me a dining room suite, I bought that wood heater, and I bought me some clothes."

Sadness touches her life now. Although it is impossible to guess by looking at her attractive frame and the glow on her face, her health has become a problem. "We're both retired. I would have been working now but I took sick. In 1983, I had the pneumonia, so I just ain't been able to work no more. When I went to the hospital for the pneumonia, I found out I was diabetic, and I already had pressure. It did me kind of bad. I tell 'em all that it's easy to make that first fifty, but after you pass fifty and go for making the other fifty, it's uncomfortable. Thank God I'm still able to move about, but you don't feel as well all the time. My Mama just got to be sixty-five and she passed. That sugar and pressure makes you weak. I'm taking pills for the sugar and I'm taking pressure pills and strength pills, but I'll never believe I'll make the other fifty."

With only one son, Rufus, a dock worker in Mobile, Mrs. Bennett is not surrounded by younger women to be taught her fine craft of art with a needle. That, too, gives her sorrow. "You know, I would teach 'em if they would come and ask me. But there's nobody coming to ask me." Also, she regrets, still, that she isn't able to farm. And she is swept with bittersweet memories just in glancing across the road to that unruly, misbegotten thicket. It is a stark reminder, along with nearby tracts of pine trees sponsored by MacMillan Bloedel, a giant paper company strongly established on Wilcox County land, of a thriving Alberta that used to be. As she tells it:

There ain't many houses anymore. Now, right across there, that belongs to colored. When I first moved up here in 1960, they used to farm right out across there. An old house is sitting out there and they don't farm it or do nothing with it. The one own it, I don't even know where they at, and I don't know whether they paying tax on it or not. I just wish sometime that we could buy it and sell it to somebody to build houses. There used to be a lot more people round in the country than there is now. I guess they had to leave, go to the city. Some in Mobile, some in Detroit, some in New York, and some in Boston. Some that done retired that had somewhere to go done come back home and built and staying in the country. Would be a lot more of 'em down here now if they had somewhere to stay. They ain't got nowhere to stay.

These passions seem uncharacteristic of someone who exhibits happy quilts for the travelers on Highway Five. "I don't be happy all the time," says Polly. "Sometime I kind of worry." But she doesn't dwell on problems. "I just go to thinking about something else. I just love to sew and I love to make quilts. My favorite color is brown. I love brown and beige. Now, I don't care too much about sewing on red. It kind of bothers my eyes. I like solid brown with other colors mixed with it, or a brown background with flowers in it, but solid brown and solid beige, I likes that! Most all of my sisters like to sew. I got a sister in California. She can make most anything that a lady can wear except stockings. She can make hats, suits, men's suits, pantyhose, brassieres, most anything. She likes to do that but she don't like to make quilts. And I got a sister in Selma who likes to sew, but all she makes is men's suits, suits for women, and dresses. She can't make hats. I can't make them hats, either. I can make clothes but I don't like to make 'em. Making quilts is all I like to do now. I *love* to make quilts."

Mrs. Bennett always has a project in hand. She needs to get busy soon to answer a letter from one of her customers in Birmingham. "I just don't like to write, and I don't like to read much." Usually, when she gets a letter that requires an answer, she recruits a young woman living there in the community. "I let her read 'em for me, then let her answer 'em for me. My Mama always raised us up to help people. 'Don't charge people for every little something you do for 'em. Do something for somebody for nothing, just to help somebody, because you don't know when you gon' need help.' That's still in me, to try and help somebody. "When I was growing up, seem like it was more love back in that time than it is now. Seem like to me most of the people these days is all for self. It just seem like if you is in a tight and I see where I can come help you, well, I won't do it. But I always want you to come and do for me. I love to help people. A lot of time I let my own work go undone to go over there to help somebody else, I reckon 'cause I was raised like that. Some people got something to do in the house, want me to come help 'em. Well, I quit doing what I'm doing to help somebody. And somebody wanting me to take 'em to Selma. Some peoples charge one thing to go to Selma. I just charge enough to help buy gas. I don't try to be so hard on people. I ain't much account, I reckon. Look like I do a lot more for people than I get credit for, but it don't bother me at all. The way some people act, I say, I ain't gon' help them do nothing.' I say, 'They don't ever need to come to me to help 'em do nothing,' and in the next two or three hours they come here to the door, and I done forgot I even said that. I just go and help. And I ain't got no certain person to help. I would do for the white just as quick as I would the black."

Polly Bennett wants to be remembered not for the beauty of her quilts or the grace with which she fingered a needle, but as a woman of her word, willing to help a soul in need: "I want people to remember that I would help them. And then, if I tell you I'm gon' do something, then I'm gon' do it. And if I can't do it I'll let you know that I can't do it. A lot of people would say they gon' do something. Then they go ahead on and don't do it and don't tell you nothing about it. But if I tell you I'm gon' do something, I'm gon' do it. If I see I can't do it, I'll let you know, because my Mama always told me, 'A person without their word is ain't no good.' I always like to be truthful. That's the way I live."

Mama
Willie
Abrams

"Call me 'Mama Willie.' That's what everybody calls me, 'Mama Willie.' " A quick-paced and perky shadow emerges from a back room at Estelle Witherspoon's home on Alberta's Route One. She is Mrs. Witherspoon's mother, who has just washed her hair. In tones of gray and white, it is a fresh fluff of tiny curls, half hidden under a man's black felt hat.

It is no ordinary hat, for it was given to Mama Willie years ago by a Catholic priest from Selma, Father John Crowley, who was Southern regional director for the Fathers of St. Edmund and president of Good Samaritan Hospital. Mary McCarthy, who held an art degree from the University of Georgia and was manager of the Freedom Quilting Bee in 1967–68, stitched a colorful design one inch in depth around the part of the hat just above the brim.

Mama Willie, or "Ma Willie," as she is called by some, has on glasses and wears an apron over her dress. Drawing even more attention, however, is her soul, which she wears in her eyes and her smile. It is like a bright sign saying "Welcome!" It registers glee upon making contact with those who come to her home.

Although well into her eighties, Mrs. Willie Morgan Abrams still quilts and willingly displays her current and recent projects. One is a festive Grandmother's Dream, executed both with polyester and Sears, Roebuck corduroy, highlighted with patches of red. Her selection of material is intriguing. There are squares not only in bold, solid colors, but in stripes, plaids, checks, paisleys, flowers, circles, dots, batik abstract, and one scheme of children at play.

As Mama Willie herself says of the rendering, it looks as though whoever made it was having a dream. The quilter takes a particular swatch all the way around, she adds, then has a dream in which she decides on another theme

One of the oldest of the quiltmakers is "Mama Willie" Abrams, whose daughter Estelle Witherspoon kept the Bee alive over the years. (Photo by Nancy Callahan)

to carry along the same route. The result is a completed rectangle of pieces that run the four lengths of the quilt. Told another way, "You start here in the middle. There's a little block in the middle. You go all the way around it till you get it big enough for the bed."

Mama Willie shows another quilt. Less complicated in design, it is a Nine Patch in large squares, mostly blue. As with the other, though, it has a dreamlike quality, for the solids, stripes, and arrow figures are interspersed with patches bearing all or parts of from two to four horses whimsically prancing through clouds.

Mrs. Abrams is a woman of few words, whose far-ranging reputation and quiet accomplishments tell her story more fully than she, herself. For instance, during the winter term of 1976, Oberlin College offered a special seminar on women and art. The weekly topics ranged from art forms used by the women of ancient China to various European styles. On February 6, 1976, the speaker was Dr. William Hood, who had enthusiastically followed the first few years of cooperative handcraft ferment in Alberta/Gee's Bend. His subject was the Freedom Quilting Bee of Alabama.

During his lecture, the former Birmingham resident showed a series of slides depicting the quilters and their products. "These women in the Deep South of Alabama love pattern," he declared. In explaining that point, Dr. Hood displayed a slide scene to his Ohio classroom that featured a small, humble home in Alberta. "This is Ma Willie's house, at least her former house," Dr. Hood indicated to his students. "She has another one now but it's about that size, and the inside is a patchwork quilt. Every single mural surface including the floor and ceiling is covered with photographs carefully selected and cut from magazines."

Dr. Hood believes such a setting provides a highly significant clue to Mama Willie's personality. "Notice here a crucifix with a guardian angel hovering nearby." He noted the ecumenical outlook of the black people of the area, for, though they are Baptist, for decades they have enjoyed relationships with Catholic establishments from Selma and Mobile.

"Here's Martin Luther King," the professor said as he pointed to a picture on the slide. "Here's Jesus, and a typical Sunday school poster. Here's Dr. King again. These are not randomly chosen. Ma Willie chose every one of these photographs because she liked it and just pasted it right up on the wall. So when you go into a room in Ma Willie's house, the walls and the ceiling and the floor are covered with photographs. And then the beds, of course, are covered with the quilts. It's really a lovely pattern and it really has come from deep, deep roots in their visual consciousness."

The roots of Mama Willie's visual consciousness have been nurtured in Alberta's history for possibly a century and a half. She was born there on November 9, 1897, and has lived in the community all her life. She was raised by her grandmother, Mrs. Jennie Walker, who was born and reared in neigh-

boring Dallas County but came to Alberta after she married. Jennie Walker
was a quiltmaker who began to train little Willie by the age of ten or twelve.

"I just really couldn't give my age," Mama Willie states as she sits calmly
on a couch and tries to remember. "I ain't no size now, but I was really small
when Grandmother raised me. I was the only child she had. She was a good
quilt-piecer and if she got her pieces, I got mine. Put 'em in my lap. Gon' do
just like her. She'd get her pieces and sew 'em and do 'em right, and I'd get
my pieces and mess up. But that I did, it done me good."

Mama Willie grew up on Grandmother's Dream, Monkey Wrench, the
Lock and Key, and a pattern simply called T:

That's about as fer as I could remember back. She
pieces some more but I forgot all of 'em near about.
Make 'em in the daytime and if you feel like it, make
one or two blocks of it at night. They throwed logs in
the fire, lighted knots in the fire. It did last a long
time. Probably had a little oil lamp. Didn't bother my
eyes. I used to hear my Grandmama talk about her
eyes be burning and worrying her sometime. But it
didn't do nothing to mine.

Mostly we'd piece it with the white thread. The
thread didn't show so bad. They used to carry some
cloth back yonder when I was a child called "calico."
Cloth then along in them times was pretty reasonable,
five cents a yard. Real cheap.

What she learned from her grandmother was refined a bit when the
Freedom Quilting Bee came to fruition and Mama Willie was advised to
shorten her stitches. "Up at the quilting bee they say, 'You got to have stitches
that are long enough for old Grandmama,' " she quotes the way they talk
about her. " 'Then, you get your toe hung in 'em on the bed.' So that's why
we had to come down and make 'em kind of short."

In comparing her brand of quiltmaking with the kind used at the Bee,
Mama Willie makes this comment: "When I been fooling around making
on quilts, I sticks on to the old part, sticks on to the safe part. If you can't
get nare machine to work on, you already know how to do it yourself with
your hand. Just take it on and do it. The biggest of my work sewing and
piecing quilts, I do it by myself by hand." Granted, she knows how to use a
sewing machine, but hardly ever touches one. "I do it with my hand."

Although Alberta is the only life Mama Willie knows, her name has
traveled the country. A discussion of the inside of her home in an Oberlin
College art class is one case in point. There are others. In July 1968 her name
was in *The New York Times* when an article about the Freedom Quilting Bee
mentioned that she was the co-op's maker of ruffled sunbonnets. In June 1969

Good Housekeeping's story on the quilters said she enjoyed sewing sunbonnets and pot holders on her front porch rather than in groups with the others. At age seventy-two, she was quoted in that feature as saying 1969 was the first year in her recollection that she did not have to work in the fields, a place where she had picked a hundred pounds of cotton daily for the sum of two dollars.

She and her husband, Eugene Abrams, who died in 1962, had been tenant farmers. But, through the Freedom Quilting Bee, she exchanged her life as a picker of cotton for one as a maker of bonnets, earning two dollars for each creation and crafting as many as three per day.

Lois Deslonde Ruth, of Rosharon, Texas, the first manager of the Bee, well remembers the vital role Mama Willie played during her work with the co-op in the summer of 1966. Fresh from New Orleans, the new staff member did not know the location of the quilters' homes; Mama Willie did. "Often, I would go on trips and would not know the way. They would say, 'Ma Willie would enjoy going with you.'" Thus, Mrs. Abrams would get in the jeep with Lois and show her where to go.

"Ma Willie would always dress up in her dressy dress and put an apron on top of it. *Always* an apron on top of the dress. I don't know why." Perhaps for the same reason, whatever it may be, the wispy figure always wears her man's black felt hat. According to her daughter, Estelle Witherspoon, she puts it on as soon as she gets up each morning and doesn't take it off until time to go to bed.

"Ma Willie was always a very delightful person," says Dr. John Crowley, once active with Selma's Catholic community and now a clinical psychologist in Santa Rosa, California. "I knew she liked hats and I'm kind of a hat freak, myself. So she and I hit it off and I just gave her a hat. She thoroughly enjoyed receiving it and it gave me terrific delight that she enjoyed it."

Through his work in Selma, Dr. Crowley made trips from time to time to Alberta/Gee's Bend. Visits to the Freedom Quilting Bee as well as the homes of Mama Willie and the Witherspoons were always on his schedule. As he recounts:

After that first visit, I was always going. I think it was because of the wonderful simplicity of the people, particularly Ma Willie, Mrs. Witherspoon, and her husband. They certainly welcomed me and there was no pretense. To me, it was a little oasis and I always looked forward to the chance to go out and relax and feel very much at home.

Some of the things they had reminded me very much of my childhood. People never think of Long Island as farm country, but I was raised on a farm. One day we had a pig-killing out at the Witherspoons

and they were really surprised. I think they thought I
was a city slicker but I was quite at home out there,
taking the hairs off the pig and dropping him in boiling
water.

When Dr. Crowley knew the family, Mama Willie was in her seventies
and lived by herself in a tiny house within yards of the Witherspoon home.
Crowley, who left Alabama in 1977, says:

It was like a grandma's annex. Only it wasn't an
annex. It was very close to the main house.
The things that always impressed me about the
homes of the poor in the black community were their
patron saints. One was a picture on the wall of the
Sacred Heart of Jesus. Quite often, the wallpaper
would be newspaper used as wallpaper. But it also was
usually a picture of John F. Kennedy and his brother
Bob.
Ma Willie seemed to be quite content in her home.
She wanted to be close to the family but certainly
felt independent enough to want to live alone. She
delighted in company and her simplicity was a great
virtue as it was with the whole family. They had a
grace of simplicity and were very intelligent people.
There are some people you can just feel comfortable
with. There's no guile. I felt comfortable with Ma
Willie and the whole Witherspoon family because they
had some of the fundamental virtues. They had good
senses of humor. They were very honest people, very
straightforward, very uncritical. I don't ever recall
them saying anything of any negative fashion about
anyone.
Ma Willie was not that active at that time. I only
saw her in the framework of her little house and the
Witherspoons' home. I don't think I ever saw her at
the co-op itself.

The fact is, Mama Willie never worked *at* the co-op, though she is its oldest
dues-paying member. When the Bee began, instead of mixing with the
groups of workers, she elected to sit on her front porch and make sunbonnets
or work at her home on other assignments that came her way, including the
Gentleman's Bow Tie, for which she was Alberta's expert-in-residence.
In 1967, when the co-op was commissioned to execute that pattern as
upholstery in the Amanda Burden project for Parish-Hadley of New York,
Mama Willie served as supervisor. The Eight-Point Star was another of her

specialties. She was also appreciated for making quilt blocks and giving them to the others to enable them to learn a particular pattern. She remembers that at least a couple of her quilts went to New York in those early times: a Grandmother's Dream and a Lock and Key. "Said they was glad to get them quilts."

Perhaps Mama Willie's most noteworthy contribution to the Freedom Quilting Bee, though, is her only daughter, Estelle, the co-op's backbone, whom she infused with an interest in quiltmaking from childhood. "I used to show her how to make a block on a quilt you could call Nine Patch. See, you put nine pieces in the block. After a while, she got to where she'd beat me. She could piece up mostly anything if she'd put her mind to it." As a youngster, Estelle assisted her mother's quiltmaking just like Mama Willie had helped her own grandmother.

"When I was a little girl," Mrs. Witherspoon explains, "I would hold a little tin lamp for my mother to see how to quilt. We didn't have electricity. Just a little lamp. We had bigger lamps but you could hold this little tin lamp over the quilt and let your mother see how to thread your needle, or you'd thread it. And Mama would hold the needle over the lamp. It was very exciting!" Estelle began to make Nine Patches at age twelve. "I teached her a lot at home before she left," says Mama Willie, "and she took it in. At the quilting bee she's the best one there." The octogenarian lets out a laugh, then repeats her statement: "She's the best one there now."

The mother of five sons, Mama Willie is obviously proud of having produced an executive daughter whose skills hold considerable respect in national cooperative circles. "She doing mighty well. She got a mighty good head in her. The Lord didn't give me but that one. All the rest of 'em was boys, and my back log plumb started!" She laughs once more.

Mama Willie no longer lives alone full time in the dwelling whose interior decor was once discussed at an elite Northern college. She spends her days at home and her nights next door with Estelle. Not in the best of health, she is highly content to spend time with her daughter, work on her sewing projects, and entertain her dog, Jim.

She admits she has no education. "Went to school a little. My grandmother, she didn't have much. No money much to send me. Back in them time they'd pay it, pay a child to go to school." Chances are, if the qualities she gave her daughter are any indication, a proper education would have enabled Mama Willie to go far. But in what direction? "I just don't know," she reflects for a moment. "I'm sewing. That's a good job. Piecing quilts. That's all I know to do. I would do that anyhow."

Estelle
Abrams
Witherspoon

On March 25, 1984, Estelle Witherspoon was honored by her church, Pine Grove Baptist, with an Appreciation Day. On a Sunday afternoon, it was held one day before the eighteenth anniversary of the meeting convened by Reverend Francis Walter at Antioch Baptist Church in Camden, where more than sixty Wilcox County quiltmakers adopted a charter and elected officers for the new Freedom Quilting Bee. Indeed, it was cause for celebration. But it was not the first such event in Estelle Witherspoon's busy career as co-op manager.

Two years earlier, on March 28, 1982, Pine Grove had held its first Appreciation Day for Mrs. Witherspoon. Invitations had been issued across the country. One of the recipients was Deirdre Bonifaz, of Artisans Cooperative. She was unable to attend, so she held her own day of tribute for Freedom's manager during an Artisan board of directors meeting later that year.

On this third time Mrs. Witherspoon is to be honored, heavy rains hours earlier have produced a slip-sliding dirt road to the church, challenging the best of drivers for the two-mile trek, which starts at a turn-off near the sewing center. But the sun is shining, the dogwoods are in bloom, and the new growth of springtime backdrops the isolated country church.

Minutes before the ceremony, set to begin at one o'clock, Estelle Witherspoon walks into the sanctuary, where a few of the early arrivals are seated. Like a politician, a minister, or one who is simply aware of the etiquette dictated by such an affair, she speaks graciously to everyone present.

Less than five feet tall, she holds her head high and her shoulders straight. She is clearly a woman of distinction. Her short, curly hair is perfectly coiffed. A plump woman, she is wearing a pink skirt and a pink blouse. Draped across her shoulders is a mink stole. She explains in a private moment later that it is much too hot to wear mink, but the stole was a gift from "a friend in New York" and it had arrived only the day before. "I just had to wear it!," she beams. The giver of the gift could have been one of a dozen or more persons, for, if anyone in the Black Belt has friends in New York, that person is Estelle Witherspoon.

But who is this good-natured, country woman, a product of one of the most obscure places in the South, whose leadership changed the course of history for a group of her peers and their families? Francis Walter contends Mrs. Witherspoon already held a position of leadership before she became manager of the Freedom Quilting Bee because of the kind of person she was. He says:

> She and her husband were respected. They both
> could read, and people knew that if the Witherspoons

Estelle Witherspoon displays the presentation quilt awarded to her on the day in 1984 when she was honored by her fellow co-op members. This lavendar-on-white Bear's Paw was the first Freedom patchwork she has ever owned. (Photo by Nancy Callahan)

read a document to them, they would tell the truth.
There is so much back-biting and deception in all
small, ingrown communities, but the Witherspoons
managed to overcome that.

I don't know exactly how she does it but Mrs.
Witherspoon could wade through cliques and disa-
greements that would tend to tear organizations apart.
She could work and mediate among the Gee's Bend
ladies, the upper-Alberta ladies and up-the-highway
Alberta in an incredible way. Yet she also could see
to it that competent people she was related to and
owed things to were rewarded. She just has exquisite
tact.

As an example of her tact, Father Walter cites a disagreement he once had
with her about the local mail carrier, a white man who began to resent the
mail coming into the area that resulted from the growing national knowledge
of the Freedom quilters:

Doris O'Donnell sent a ham from an expensive
New York chain as a thank-you after having been
down. Their postman threw it over in the field on the
side of the fence where he knew the hogs would get it.
The hogs got the ham and ate it. The Witherspoons
were complaining about that. Then we noticed some
mail to the Freedom Quilting Bee had been opened. I
was incensed. I knew you didn't tamper with mail.

So I drafted a letter to the postmaster general. But
Mrs. Witherspoon said, "Now, Reverend Walter, we
grew up with those people. We picked cotton together
and they're just as poor as they can be." And she said,
"You know, we've all got to live together down here. I
believe I can talk to him and just work it out without a
confrontation."

She was appealing to their common bonds and to
the fact that they were human. But then I learned that
when that white man wanted to go out of town, the
Witherspoons were the only dependable people he
could get to deliver the mail because they could read
and write well. They were the only people down there
white or black he could trust. So they would run the
route for him and he would pay them a small amount
of money.

They had a religious reason but they also had a
practical reason which they did not disclose to me.
They realized if they really wanted to make a success

of their quilting bee, they would have to enter alliances
with people who didn't share their values or who
might exploit them.

Father Walter also observed that Mrs. Witherspoon was incapable of being
offensive in a social setting:

If she was told she was going to have five minutes
to get ready to be on national television with Ronald
Reagan, it wouldn't bother her. She wouldn't be so
overcome with self-importance that she would goof
up what she was to say. She would be herself.
Both Ma Willie and Estelle have the gift from God
of hospitality. To be made welcome in someone's turf
is a gift, and it isn't the same thing as just giving
somebody something. They could make you feel
welcomed.

Bob and Joyce Menschel remember the hospitality they received the time
they visited the Bee and stayed in the Witherspoon home. As Bob says: "The
Witherspoons insisted we sleep in their room. We had dinner with them the
first night and they brought all the neighbors over to meet Joyce."

"It was a real party," Mrs. Menschel adds, "and the food was delicious:
potato salad, fried chicken, sweet potato pie, and fried fish. Bob had never
seen a catfish before and while we were there, one of the men brought in a
catfish in a gunny sack and just put it on the floor. The catfish went 'wuh.'
Bob looked at it for a long time. I don't think there was any refrigeration in
her home then, a freezer but no refrigerator."

Deirdre Bonifaz has watched the way Freedom's manager relates to all
sorts of audiences: "Mrs. Witherspoon is a terrific politician. I have been with
her to senators' offices in Washington and seen her walk right up and say
what she needed to say. Once we had educational television interviewing
Mrs. Witherspoon and some of the other quilters on one of their first trips
to Chadds Ford. Mrs. Witherspoon particularly would talk into the camera
as if she always had."

Mrs. Witherspoon has traveled widely. She was once a major speaker at an
Urban League dinner in New York City. She has attended Smithsonian
folklife festivals in the nation's capital as well as similar events from West
Virginia to Missouri. She has been in Atlanta uncountable times on business
affecting the Federation of Southern Cooperatives. The Philadelphia airport
is practically her second home as a step en route to Artisans board meetings
in Chadds Ford.

In 1982 she was in Fayetteville, New York, a community near Syracuse,
where she quilted for three days as part of an exhibition to open a crafts store

called Bear's Paw—a name inspired by the pattern made famous by one of the store's suppliers, the Freedom Quilting Bee. She was joined by longtime friends from Rochester, New York, Myron and Emma LeFebvre, Mennonites who had once spent time with the co-op. Mrs. LeFebvre quilted with Mrs. Witherspoon, who had brought along jars of homemade jam from Alberta and cooked biscuits for those who came through the store. "Are you a good biscuit maker?" "I don't know, but everybody thought I made a pretty good biscuit. They ate 'em like they was good."

During an earlier conversation in the living room of her small home on Alberta's Route One, her mother a few feet away, Estelle Witherspoon explains herself. She is responding to a question: "If the story of your life were written, what would you like other people to know about you?" She begins: "Everybody alreadys knows this just about. I would like for peoples to know that I love peoples and I always like to try to treat people like I want to be treated. I always wanted to be nice and friendly and loving to peoples. That's my method. And I ain't got no color or no what-not. I'm just plain Estelle. That's all I am. And when you be a plain person, you'll try to love everybody and treat everybody the same."

Mrs. Witherspoon was born Estelle Abrams on January 20, 1916, in Alberta, or Rehobeth, as it was also called, the second of six children. Known as "Stella" to many of her friends, she was once dubbed "T Stella" by the children of Alberta and often responds to that name.

Her childhood memories include her great-grandmother, Jennie Walker, whose home was next to what is now Pine Grove Baptist Church, and who raised and taught Mrs. Witherspoon's own mother the art of making a quilt:

> I was a little child but I remember her well. Back in
> my time it was really hard and people didn't have flour
> bread but maybe once a week when you got some
> chicken and biscuits and things like that. We called her
> "Ma." She used to go down to her daughter Liza Jane's
> house, wearing dresses with pockets in the sides. She'd
> come back with biscuits in one pocket and teacakes
> in the other for my brother Mirie and me. We would
> almost be knocking one another down to get to my
> great-grandmother 'cause we knowed she had some
> biscuits or teacakes for us. The children have a good
> time now for what they want to eat, but we were
> so glad to get that biscuit.

As a child, Estelle Abrams thirsted for education. She attended Pine Grove School; some of the classes were held in the church and others in the adjacent school building. "The parents would pay 'em, sometimes in sweet potatoes, peas, and meat out of the smokehouse. Lots of times we used to kill hogs. That's the way she got paid and she accepted it."

Estelle's main teacher was a Mobile woman, Irene Bryant, who boarded with Liza and Andrew Mingo. "You see, teachers were teaching for little or nothing then, and the people would take 'em in for little or nothing." Miss Bryant was supposed to teach only through the sixth grade, but offered three more years of learning to those who wanted it. "About fifteen or twenty of us—some of the preachers' sons and deacons' sons and all of 'em—wanted to go to school so bad. We just had to go in on 'em. So she taught us."

Estelle went through the ninth grade, receiving what she believes was equal "back then" to completion of the twelfth grade or even early college. "After I finished the ninth grade I went to school three more years in that same grade 'cause my Mother and Father wasn't able to send me to a high school and I just wanted to go to school." The closest high school was at Prairie, a community down the way. Another was in Miller's Ferry and still another was at Beloit:

But my peoples just wasn't able to send me to school
so I just went on to school at Pine Grove. But how I
got through the ninth grade, this teacher would bring
her books herself. The county wasn't giving you those
books and the parents wasn't able to send us to school.
So she brought those books from Mobile and taught
us. She was one of the best teachers I have ever known
and a real good songster.

She taught me how to sing and if I was going to
lead a song, I would be on the stand and she would be
in the door. If I made one error, she'd hold her finger
up and I'd have to go back and get that song straight.

I'm an old lady now. I'm sixty-six years old and
I'm not ashamed of it, and this little what I've got, I'm
proud of that.

"Did you ever wish you could have received more education?," Mrs. Witherspoon is queried.

"Of course, of course. I would like to have received four years of college. If my folks had been able, no doubt I would have."

"Is there a course of study you would like to have pursued?," she is questioned further.

"I reads pretty good and I likes math, and then English or something like that. Maybe I can make better English and speak better. I'd like it. Yeah, I'd like it."

"With four years of college, what career would you have chosen?"

Well, I tell you, I did like to be a school teacher back
when I was going to school, but nowdays if I had to
say, I wouldn't like to be a teacher. The children nowdays aren't like they were when I came along. Back
when I was going to school I taught school for my
teacher when she would be out when her mother was
sick. I could just go right through there and hear those
lessons for those children just as good, and they was
obeyable to me.

The parents of some of 'em got mad about it and
said they would not send their children out there.
Really, I'm telling the truth now. I was going to school
and the parents would say, "Oh, she don't know how
to teach them children." And that same lesson what
the teacher was teaching 'em, I could teach it, too.

"It sounds like you got mixed up in politics at a very early age," comments
a guest. "I think so," she laughs. "I think I did. If I had to go back to school,
I'd like to take up accounting because of a lot of the work I'm doing now. I
do a lot of figuring." She says she would also enjoy knowing how to perform
the varied skills of the Freedom Quilting Bee secretary, including typing.

One of the students Estelle met during her time in the ninth grade was
Eugene Witherspoon. Born on March 18, 1907, in Rehobeth, the young man
lacked two months of being nine years her senior. They were married on
February 26, 1936. He was almost twenty-nine; she was twenty. "He was
almost 10 years older than I was but he was a dear husband. I liked him."
During their forty years together, Mr. Witherspoon, a farmer, not only
sought to bring out the many talents of his wife but was also her strong
right arm as she supervised the first decade of the Freedom Quilting Bee.

Father Walter, who spent most of his Wilcox County nights in the Witherspoon home, recalls:

Eugene was very interesting to me because I was
learning with my male workers at the Selma Project
about radical feminism, something we never bothered
ourselves with. Eugene cooked. Estelle would be
working at the Freedom Quilting Bee, she'd come
home, and Eugene would have supper already cooked.

I talked to him about why he didn't resent that and
stand on his privileges as a man. He told me he had
fallen out of a tree and broken his hip when he was so
young that he had not been able to go out in the field
and work as a man. His mother often left him at home
and he would cook the meals. He said he had come to

understand what it meant to be a woman. Being crippled had somehow given him an appreciation of a
woman's role because he had been thrown into that
role. He said that when he got married, he supposed
some of that was carried into his marriage.

A slightly built, good-humored man who was always smiling, Mr. Witherspoon was a self-sufficient sort of person. He fashioned a turkey caller
from white oak. He made palmetto brooms. Despite his physical handicap,
he single-handedly built a mud chimney for his house. He was an outdoors-
man who loved hunting and fishing. Guests from the outside, hosted by this
only male member of the Freedom Quilting Bee, would be treated to such
gustatory delights as chicken hawk, beaver, turtle, raccoon thigh with yams,
or fried eel and catfish. Some people were served portions from catfish
weighing as much as thirty-five pounds. Others would take home squirrels
that this man of the woods had killed and dressed.

Mr. Witherspoon often entertained visitors with an account of the proper
way to catch a catfish in mating season. During springtime at Chilatchee
Creek, he would explain, indisposed catfish could be captured with one's
bare hands. They would lay their eggs in hollow logs, sit on them, and refuse
to move. A careful person could catch them, he noted, if a helper were on
hand to block the other end of the log, because a catfish would not live in a
dwelling having only one entrance.

Mr. Witherspoon said he would stick a hand in the log. If he did not get
bitten by the catfish, he would feel around gently until he could snatch it at
the gills. If the fish were to bite, he would pull it out by the mouth. He was
quoted to have said that fifty-pound catfish had been hauled out of rotten
logs in those very waters. Pointing to the strong social conscience of that
species, he would end his discussion by suggesting a return to the same log
every other day because catfish would not allow eggs to remain uncovered.

A civic-minded man, in 1969 he was part of a local delegation who traveled
to the northwest Alabama town of Fayette to talk telephone officials into
providing service to Alberta/Gee's Bend. In January 1972 the Alabama League
for the Advancement of Education called a meeting of selected leaders of the
Wilcox County black communities to consider problems affecting black
students in the Wilcox schools. Mr. Witherspoon was one of thirty-one in
attendance. He was always willing to talk to newspaper reporters who came
to cover the co-op and to other out-of-towners who were there on quilting
bee business. One he received was Tom Screven, who remembers, "When I
was there once we rode over to the river and got a good sense of the
community's horseshoe geography and the isolation of the people living there.
Mr. Witherspoon rode with us. He did a lot of talking about hunting and
game in the area. He also talked about the mussels in the river. When he

needed funds, he would sell mussels. If anybody ever taped him that would be a prize. He had a terribly heavy accent."

Mr. Witherspoon was a church man. As a deacon at Oak Grove Baptist, he would give the "deacon's prayer," a long, inspiring chant not unlike the Catholic versions from the earlier centuries of Christendom. His prayers were among the best in the area. "Mr. Witherspoon literally ran the Amen Corner," declares Martha Jane Patton, a Birmingham attorney who once was the Selma Project staff liaison to the Freedom Quilting Bee. "People referred to him as 'Colonel' Witherspoon. There's a real hierarchy there so when the preacher started preaching, you didn't say 'Amen' before Colonel Witherspoon did, and when there was singing he was the first to start the verse. During conferences at the Freedom Quilting Bee some of the quilters would ask the men to sing. He had a wonderful voice and would lead the singing."

On April 8, 1968, Mr. Witherspoon rode with Father Walter to Atlanta, where they represented the Freedom Quilting Bee at the funeral of Martin Luther King, Jr. While there, he presented Dr. King's widow with a king-sized, multicolored Double Star quilt, a gift from members of the co-op.

Elizabeth Walter came to know Eugene Witherspoon well while she aided Francis Walter in his work as adviser to the Bee. She comments:

Mr. Witherspoon was the only elderly black man I
ever had a close relationship with as a human being,
not in a child-servant relationship. He distrusted me
because I read things in books. Any time I or anybody
would make a certain kind of comment, Mr. Witherspoon would rare back with his pipe and say, "Did
you read that in a book?" If you said, "Yes," he'd say,
"Huuuuuh. That's what they say." But he might know
differently.

In the United States we have the glamorized view of
mountain men out in the Rockies. Mr. Witherspoon
was a river man from the Alabama bottoms. Almost
everything he knew reflected his ancestral education
from his grandfather's slavery. These children had the
tradition of slavery for their education because it was
their parents who were freed.

He had a touch with nature unlike any person I've
ever known. He could read tracks, smell the wind and
sense shifts in nature so subtle that it almost took the
guise of prophesy, it seemed to me.

He was mechanical. He could repair anything out of
nothing although he had very limited formal education. He was highly intelligent and had an uncanny
sense of appropriateness and brightness both in social
situations and in nature.

Once we were going down the road and he mentioned a family's name up in the woods where "there's
haints." I said, "Now, Mr. Witherspoon, do y'all have
haints down here in this part?" And he said, "Oh,
weeeeelllllll, you know." It didn't take much to get him
started on stories. I do believe there was a palpable
sense of the spirit world down there and I'm sure it
must still exist. It was very strong in the sixties.
    In the Bend, vestiges of African lore still persist that
he was able to transmit, and occasionally Mrs. Witherspoon would corroborate these stories. But when
you got right down to it, there was reserve. They
mostly were stories to entertain but underneath that
entertainment veneer was a lot of reality, I think, and
belief in the spirit world.

Did Eugene Witherspoon believe in "haints" himself? "I think he enjoyed
telling the story," says Dr. Walter. "What he was doing was mocking slightly
those who still retained the degree of belief in what I say is African lore."
    Dr. Walter contends that his lameness also figured in his character:

When you talk about Eugene Witherspoon, you're
talking about Greek tragedy. He covers the spectrum of
archetypal human experience because when Eugene
fell out of the tree, there were no doctors to set black
folks' bones. So it went unset except for the primitive
medicines, the asafetida bag and almost voodoo level
of medical practice. As he aged—and he was elderly
when I knew him—a terrible arthritic condition had
set in and caused him great pain. But he never complained about the pain.

Dr. Walter says that an anesthesiologist from the University of Minnesota
Medical School who worked in the civil rights movement heard of Mr.
Witherspoon and his hip injury. The doctor and his wife offered to raise
money to fly him to Minnesota so that he could have an artificial socket
placed in his bad hip and his leg straightened, all expenses paid. "Eugene
made the conscious choice not to have the hip repaired. He said, 'I have had
it all my life and I have learned to live with it.' "
    In 1972, because of a change in quilting bee personnel, fifty dollars a month
became available, and Eugene Witherspoon was put on the payroll as driver
of the van. His duties were to pick up and deliver goods, which he had been
doing anyway as far back as 1966, when he would make trips to Coy,
Gastonburg, and other outposts to collect quilts to be sold by the Bee.
    He died on July 13, 1976, at a hospital in Selma. He was sixty-nine. A

Among the men allied with the Bee, which is primarily a matriarchal enterprise, were Eugene Witherspoon, left, and his brother Nero, shown here in 1969. (Photo by Nancy Redpath; courtesy, Reverend Francis X. Walter)

lengthy obituary in the *Wilcox American* at Camden said among other things that he was a Mason; a member of the Wilcox County Democratic Executive Committee; a well-known storyteller; active in the local burial society, the Preachers and Deacons Union; and one of the founders of the Freedom Quilting Bee.

The quilters feel that, since his passing, the void he left at the sewing center never has been or ever will be filled. His widow states:

I tell you what he did. He did anything to help
eliminate a problem that I had to cope with. He was
always there. If I had to go away, he would take care of
everything I had to do around there. We didn't have a
UPS man coming down here at that time. He handled
all the quilt shipments. He would pack 'em the way
they were supposed to be packed, tape 'em and take
'em to Selma to UPS. He'd go to the post office. He'd

go anywhere to do anything to help with the quilting bee.

Some husbands would have fussed at me all the time saying, "You got to do this and you got to do that. You've got to go home. You're gon' have to cook." We didn't do that. If I wasn't able to get here and cook, I didn't have to be worried 'cause he was gon' see after it.

And if I was going from here to Philadelphia or wherever I had to go, he would say, "Baby, you go and tend to this business for the quilting bee 'cause we got to try and keep the door open. And if you have to stays there, I'll take care of your mother and I'll take care of Louise, so don't you worry about it." He was a dear husband. I give him praise in his grave today.

"It sounds as though he was a liberated man," declares someone who had never met him. "He really was," Mrs. Witherspoon agrees, as laughter streams from her face like sunshine. "Did you ever see his picture? That's him up there." She points to a living room wall where her late husband's memory is prominently in evidence. "Sho is where we started from. That's the beginning."

In one frame is a huge black-and-white photograph showing Eugene from the shoulders up. His beard is a fuzzy white bush spread across the bottom portion of the picture. His eyes shoot through the frame and into the Witherspoon home. Another frame holds two photos. One is of Mrs. Witherspoon in a quilting scene. The other depicts Eugene sitting on the porch of his former home, hat on head and pipe in mouth, while three women brush a display of quilts on a nearby clothesline. That picture appeared in *The New York Times*.

"This is the old house we were in," Mrs. Witherspoon explains the photographs. "That's Eugene sitting on the porch there, and that's where we had the quilts hanging out in the yard. They're some of the first quilts we made. I'm inside the house, cutting off some material." Mrs. Witherspoon laments again, "He was a dear husband." One of those present says, "He looks like someone who enjoyed having a good time." The laughter of "T Stella" fills the room.

Speaking of his ties to the Bee, Mrs. Witherspoon declares:

I'm telling you, he was really devoted to it. In his last days he devoted his life to it. He really was a devoted husband all the way through, but down to the quilting bee—sometimes I didn't get a dollar and a half. Sometimes I didn't get nothing, but Eugene said, "Let's keep on 'cause one day we will get something."

Most of those mens would tell 'em, "You ain't done
nothing; you going up there and you ain't getting
nothing and the quilting bee never will be nothing.
Why go up there?" Well, Eugene never told me that.
He said, "Let's go!"

Estelle illustrates her late husband's loyalty to the co-op and his belief in
its potential:

Somebody called me from—I'll say California.
They was going to Florida. They said, "Mrs. Witherspoon, I've heard of your quilting bee and I would like
to go in and see it but I can't get to your place until
about nine o'clock tonight," or whatever night. "Would
you let me go in?" I'd say, "Yes, of course. I'll take you
up there."
Eugene would say, "When time come for us to go
up there, if we're in the bed, we'll get up and go up
there. Let 'em look at it."
We used to farm, you know, and he was just that
way when he was farming. He would try to give his
best attention to whatever he had to do.

By the time Estelle Abrams was married, she possessed four quilts, including Pig in the Pen, Grandmother's Dream, and Monkey Wrench. She
proudly asserts:

I made 'em myself. Mama made me make 'em.
Mama and Aunt Liza Jane and all of us got together
and quilted. When I got ready to marry, the quilts that
was still good, they gave 'em to me. We put everything in 'em—old dresses, old shirt-tails, and old
everything. We didn't care what color they were. If you
got a new dress, you'd put pieces of that in the quilt.
So I wasn't picking no colors then. I was just loving
everything. Just wanted me a quilt.

Mrs. Witherspoon laughs again, reflecting on what she has said. Now, she
tells what constitutes a good quilt: "A good quilt is in the quality of it. You
have some nice material to make it out of. If you're going to put two or three
colors together, use *matching* material. You cut it right and sew it evenly.
When you quilt it, make the stitches just about the same length. Don't have
no whole lot of long stitches and short stitches. Better have it geographical,
with all the stitches just the same. If you have it like that, you have a good
quilt, but less than that"—She makes a funny face.

Mrs. Witherspoon can look at a woman's hand and tell whether she is a maker of quilts. She says that over time, the little finger takes on a darker color than the others, in the shape of a strip. "I can tell whether she been quilting or not. I've did it so much myself. Of course, I don't have time to do it much now."

Mrs. Witherspoon's current life is focused on managing, promoting, and seeking sales outlets for the cooperative. But her time is not spent entirely on those efforts. "I have heard you are a community leader," declares a questioner from out of town. "I do my best," she quickly responds. "I go into everything that I do to help upgrade things. I don't like to go into things they're going to tear down. Whenever I see it's going to be torn down, I've got a way I can go in and say, 'I think you're going in the wrong direction. Let's sit down and talk about this and see if we can't solve some of these problems and solve them in a nice way.' That's the way I feel like going into it. That's my method."

She devotes much energy to caring for her mother, Mama Willie. And then there is her church life. "She used to go from church to church to sing," says Luella Pettway, of Gee's Bend, one of the original co-op members. "You talk about singing! She used to do that. I learned her as a singer before I did a quiltmaker."

When she was young, before printed choral arrangements were part of her church, she was "chorister" of the choir: "That's leading the songs, you know. My uncle, my husband and my brothers-in-law would really back me up in singing. I could lead them songs just one right after another. Of course, I can't do it now but I try. I still sing in the choir."

A soprano, Mrs. Witherspoon is a member at Pine Grove, but is known for her singing and other forms of Christian leadership at many area churches:

I be to Oak Grove on a first Sunday and Pine Grove
on the second Sunday, if I'm not away and the Lord
blesses me not to be so sick that I couldn't get there. I
thank the Lord for that, too. I've spent my life singing
and praying and working in the church whatever to
be done.
    "I'm also Mother of the Church. A Mother of the
Church is the one who takes care of the wine when
you have sacrament. I take care of the tablecloths and
all the dishes for the wine, then make the wine and
bring it to the church.
    They call me a Mother. I was ordained a Mother. I
didn't want to be one but look like the Lord just put it
on me.

Because the couple were not members of the same church, the deacons had to ask Mr. Witherspoon's permission for his wife to be Pine Grove's Mother of the Church. "He was so happy. He said, 'Yes, Lord. She'll make a good one.' That's all they wanted, for him to say I would make a good Mother. I cried because I didn't want to be a Mother. It could be such a big responsibility, you know." Regardless, it is a role church members say she carries yet with dignity and grace.

Mother of the Church has not been Estelle Witherspoon's only acceptance of public responsibility. After working tirelessly to achieve voting rights for black people, she is also a poll worker. "Have you ever thought of running for public office?," she is asked. "I've been a constable," she answers brightly. "I was a constable for four years. I didn't drive my car so my husband would always take me around. When he passed I resigned." In addition, she is one of the secretaries of the Sisters and Brothers of Charity Society, which gives aid to the needy and provides burial insurance to area black people.

In the early 1970s, U.S. District Court Judge Frank Johnson ordered sweeping changes in Alabama's mental health system. When he appointed a human rights committee to oversee the changes he had mandated for Partlow State School and Hospital, a Tuscaloosa facility for the mentally retarded, Mrs. Witherspoon received a letter from him asking her to serve on the committee. "When I got the letter, I said, 'Well, this is a way I can help peoples, and that's my philosophy, to help peoples." So her appointment took effect on April 14, 1972. She served for seven years, until the committee was disbanded. "There's still a lot to do, but Partlow has come a long way since this committee was formed."

Minnie McMillian Williams, who grew up under Mrs. Witherspoon's careful guidance and once worked at the co-op, tells of the time she drove her to Tuscaloosa for one of the human rights meetings:

They gave us a tour of the hospital and then we had to go into the board room. I wasn't on the board but I was listening in. She said, "Well, I've been sitting here thinking about the people and I can't see why humans are treated that way." She mentioned certain incidents in which they told us they had to use restraint and other measures for whatever reasons.

She said, "You know, we are all God's children and I just don't understand why they have to be treated that way. Can't you find some easier solution than tying a person up, letting them wander around in a hallway and go to the bathroom on themselves?"

Everybody else was more or less ignoring the situation, pretending it didn't happen or they didn't see it. *She* brought it to their attention, and after she finished

speaking, the head of the board or whatever he was
said, "I was just wondering when somebody was going
to mention that."

When Minnie Williams was a child, her mother died. Mrs. Witherspoon's
uncle was Minnie's grandfather. Although Minnie and her sister, Annie, did
not grow up in the Witherspoon home, they were raised by Mrs. Witherspoon, an aunt, and another cousin. Mrs. Williams, a checker with General
Motors in Detroit who attended Wayne Community College there for three
years, says:

> She taught me never to take people at face value and
> not to believe rumors or first impressions. One of her
> favorite expressions was, "You can always judge a
> person if you observe, listen to, and are around that
> person more than a day. That way, you would always
> know what type of person he or she is."
> I do a lot of observing even now and that way I can
> pick my friends. She always said, "Be polite to every-
> body. Don't look down on anybody for any reason,
> but don't just be friends with anybody. Pick your
> friends." I've taught my kids the same thing.
> She conducts business the way you run a family.
> People open up to her. Everybody has their say. And
> when she approaches a person, it's as if "This is a nice
> person" or "I've known this person for a while." Even
> if a person mistreats her, she's still the same. She'll say,
> "Well, you never know why that person said or did
> what he did, so you can't say he is terrible or no good."
> That's one of the things she taught me, too: "Don't
> jump to conclusions about people."

Another Estelle-watcher was Lois Deslonde Ruth, Freedom's first professional helper, who says the Witherspoons were good managers and did not
place great importance on material things. "I will never forget one night
when we were sitting on the Witherspoons' front porch," she states as she
reflects on a summer incident of 1966 when the quilts were selling for thirteen
dollars. "Mrs. Witherspoon said, 'I wouldn't take a thousand dollars for the
life I'm living now.' I was so impressed with that statement because of how
little materially Mrs. Witherspoon had. If anyone had a problem, especially
of a financial nature, they would go to Mrs. Witherspoon."
According to Elizabeth Walter:

> Mrs. Witherspoon is an astute student of human
> nature. She is able to meet someone and immediately

size up that person as to his or her trustworthiness and
honesty. She can spot bumming at twenty feet but
can still smile and allow that person to feel wanted
and needed without making anyone feel uncomfortable. In another day she would have had a degree from
the Jung Institute in Zurich and would have been a
first-class psychiatrist. She has a very sophisticated
sense of people's souls. She is a reader of souls.

Dr. Walter saw Mrs. Witherspoon in action during times of friction and
controversy that surrounded some difficult decisions, especially when the
money factor and the collective emotions of the co-op members were brought
together to foment the "creative design" of the quilting bee. "She had to have
the consummate negotiating skills of any man in the State Department
negotiating at this point a settlement between Israel and Syria." From Dr.
Walter's perspective, Mrs. Witherspoon provided leadership that changed the
economy in her part of Wilcox County. "She's an economic heroine."

Part of the strength of her leadership, Dr. Walter feels, was her ability to
believe anything was possible:

She never once said, "It can't be done." She'd say,
"Well, it might be kind of hard. But we'll see what we
can do, the Lord being my helper." I'm talking about
a deep Christian commitment transcending anything
the white, middle class, bourgeois denominationalists
know anything about. It's a living spirit of self-sacrifice
but not maudlin altruism. She's genuine. And on a
small scale or in a microcosm, she is the embodiment
of everything Martin Luther King wanted for the
emerging blacks.

The subject of Mrs. Witherspoon's living room conversation changes to
her activities before the coming of the Freedom Quilting Bee:

You know, we haven't been here all our life. We used
to farm. When we got married, he was working in
the field and I worked, too. He was working on Mr.
Hardy's plantation in Alberta, so I joined in with him
on the farm. We worked until he got disabled and I
did, too, from farming. I had three operations. I really
had four but one was since Eugene died. And then
with his arthritis he couldn't walk and plow like he
used to, so he just stopped farming and we just rented
the house from Mr. Hardy.

Mrs. Witherspoon feels fortunate because she and her husband were never asked to leave the land they rented at a time when large numbers of black people in Wilcox County were evicted from their home sites because of their work in civil rights. Unlike most landlords in the area, S. J. Hardy, Sr., did not require his black tenants to leave during those times. In fact, when the Witherspoons were no longer able to farm his land, he allowed them to continue to rent the house in which they had been living. It became the structure from which the Freedom Quilting Bee took root. "He was really nice about letting us stay there until we got ready to move," she declares in grateful tones.

In the late 1960s, the Witherspoons reached the point where they wanted a place of their own. Mr. Witherspoon's sister became ill and was sent to Mount Vernon, a state hospital near Mobile. When she returned, because her husband was working, he was unable to care for her. So she stayed with the Witherspoons for two years under her sister-in-law's charge. "I wouldn't take no pay," Estelle explains. "Her husband said he wasn't gon' let us be no better to him than he was to us, so he gave us this two acres of land." After they acquired the land, the Witherspoons heard about a small house for sale. They bought it and moved it to their new land, which they had begun to farm. That was 1968.

Three years later, when most of the nation considered the civil rights era to be part of history, in Wilcox County the campaign was at its zenith. Estelle Witherspoon was a vital part of it. Voting rights had come to black people in 1965 and Martin Luther King had been killed in 1968, but in 1971 only a small number of blacks was attending the white schools of Wilcox County and no whites were attending the black schools. In September 1971, black students across the county went on strike.

According to the Selma Project *Newsletter* for August 1972, the reasons for the strike were inadequate books and equipment, low morale among the teachers, lack of real integration, the absence of blacks on the county board of education, poorly heated buildings, and no accountability to the community for the federal Title I education funds. The superintendent of education had refused to give anyone a copy of the Title I budget and program, clearly a violation of federal law.

As a result, black students stayed out of school in protest. Also, during that autumn, county blacks had been boycotting stores in downtown Camden. Those stores had been supported primarily by the blacks because the whites shopped in Birmingham and Montgomery. Yet the owners refused to hire blacks to work in their businesses.

By November 1971, a series of marches was held to make known the grievances of blacks against the board of education. "All the big marches, Selma-to-Montgomery and the Mississippi killings were gone, but this was the *real* civil rights movement," says Martha Jane Patton. "This was not the movement created for the media. This was where it started happening. Some leader such as Martin Luther King was not coming in with a big visit to motivate people. This time they were on their own saying, 'Look what's happening. Here are these rights we have. Let's get on with it right here.'"

During the third week of November, 429 men, women, and children, ages nine to eighty-five, were arrested for parading without a permit and spent time in jail. On November 18 alone, 347 people, including Mrs. Witherspoon, her daughter, Louise, and Ms. Patton, were arrested and jailed. The occurrences that week involved the placing of 116 children behind bars. It was one more opportunity for the leader of the Freedom Quilting Bee to show the fiber of her soul.

First, though, Ms. Patton recalls the incidents leading to the arrest of Mrs. Witherspoon and the others and notes how she and Louise Moody, another young staff member with the Selma Project, became involved: "In our work with the Freedom Quilting Bee we knew there were marches going on in Camden but I can't say we were right in the thick of things. We were just there hearing about it. One time Louise and I went down there with a bit of apprehension. We knew white people who ran the city didn't like what was going on. Mrs. Witherspoon said, 'Let's go to the church meeting.'"

A gathering at Antioch Baptist Church, in downtown Camden, had been convened so the blacks could talk about the economic boycott then in progress:

Several hundred people were there. Of course, Louise and I didn't know about the march. We knew there was a meeting at the church. We were invited, so we went and were given seats of honor. We listened to the speeches and the reasons for the marches. The people really were keyed up. They would come up to us and say, "Do you have your toothbrush? We're going to jail, you know." And we'd say, "We're just here at a church meeting." They'd say, "Well, we're gonna march." Louise and I would kind of look at each other. So far as we could see, we were the only white people there.

We were there with friends, people we knew, so we didn't feel afraid to be where we were, but the idea of all of us going out and marching downtown to Camden was a little frightening. But we said, "We're really going to embarrass our friends if we sit here instead of march with them. We're here because we're for them. So we should go out and march."

We positioned ourselves three-quarters of the way

down this long line of people. SCLC workers were
going up and down the line, organizing people, making sure nobody had knives or other weapons, and
that they were four abreast. They were telling them to
stay orderly despite what happened and to be non-
violent. They also showed them how to lie down and
curl over to protect their heads. It was the time of
real non-violence.

   The SCLC people were the ones responsible for
organizing those things and they were good at what
they did. So somebody found Louise and me way
in the back of the line. They put us on the very front
row, with four or five hundred people behind us.

   Of course, everybody believed afterwards we were
the outside agitators responsible for all this, and the
Selma Project was the group that had started it all. I
remember holding hands with Louise. There was a
black man on the other side of her and a black man on
my side. White women and black men holding hands.
When I think back, that must have really incensed
the people of Camden. Even beyond the issues involved, here was their greatest fear—blacks and whites
intermarrying. With these white women coming down
here, that's what was going to happen, no doubt.

   So we went on down the street and met the sheriff
face-to-face. Louise and I didn't say anything. The
black leaders talked with him briefly, and he said,
"Well, you're all going to jail."

   The march had violated the town of Camden's parade permit:

   I remember this big uprising from behind and
   everybody rushing toward the jail. They knew right
   where it was; they had been there before. We were just
   caught up in the big rush. The jail was probably designed to hold ten people. Here came three or four
   hundred.

   They put most people in school buses and took
   them to a county work camp because there wasn't·
   room in the Camden jail. People were divided and
   there seemed to be some real reasons for the way they
   did it. Louise and I were separated for a while. She got
   with the downtown group. Later on, they brought
   her back to the county work camp. She may have had
   to go on the schoolbus to help Mrs. Witherspoon take
   care of the children.

There were quite a few children. Most were twelve
or thirteen. Those old enough to understand what was
going on were there and they had their toothbrushes.

Eventually, Ms. Patton was placed in the same unit with Mrs. Witherspoon:

When they took us all to the work camp, they lined
everybody up, put the women on one side and the
men on the other. We could hear each other. There
was singing all night long. They sang civil rights songs
and old black gospel tunes. Some of the younger children sang school tunes and braided each other's hair.
It was pretty uncomfortable. Nobody could sleep
because of the concrete floor and no mattresses. So
most people just sat up all night, singing and talking.

During the night, Ms. Patton discovered that two whites had been jailed
in addition to Ms. Moody and herself. They were Rhoda Salz and Jerry Kelly,
former VISTA workers who lived in Wilcox County.

Mrs. Witherspoon "was like the mother hen," Ms. Patton declares. " 'Now,
you go over here and do this.' And she would lead the songs. Her sense of
humor went on forever. There was always a twinkle in her eye. You had the
sense she was thinking of something funny all the time, even in the darkest
of situations."

Adds Louise Moody, who promoted day care for the Selma Project, "Mrs.
Witherspoon, Minnie, and I stayed with the children. They packed us on
buses like sardines. I had heard stories about Southern police mobsters doing
that and then throwing tear gas onto the buses. I was terrified, but Mrs.
Witherspoon never seemed to be the least scared. If she was, I didn't see it."

Sitting at her desk in the manager's office at the Freedom Quilting Bee,
Mrs. Witherspoon relates her account of the time she went to jail: "They said
they were going to put everybody in jail who would come over there and
march. My husband, my mother, my daughter, and I decided we would go
on over there, get in the march, and go to jail. We were trying to protest on
behalf of the interests of ourselves and our children." At that time daughter
Louise was thirteen; Mama Willie was seventy-four.

Estelle continues:

They didn't have too much legal reason to put us in
jail. They didn't just handcuff us and put us in jail.
When they set that bus up there, we walked on the
bus and went to jail ourselves. They had said they
were going to put us in jail if we marched so we just
decided before we left home that we would go along.

We was marching for our own rights and if everybody
else was going to jail, we was going, too.

We decided Mama and Eugene would go back home
to take care of the business at home, and my daughter
and I went to jail. When we got over there, they carried
us to the penitentiary instead of the jail, the prisoners
camp where they put the prisoner folks. There were
four hundred of us from Alberta, Gastonburg, Catherine, Gee's Bend—it's Boykin now—and Safford, and
some from other counties. We was just from all
around.

The county law enforcement officials collected enough school buses to
transport all the marchers:

We stepped up on them buses and went to jail. We
was singing and praying and shouting and doing
everything on there. We sung about how we're going
to keep on marching. We ain't going to let nobody
turn us around.

I spent one night in jail. A lot of 'em stayed over
there three or four days at the prison camp. I stayed in
the jail because we had the children over there in jail
and they was upstairs. Somebody had come over to
the prisoners camp and told me they had turned the
hot heater on and were burning the children up. They
were so hot they couldn't rest. So finally, I talked to
the judge and the sheriff.

At that point, Mrs. Witherspoon was allowed to go to the jail to see about
the children:

When we first talked to the sheriff, we was trying
to get in the courthouse. When he didn't let us go in,
we stood there in front. We sung and prayed and talked,
and told 'em what all we was going to do. We was
going to get us a new jail, a courthouse, and a new
sheriff. We just told him all that stuff we was protesting
for and trying to do.

We asked him could we go in the courthouse jail
and he told us we couldn't go in that courthouse 'cause
we were like a gang of mob peoples. He didn't want
to let this crowd go in. So Mrs. Callie Young told
him, "Well, we're not in a hurry. We'll wait till the
circuit comes up 'cause we mean to go in. We gon' tell
y'all what to do." We was protesting, trying to get in
then to talk to the peoples.

I'll tell you what happened. When I came back to
the jail, I wouldn't sign no paper to say they could let
the children come out. The children didn't want to
come out. I was under the impression they was upstairs
there all heated up, that they had turned the hot heater
on. Well, somebody had brought that false alarm out
there to the prisoners camp. They never did that.

When all the children came downstairs my daughter
said to me, "Mama, why did you send for us to get
out of jail. We don't want to get out of jail. We want to
stay here." They all went home that afternoon. The
next day the children came back and marched but
nobody said anything.

The children were out of school every day. Most of
the teachers was still there with a few of the students
but most of the children who could walk a half a mile
was marching. We was just trying to help ourselves.

Francis Walter says that, when he learned two of his Selma Project staff
members and huge throngs of local blacks had been imprisoned, he called
the jail to see if he could help. Answering the only telephone was Estelle
Witherspoon. She laughs at his recollection and says:

Yeah. I was happy about doing what I was doing
'cause I was doing it for our peoples. I wasn't trying to
do it just for blacks. I was trying to help everybody.
So I just had to do it. I wasn't afraid 'cause I had the
Lord on my side. I know the Lord knows just what to
do and what not to do, so I was trusting him. I was
going on out there in his name.

Three of us spent that night in jail at the courthouse.
It was Louise Moody, my cousin, Minnie Williams,
and myself. They was really nice to us, too. They gave
us some nice mattresses to sleep on and cover to put
on our mattresses.

Those at Camp Camden were not issued the same courtesies. "They was
just laying on this hot cement. They stayed there three or four nights."
According to Mrs. Witherspoon, while the children were confined, they had
nothing on which to sleep. "They were up there singing and jumping and
enjoying themselves. 'Keep on walking, keep on talking, won't let nobody
turn us around.' "

Father Walter tells how some of the women began to yell and scream when
someone entered their cell while they were changing clothes. "So much went
on," Mrs. Witherspoon responds, "I can't remember all of it. Reverend Walter
helped all he could, yes, sir. When he called and I answered the telephone, he

237 Estelle Abrams Witherspoon

was very happy about that. You know, I was just trying to help them." Tales continue to be spun about the moment Mrs. Witherspoon finally was able to lie down on her mattress and go to sleep. Someone had to remind her she still had on her hat. She was so busy, says local lore, she had even forgotten she was wearing it.

"I got up the next morning and cooked breakfast for everybody in jail." She says she fried eighteen dozen eggs. "I fried more eggs than I've ever fried in my life and cooked more grits than I've ever cooked in my life. But I enjoyed doing it because I was just over there trying to help ourselves, that's all."

On the morning after their night in jail, the two SIP associates were released. According to Ms. Patton:

Louise and I decided to pay our ten-dollar fine and
forget it. Other people refused to do that but we didn't
feel we were part of the community and should not
get involved in an ongoing lawsuit. We might as well
plead guilty and pay our fine. We were guilty. We
knew they didn't have a parade permit and we marched
anyway.

Around noon the next day Francis came down and
sprang Louise and me. We went on back to Tuscaloosa,
dirty, tired, and ready to get home.

Everyone arrested was found guilty; most of them appealed. The issue was in litigation for months.

By the time of those November marches, Estelle Witherspoon was an old hand at that sort of thing. Her active efforts in the thrust for civil rights had gone back as far as 1965 and the Selma-to-Montgomery march:

I didn't march the entire way. My husband and I
drove part of the way and then walked a little. He
didn't walk none very much because he was crippled
but I walked some. We didn't stay all night up there.
We drove back, and the next morning I got in the
march near Montgomery. My husband was driving
along with me.

I know I was in need and we as poor peoples was in
need. If there was any way to help upgrade our living
standard any way I was just ready to try. That's all.
Wasn't trying to be no racist person or nothing like
that. I just thought I could do anything to help not
only black peoples but *peoples,* 'cause I just love people.
I don't just say I love colored. I love peoples. So I
thought maybe we could just do something to help
get things going for everybody.

In her own county, Mrs. Witherspoon marched for civil rights several times under the leadership of Dr. King. She recalls one day when he came through Camden in a motorcade. She was in a group marching behind Antioch Baptist Church. Following the march, participants entered the church to hear a speech by the black leader. "Some of 'em was saying, 'You better get on down to the church where your God at.' We knew he wasn't no God but we was saying, 'Yes. He's there.' Why? Because I know God is here and there and everywhere. We weren't thinking Martin Luther King was God, but he was one of the best leaders we've had on earth."

Estelle had met Dr. King earlier during one of his missions at Pleasant Grove Church, ten miles from her home: "When he went to Boykin, I went down there. I shook his hand and admired him for coming down because it was raining so that night when he did get down, and the roads didn't have no black top all the way down there then like they got now. We was slippin' and slidin' but we went on down there. And I spoke to him in Camden, too."

Was her time in civil rights worth it? "I'm not altogether satisfied but we've come a long ways with the Lord's help and I'm just thankful to the Lord. Just in this area the quilting bee has come from selling quilts for $10. Now we can sell 'em for $400 and $450. An average job is $300. We can make $300 like that." She snaps her fingers. "But we was really glad to get that $10."

Mrs. Witherspoon considers her travels as Freedom's manager among the highlights of her life:

> I've gone places I thought I would never have gone.
> I've even become a board member of the Artisans
> Cooperative up there and chairman of the board. The
> biggest contract we have is with Artisans. They've got
> board members from different parts of the country,
> from Boston, Maine, and Los Angeles. Some are from
> Atlanta, one is from South Carolina, but I'm the only
> one from Alabama. Nobody from this far down is
> on it but me.
>
> Being chairman is one of the best honors of my life.
> I was surprised they would keep bugging me to be
> chairman of this board way up there. I looked for
> being a chairman of boards in Alabama but never
> thought I would become a chairman of the board up
> there. I'm the only black one on that board. So I
> thought they would pick somebody else. But they all
> seems to be happy about it.
>
> I fly to Philadelphia four times a year. They'll have a
> limousine there waiting on me. Then they takes me
> on a limousine out to Chadds Ford. A lot of us be
> coming in on the same flight so they pick us up maybe

five or six at one time. I mostly fly on Delta. Some
come in on Continental and some mostly be on
United. We know who's coming and where they're
coming from so we just wait on the others till they get
there to keep from making so many trips.

I never would have had a chance to travel so much if
it hadn't been for the quilting bee, and then when I go
to these places some company will always bear my
expenses. I would never have been able myself just to
take these flights like I do 'cause it costs so much.

One of Mrs. Witherspoon's first major journeys away from Wilcox County
occurred in 1969, when she and her daughter Louise were flown to New
York by Stanley Selengut to show the wares of the back-home artisans to
potential buyers at Saks Fifth Avenue, Macy's, and other marketers. She
exclaims:

I enjoyed it so very much. It was just a pleasure to
do those things and see the excitement. It was in July
when we went the first time. The next time was the
next year in December. The Christmas trees was all lit
up. Seeing all those beautiful sights, I didn't know
how to take it. And my daughter was very excited.
You couldn't hardly get a taxi or nothing to take you
nowhere. We would be out there flagging, trying to
get a ride, and they would be just flying by. I said, "It's
just too close to Christmas for me." A busy place.

When the Freedom Quilting Bee was chartered, Estelle Witherspoon was
pushing fifty. "You know," she says as she looks back, "that was kind of old
to try to help start a business. See, I was willing and the Lord just gave me
the courage to go on, and I had a husband who would push me. He was
willing to help me with anything he thought would uplift fallen humanity.
So that's just the way I felt about it."

It's twenty minutes past one now and a churchful of people, mostly from
local communities, but a few from Birmingham, Atlanta, and elsewhere,
have filled the pews in the sanctuary at Pine Grove to honor "Mother" Estelle
Witherspoon. It is a grand and well-planned service that begins with the
traditional deacon's prayer. Led by one of the men of the church, the prayer,
possibly fifteen minutes in length, is a soul-stirring plea to God for his favor
on those present and for his blessings on the state of the world. Kneeling
before the altar, the deacon delivers his prayer in the style of a chant. It is
highly charged with patterns of jazz, the kind heard in New Orleans and

Memphis. Above the choir loft a crucifix hangs from the pastel wall and looks downward on the bowed human figure, in a light blue suit.

After the prayer begins, a woman sings "Amazing Grace," sitting at her pew. Others follow her lead. The chanter continues to pray. "Amazing Grace" fades away. Moments later, it is replaced by "Come and Go to That Land." It, too, runs its course. Feeling led, those in the pews come forth with other hymns and are joined by the seated assembly. It is a shame Eugene Witherspoon cannot be here to render his version of the deacon's prayer.

Minutes pass in this deeply ritualistic form of worship that typifies the black Baptist way in Wilcox County. The deacon concludes his prayer. Father Walter, a "special guest," reads from the Scriptures. His text is the thirteenth chapter of St. Paul's first letter to the Corinthians: "Though I speak with the tongues of men and of angels, and have not charity, I am become *as* sounding brass, or a tinkling cymbal. . . ." The words form a portrait of Estelle Witherspoon, one whose own charity has been the prime reason for her human success.

At this point, Mrs. Witherspoon and a group of church and co-op leaders, those who are part of the agenda and guests from afar, leave the sanctuary. As more music is sung by the congregation, they reenter in a procession and take their places. A series of speeches follows, paying tribute to the guest of honor. They are interspersed with music by the church choir, soloists, and a family of singers.

One person remembers how the honoree taught him about loving people whom it would have been much easier to hate. Another calls her "a star on earth." Her own daughter Louise, attractive, articulate, and fashionably dressed in gray, says she is thankful Estelle Witherspoon is her mother. Someone else notes that, in 1983, the Freedom Quilting Bee books showed $200,000 in sales, three-fourths of which came back home in wages. That fact alone is reason enough for appreciation. As Elizabeth Walter had commented on an earlier day, Estelle Witherspoon is "an economic heroine."

But that is just one of the reasons why Pine Grove Baptist is full this afternoon. People are here because of how her light has shined into the hearts of so many individuals and inspired them in a multitude of personal ways. In line with the Scriptures, she has given them faith, hope, and charity.

It is after four o'clock now and those with whom Estelle works come forward to present their manager a gift. It is a show-stopping Bear's Paw quilt, made by the Freedom Quilting Bee. The paws are of a lavender print. The background is off-white. They spread it out and hold it up to the delight of the lookers-on. The names are read of those who pieced the quilt, of others who did the quilting. Pictures are made of Mrs. Witherspoon and her quilt along with the ladies who had a hand in its production.

Obviously touched, "T Stella" finally has the floor. "I've always wanted a quilt made by the Freedom Quilting Bee," she says in response to the big surprise, "but I never could afford to buy one." Someone announces that the market value of this quilt is $450.

Mrs. Witherspoon thanks everyone for coming and gives lots of credit to others for the success enjoyed by the Bee across the years. "Y'all keep on praying for me and I'll do the same for you," she concludes as she looks across the crowd. A benediction is pronounced, and the celebrants move into other rooms for refreshments of fried chicken, potato salad, English peas, sweet potato pie, cornbread, rolls, cake, and punch.

"My only regret is that Eugene couldn't be here with me." There is sadness in her voice but still a smile on her face as she makes the comment to a table of people who are about to eat. Minutes later, she pulls together her family: Mama Willie, dressed from head to toe in yellow finery, who could easily have led an early Easter parade; daughter Louise, twenty-six now, a graduate of a Mobile business college, a wife, and mother of twin baby girls; Louise's husband, Eugene Jerome Williams, stationed at Fort Rucker, in southeast Alabama; and their daughters, Tamika Reneé and Jamika Nicole, only four months old.

They get in a car with the $450 quilt, and "just plain Estelle" goes home.

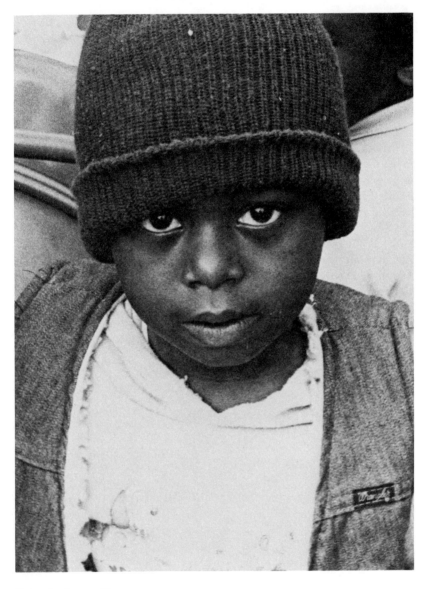

Co-op leaders say Free-
dom's future depends on
the willingness of the
young, such as this child
at the day-care center,
to keep it alive. (Photo by
Nancy Callahan)

Epilogue

In the village of Alberta, Alabama, a small, white house sits a few yards across the road from Hicks's Gin. On sunny days, a half dozen or more quilts are out for a breath of air. They hang on a clothesline to the side of the house, on a bush hedge at the front, and wherever else they can find a spot to soak up the sun.

The house lot is small, so each slice of space must count, and it does: a corn patch, pecan trees, canna lilies, and quilts. It is a place of enchantment, for the patchworks are not the typical, off-the-rack variety. They are strong, assertive designs—car stoppers—that run the geometrical gamut. One is a sky of stars in black, aqua, and white. Another is a canvas of yellow, aqua, and wine. A third is a fanciful jumble whose zigzag rainbow has one lone swatch of black.

Because the Freedom Quilting Bee and its perfectly put-together renditions are only a few miles down the road, the scene almost seems out of character— like a giant step backward in time. It is as though the years have been frozen since Francis Walter noticed a similar clothesline filled with sensations equally as strange and hauntingly beautiful in another part of the county during the Christmas season of 1965.

But history has not stood still, for either the Bee or the participants in its story. Father Walter has not been an active part of the organization since the end of 1972, when he resigned as executive director of the Selma Inter-religious Project. Under his leadership, it had made great strides. It gave hope to those evicted from their homes during voting drives and distributed food and clothing to those in need. It had a hand in a rural health project, a self-help housing venture, a new Brickcrete industry, a large and at times controversial co-op called the Southwest Alabama Farmers' Cooperative Association, and day care for the children of welfare recipients.

Father Walter's network provided technical and legal assistance to many individual blacks and black groups; boosted job opportunities among blacks and whites through a pulpwood association; and put scores of blacks in positions to learn leadership, handle money and power, and relate to social forces from outside their counties. Today, numbers of Alabamians and other Southerners, black and white, are engaged in creative, beneficial causes that directly or indirectly were brought on by their liaisons with the Selma Inter-religious Project.

But, by the conclusion of 1972, the civil rights movement and its funding had passed their peak. New social issues arose that could not be focused so easily as those stemming from the aftermath of the Selma-to-Montgomery march. The Selma Project had become large, diverse and without clear image or direction. A couple of years later, it was no longer in operation.

Father Walter exchanged his role in civil rights for one in mental health. In Tuscaloosa, in 1973 he became the first project manager for the first group home in the state's new plan to deinstitutionalize its mental health facilities. In 1974 he became executive director of the Saint Andrew's Foundation, a nonprofit corporation and adjunct to Saint Andrew's Church, in Birming-ham. Its mission is to provide housing and training for mentally retarded persons, under contract to the Alabama Mental Health Department. Father Walter was also named as priest associate at that church, known citywide for its projects that epitomize the social gospel. On May 16, 1985, he was instituted as rector of Saint Andrew's. Since 1977 he has been married to his second wife, Dr. Faye Walter, a Birmingham clinical psychologist.

After the passage of so many years since he sculpted a quilting co-op, what are Father Walter's thoughts now about the Freedom Quilting Bee? He believes the reason a co-op was begun had to do with people deciding they wanted to make money and control their own lives. As he sees it, the approach was a threat to the economic and social structure that had controlled them for generations and had not given them any say in that control: "In a tiny, politically-insignificant way, the Freedom Quilting Bee was this little spark of a protest or a movement or another way for society to be organized in our country. I just wish the co-op movement and what we call 'community organizing' were a more potent force for social change in the United States. I still see the co-op concept as a flea that's not giving this big elephant country of ours very much trouble."

That may be the case, but, especially during its first few years, this one cluster of uneducated, impoverished black women, determined as they were, became a structure that produced a powerful, almost born-again effect on its individual members. Moreover, the Bee spawned and nurtured a nationwide renaissance of interest in quilting as an implement of interior design. It lives on as a home of hope for cooperatives of lesser significance across the nation. It is a shooting star from civil rights that continues to brightly beam.

Father Walter watched firsthand the transformation of the women. "I don't think it was so much a change in personality as a broadening of horizon," he points out:

> We would tell them all the nice things Henry Geld-
> zahler had said about them and that he was with the
> Metropolitan Museum of Art in New York. That
> didn't mean a thing to them. When Lee Krasner came
> for a visit, we told them she was a famous painter.
> That didn't mean anything either. We would bring
> down those *New York Times* articles that had been
> written about the ladies, but they had never before
> seen a copy of the *New York Times*. They would have
> been so much more impressed if a story had been
> done about them in the little *Wilcox Progressive Era* at
> Camden.
>
> I think at first the women appreciated the craft and
> beauty of quilting but only among themselves. They
> thought the only people interested were their sisters.
> But when the Alabama papers and television—the
> black person's real eye into America—began to pick
> up on what they were doing, they came to realize the
> significance of it all. When Mrs. Witherspoon began
> to go to New York and make speeches, that meant
> something to her. And when some of the ladies went
> to the Smithsonian folklife festivals, that meant some-
> thing to them. So they slowly began to find out the
> whole world appreciated what they were doing.
>
> Through the trend setting of Parish-Hadley, promo-
> tions by Henry Geldzahler and Lee Krasner and mar-
> keting by Stanley Selengut, the Freedom Quilting Bee
> made an impact on the whole country.

Father Walter believes a combination of factors caused that vast geographical impact. The black struggle in the South was popular in the North,
including the Manhattan seedbed for the commercial ideas that set the pace
for interior decor. The members of the co-op were women, viewed traditionally as harmless. Bold, op art patterns were fashionable and therefore
compatible with Freedom's quilts, whose flat, geometric quality was different
from that of those featuring a three-dimensional essence. And, finally, there
was a general approval of the church's role in the civil rights movement, an
acceptance of religious groups who sent representatives to the Selma-to-
Montgomery march.

Such were the forces, Father Walter feels, that merged and fostered the
success of the Freedom Quilting Bee. That the food-fashion editor of the
New York Times sent a reporter to Alberta/Gee's Bend was evidence to him

it was a countrywide phenomenon; the enormous size of the photographs of Freedom's quilts in leading women's magazines was all the more proof of the Bee's effect on style. "Those phenomena were perceived consciously or unconsciously by Sister Parish, Stanley Selengut, Estelle Witherspoon, myself and other people, and it just happened to work."

Father Walter also asserts the Freedom Quilting Bee has earned a place in the history of the civil rights movement. For one thing, the co-op still exists, though many similar programs established in the late 1960s and early 1970s have floundered. What's more, the Bee is a moral example of blacks exploiting white help rather than turning away from that help. And, third, it is an expression of the deep gospel values Martin Luther King tapped in black people. "The Freedom Quilting Bee women are so deeply Christian in the best way black people have of manifesting the gospel that they are very forgiving and accepting of people's differences."

Many trade-offs occurred. After the quilters' initial thrust on the American folk craft scene and all the accompanying publicity, no longer did they fill the UPS trucks with original, one-of-a-kind works of art. No longer did they offer an unlimited variety of patterns bearing whimsical names, such as Map Apple, Monkey Wrench, and XYZ. No longer did they sell quilts stored away in the closet or snatched off the bed. No longer did the material come from faded blue jeans or feed sacks. No longer did the inside batting come from lumpy, uneven bolls of cotton picked from the fields by daytime farmhands whose art was confined to the darkness of night.

To stay alive as a business, the quilters had to keep their stitches even. Quilt dimensions needed to be exact. Colors had to match. Fabrics had to be washable with nonrunning dye. Batting required not the product of a cotton field but the invention of a chemistry lab: Dacron. Confined to five or so homegrown patterns embellished by marketers from the East who were in touch with a society of consumers, the quilts became look-alikes— an unending parade of Bear's Paws in French blue and white, of Coats of Many Colors in tones of blue, green, and white.

By the same token, though, the business approach put food in the artisans' bodies, clothes on their backs, and money in their pocketbooks. It brought in telephones, furniture, and indoor bathrooms. It paid for doctor bills and light bills. It educated their children. And it gave them a sense of their human worth.

Father Walter maintains that an additional factor etched for these women a place in civil rights history: they were not afraid of psychological annihilation by an encounter with white people who might use them. As he observed the 1960s, it was a time when so many black people, particularly in the poverty pouches of the North, had lost at least a part of their self-respect. The blacks with whom he had worked in the Jersey City slums were shattered people who were ashamed of their past and whose roots were void of a culture. But the women of the Freedom Quilting Bee, as he came to know them, were members of the black race who were well-rounded, strong, and whole. They were among the last remnants of a local culture, and the possibility of that culture's greater demise made them sad:

> I remember one of the ladies saying, "Oh, Reverend
> Walter, the dances we used to have. Every Saturday
> we would have bands that went all around the county."
> That was when the black population was much larger
> there and it thrived on a whole, rich, black culture.
> She said, "There isn't a black band left in Wilcox
> County." So many churches had closed. The fields
> looked so pretty to me but were not pretty to the peo-
> ple who lived there because they remembered when
> as many as thirty shacks composed what is now one
> field. There were whole communities that didn't exist
> any more. It was just a remnant of a place that had
> literally been decimated. The Great Exodus down
> there was before the First World War but the people
> left still have their very wholesome cultural values.

This man who began the Bee thinks perhaps the history of the civil rights movement will someday record the manner whereby these women of the Freedom Quilting Bee clung so steadfastly to a faint and fading sketch of a culture that caused them to be what they became.

That the Freedom Quilting Bee has concluded its second decade—indeed, that it lives on—is a testament to Estelle Witherspoon, to her assistant, Nettie Young; to the members, past and present; and to all those caring, believing souls from the outside, some of whom made great personal sacrifices, some of whom stayed for only a week or ten days, some for a season, and a few who came or have kept in contact for years. Like a living tableau, they all did their share in making an improbable dream come true.

Does the Freedom Quilting Bee have a future? Estelle Witherspoon spends much of her time pondering that question. A part of her answer is reflected in her feelings for the past, expressed in concert with Francis Walter, and for how the past compares with life now on the rural route where she lives. She remembers the Alberta, or "Rehobeth," of years gone by: a mass of houses and many, many families. Today, the scene is only a pleasant memory.

"The houses are all gone," she sadly proclaims. "See, we as black people stopped farming 'cause we wasn't able to buy all this high equipment." Houses used to line the road from the sewing center to the beginning of Boykin, she recalls. Now it is mostly wilderness and mammoth stretches of farmland:

Houses was all out there. Houses was all along the
highway, the road down there. We were always gotten
together with the neighbors. That's how the quilting
bee started, in different homes. I'd piece my own quilt
and you'd piece your own quilt and five or six ladies
would get together and quilt at night.

It just seems so hard 'cause the families what used to
live in these houses, most of 'em has gone to town,
those that are not dead. And the younger children
don't do like us. When they get finished school they
wants to go.

Yet, this quilting bee leader lives in hope there will be a future for the co-
op she has been so instrumental in sustaining:

I tell 'em all in my saying, wherever I go, "I hope
when I'm passed on that somebody will still be able to
take this quilting bee on through. And if I'm not
passed on, when I get disabled I'd like for 'em to carry
on." It's going to take some young people to do it.

Some older peoples need to be involved but it takes
a lot of energy to do a thing. If you ain't got energy
and a will to do it, you just ain't gon' do it no way.

Except for frequent talks on the telephone and once-a-year visits home,
Minnie Williams is far removed from the handcraft co-op that unleashed her
talents and set them spinning. But she, too, ruminates about what's in store
for Alberta's largest industry. "As far as its future is concerned, I think it will
be around for a long, long time because they take pride in what they are
doing. Consumers buy their quality." Now in her early forties, she recalls her
visit to the Bee in the summer of 1982: "They were still turning out really
good work. They have more equipment now than when I was working there
so I think they are slowly but steadily going forward."

Even so, despite an active worker list of thirty-five, on some days Nettie
Young and four or five women who work under her direction have the place
all to themselves. Those days make Estelle Witherspoon take serious stock
of what may lie ahead. Still, though, the last vestige of the black Wilcox
culture continues to prevail. It may be *the* lifeline whereby the co-op forges
on. Minnie Williams can feel it yet, even at home in Michigan. "They keep
trying to get me back down there," she explains. "If the pay were better I
wouldn't mind, 'cause I loved working for the quilting bee. When I was there
all the people were wonderful. They were two communities working beautifully together. It's a family atmosphere where you look out for each other.
I was just raised up that way."

A key ingredient in Freedom's outcome is its longtime manager. Realistically, the co-op's future rides on her shoulders. When she is no longer part of its operation, what then? As past member Jensie Irby tells it, "I don't know where you gon' find a *little* Mrs. Witherspoon."

Probably nowhere. But a couple of young women are now part of the business end, younger generations are working as quilters, and the co-op can seek advice and support from the Southern Federation of Cooperatives and from Artisans Cooperative.

Aside from Estelle Witherspoon's role in the years to come, economic questions are involved. How long will the Sears contract continue? How long will the American economy enable consumers to spend upwards of $400 for enough patchwork quilts to ensure survival of the Freedom Quilting Bee? And how long will an arts-and-crafts intrigue for this age-old phenomenon be sustained?

Mrs. Witherspoon daily copes with the questions. Mostly, she does not know the answers. "We're gonna make it, though. I just feel like we're gonna make it." Words of the ever-confident, never-say-die mother hen of it all. "I got that faith in the Lord and I got the strength and the courage to try to keep on, to make it. You can't sit down now 'cause the Lord ain't gon' step down here and hand you this one in your hand. You gon' have to get up and go get it. *Get up and go get it:* That's the way I feel about it."

In 1977 Father John Crowley, a favorite of the people of Alberta/Gee's Bend, retired from the Edmundites, married, left Selma, and became a clinical psychologist on the West Coast. As a wedding present, the Freedom Quilting Bee gave Dr. and Mrs. Crowley a blue patchwork that covers his office couch. He states: "Quite often people remark about the quilt. It gives me a chance to say, 'Oh, that's something very special. That's from my friends in Alabama.' Let me assure you that no one out here knows where Alberta, Alabama is. They would hardly have any understanding of what that quilt means to me now."

Today, multitudes of people own quilts produced by the Freedom Quilting Bee. For a few, such as Dr. Crowley, the Bee evokes strong and passionate glimpses of the past. Most are not so fortunate as to have been directly involved with this unique assembly of women.

During the early years, some of the customers heard of the group through the civil rights movement and ordered portions of its artistry through allegiance to that cause. Others learned of the co-op through national pipelines stemming from the Selma Inter-religious Project and requested quilts for religious reasons. In the late 1960s and early 1970s, buyers from another realm were bedazzled by all the magazine photographs and wanted to be part of a countrywide trend. As the quilts and their marketing procedures have become more sophisticated, a public enthused with arts and crafts has purchased from the sewing center through co-op outlets, catalogs, and brochures.

Some owners know they have a well-made and beautiful Grandmother's Choice, designed to match the mood of an antique bedroom. Alas, that is all they know about their quilt. Dr. Crowley and others of his bent know much more, for, whether Freedom's products are from the 1965 vintage or the version now being made, each is a patch of history. Behind every quilt is the battle for economic survival against all the odds.

Stitched into each is the full-circle story of the black race in this country, from slavery to freedom and far beyond. The fingers, the hands, the care, the love, and the skill with which a Freedom quilt has been brought into being represent the Southern black woman at her finest hour.

Index

Abrams, Mama Willie, 207, 209–13; on Estelle Abrams Witherspoon: 213, 241

Alabama Black Belt, 4. *See also* Civil rights movement

Alabama Cooperative Association (also Federation of Southern Cooperatives), 133, 134

Alabama Department of Pensions and Security, 171

Alabama Rural Rehabilitation Corporation, 37. *See also* Farm Security Administration

Alberta, Alabama, 31

Alberta, Route One, Alabama, 32

Alexander, Dr. Will, 37

American Friends Service Committee, 94

Artisans Cooperative, 132, 136–40. *See also* Witherspoon, Estelle Abrams

Auchincloss, Hugh, 52

Basch, Peter, 21, 22

Bayley, Edwin, 24, 30

Bayley, Monica, 24–30, 50, 51

Bear's Paw quilt, 240

Bennett, Polly Mooney, 196, 198–206; on civil rights movement: 200–201; on Reverend Francis X. Walter: 202

Bloomingdale's, 66, 71, 81, 84. *See also* Bradshaw, Jody

Blue-jean quilts, 29, 30

Bonifaz, Deirdre, 120, 136–40; on Coat of Many Colors quilt: 138; on Estelle Abrams Witherspoon: 138–39, 217; on Nettie Young: 139, 214

Bonwit Teller, 117

Boykin, Alabama, 39. *See also* Gee's Bend, Alabama

Boykin, Congressman Frank, 39

Bradshaw, Jody, 71, 81–86; on Stanley Selengut: 82; on Bloomingdale's: 82, 85–86, 100; on sewing center wedding: 103

Bricklayer quilt, 41

Brooks, Mary, 64. *See also* McCarthy, Mary

Brown, Lonnie, 103

Burden, Amanda, 57

Camden, Alabama, 12, 193, 233, 238. *See also* Patton, Martha Jane: on civil rights movement (in Wilcox County)

Cargo, Dr. Robert, 90

Carmichael, Stokely, 7

Cary, Millie, 15

Chestnut Bud quilt, 51, 57, 184, 185

Christian Century. See Kennedy, Reverend Renwick C.

Civil rights movement, 3, 5–13; in Wilcox County, Alabama: 231–38. *See also* Bennett, Polly Mooney; Mosely, Aolar Carson; Patton, Martha Jane; Ross, Mattie Clark; Walter, Reverend Francis X.; Witherspoon, Estelle Abrams; Young, Nettie Pettway

Clary, Kevin, 124–27; on Estelle Abrams Witherspoon: 124, 126

Coat of Many Colors quilt, 63, 117. *See also* Bonifaz, Deirdre

Coleman, Eva Mae, 175; on China Grove Myles: 178, 179

251

About the Author

Nancy Callahan is a freelance writer based in Montgomery, Alabama. She received her B.A. and M.A. degrees in journalism from The University of Alabama.